Committee Management
in Human Services

Committee Management in Human Services

Running Effective Meetings, Committees, and Boards

Second Edition

John E. Tropman
The University of Michigan

Harold R. Johnson
The University of Michigan

Elmer J. Tropman
The Pittsburgh Foundation

Nelson-Hall Publishers ■ Chicago

Cover Design: Sandi Lawrence
Cover Painting: *With My Eyes Closed* by Mary Curts

LIBRARY OF CONGRESS CATALOGING IN PUBLICATION DATA

Tropman, John E.
    Committee management in human services : running effective meetings, committees, and boards / John E. Tropman, Harold R. Johnson, Elmer J. Tropman.—2nd ed.
      p. cm.
    Includes bibliographical references (p.   ) and index.
    ISBN 0-8304-1291-3
    1. Committees. 2. Meetings. I. Johnson, Harold R. II. Tropman, Elmer J. III. Title.
AS6.T74   1992
658.4'56—dc20
                                                91-22103
                                                  CIP

Manufactured in the United States of America

10 9 8 7 6 5 4 3 3 2 1

CONTENTS

Preface to the Second Edition ix

Preface to the First Edition xxiii

PART I
The Nature of Committee Roles 1

▪ CHAPTER 1
The Chairperson 5

▪ CHAPTER 2
Officers 16

▪ CHAPTER 3
The Committee Member 21

▪ CHAPTER 4
The Staff Person 32

▪ CHAPTER 5
The Executive and the Board 41

PART II
The Mechanics of Committee Process 53

▪ CHAPTER 6
Getting People to Attend Meetings 55

■ CHAPTER 7
Planning and Preparing the Meeting Space....................... 61

■ CHAPTER 8
Compiling and Distributing Reports............................ 65

PART III
The Dynamics of Committee Process............................ 73

■ CHAPTER 9
Premeeting Activity... 77

■ CHAPTER 10
Regular Meeting Sessions 85

■ CHAPTER 11
The First Meeting.. 98

■ CHAPTER 12
Pulling It All Together.. 110

PART IV
Committee Types and Functions 117

■ CHAPTER 13
The Policy-Sharing Committee 121

■ CHAPTER 14
The Policy Advisory Committee................................. 126

■ CHAPTER 15
The Policy-Coordinating Committee............................. 134

■ CHAPTER 16
The Policy-Implementing Committee 140

■ CHAPTER 17
The Policy-Deciding Committee 149

■ CHAPTER 18
Policy-Overseeing Committees 155

■ CHAPTER 19
The Policy-Administering Committee (Task Force) 162

PART V
The Social and Organizational Contexts of Committee
Operation 169

- CHAPTER 20
  Committee Auspice: Public and Voluntary Committees........... 173

- CHAPTER 21
  Elected Versus Appointed Committees 179

- CHAPTER 22
  Committee Scope.. 184

PART VI
Significant Issues in Committee Life 193

- CHAPTER 23
  Representation and Representativeness.......................... 197

- CHAPTER 24
  Optimizing the Participation of Special Groups.................. 204

- CHAPTER 25
  Committee Decision Quality, Effectiveness, Evaluation, and
  Accountability 210

PART VII
Rules to Improve Committee Efficiency and Effectiveness........ 219

- CHAPTER 26
  Principles and Rules to Improve Committee Efficiency........... 221

- CHAPTER 27
  The Fraction Rules.. 228

- CHAPTER 28
  The Agenda Bell 235

- CHAPTER 29
  The Writing Rules... 240

- CHAPTER 30
  The Integrity Rules... 249

PART VIII
Committee Evaluation 253

- CHAPTER 31
  Committee Evaluation 255

PART IX
Achieving Decision Crystallization.................................. 261

  ▪ CHAPTER 32
    Decision Crystallization in Committees 263

PART X
The Voluntary Board of Directors.................................. 271

  ▪ CHAPTER 33
    The Board of Directors... 273

    Epilogue... 285

    Bibliography... 287

    Index.. 297

PREFACE TO THE SECOND EDITION

Since the initial edition, *The Essentials of Committee Management*, a great deal has happened in the field of effective decision making, meeting management, and the management of decision-making groups. The point where our earlier volume ended—the emphasis on decision quality—is the point where this second edition begins. Only modest changes have been introduced into the original text; it remains amazingly durable. Its focus on roles, on preparing the meeting space, and on the different functions of committees and meetings, holds up extremely well. However, what is missing from the first edition are a number of additional steps that would help the committee manager, the meeting chair, the administrator, the manager, or the executive to further improve and refine his or her skill at the process of decision development. Community agencies, governmental units, social planners, and policy analysts all need group decision-making skills. What has become especially clear during the intervening period is that one must always ask the questions, "Committee management—for what?"; "Meeting management—for what?" The answer is always the same: for decisions, and for high-quality decisions at that. Whether one is in the human-service sector, the government sector, or the commercial sector, the central reason for coming together in a committee or meeting is to take effective and efficient action that will be of high quality. That action, of course, is decision making.

In the human-service sector, one might assemble a committee to recommend removal of a child from its home because of potentially abusive parents; in the government sector, one might assemble a committee to decide what departments to recommend for budget increases and budget decreases; in the commercial sector, one might assemble a committee to decide which agencies should receive philanthropic gifts or whether or not a particular new product should be introduced. All of these actions are taken within a group process where the information and people needed must be assembled and present in the same room at the same time. There are a variety of ways that committee chairs and meeting managers can assist not only in the assembling of the components but in processing the various points of view as well.

The presentation of these skills represents a new section of this volume, Part VII, and consists of chapters 26–32. Chapter 26 focuses on effective principles or points of view for decision making. Chapters 27 and 28—"The Fraction Rules" and "The Agenda Bell"—focus on organizing information for the committee. Chapter 29—"The Writing Rules"— stresses the options memo and the executive summary techniques. Chapter 30—"The Integrity Rules"—stresses the importance of adhering to the timetable and agenda previously announced. Chapter 31, in Part VIII, outlines some steps in committee evaluation. Chapter 32, in Part IX, looks at ways to assist committees in actually making decisions. Finally, Chapter 33, "The Board of Directors," in Part X, helps board members—actually, directors of non-profit enterprises—to better perform their role.

A Brief History of Group Emphases

Committee, meeting, and board group activities generally have a problematic history. They are often portrayed as inept and incompetent. A bit of attention to the recent history of group emphases helps put this perspective into context.

The social science community has always been interested in the group aspects of human life. Charles Cooley's early classic on sociology introduced the concept of "the primary group," referring to the family and community groups that introduce us into the human race and nurture and develop our humanity (1920). George Casper Homans's classic of the 1950s, *The Human Group,* brought together a wide range of sociological material that sought to place group activity more centrally within the agenda of social science (1950). At about the same time, Robert Freed Bales of Harvard was developing his ideas of "task" and "process" emphases within human group interaction (1950). Group activity was celebrated by the development of the subdiscipline of "group dynamics," deriving as it did essentially out of psychology and social psychology. The focus of group dynamics emphasized the psychosocial patterns of group interaction. Implicitly, and at times explicitly, the action implications of this focus tended to be water drawn from the same well. Thus, if one "got to know" others, and "understood where they were coming from," then almost by implication group processes would be improved. But the hidden question, "Group processes for what?", still hung unanswered. It was unanswered in part because it was, in this tradition, un-asked.

Within the social work community, a similar emphasis on group processes always existed, but, as in social science, it occupied a subdominant role. Initially, the social work emphasis on groups as such began in the recreation field. Here teams naturally occurred, and a focus on working on teams was thus not unusual, but this focus did not yield any particularly startling insights. Similarly, social workers understood the family group was powerful and influential, but this understanding became crystallized with the use of groups for purposes of social treatment. In this case, the goal of group activity was the improvement of the individual's psychological function.

Group work agencies, therefore, tended to focus on using groups as a method for individual intervention. However, all human-service organizations did not take this view. The so-called "character-building agencies"—the Boy Scouts, the Girl Scouts, the Boys' and Girls' Clubs, the Y's, the Jewish community centers—viewed group processes as useful not so much to improve the psychological functioning of individuals but rather as a training ground for future social interaction. Since one would interact with others most of one's life, understanding how to interact with others and getting along with others in collective settings seemed to be a central and important feature. "Character" was thus built through interaction with others, and while the goal was not the improvement of psychological functioning, the improvement of social performance certainly was.

This tentative social emphasis on groups and their power was developed in the commercial sector as well. Businesses and firms, highly hierarchical and authoritatively oriented, had grown up in the early part of this century on the machine model of the organization, in which the individual, like the interchangeable parts with which she or he worked, was easily replaceable, one for the other. This view took substance and legitimacy from the Western tradition of hierarchy (Pascale and Athos, 1981), and was fueled as well by the influx of thousands and thousands of immigrant workers to the shores of America. Theories of interchangeability are certainly enhanced if new parts are always available. Relatively modest attention was paid to the interactive aspects of individuals in the workplace until the famous Western Electric studies done by Rothensburger and Dickenson in the mid-1930s (Homans, 1950). They asserted, to some extent, that "an informal system" existed parallel to the formal system. One could not explain behavior totally by reading the organization chart and the piecework assignments—rather, one had to understand the interactive aspects of individuals in that selfsame workplace. To some extent, it appeared that the individuals controlled their own destiny, and "decided" in some unclear way whether or not to go along with the orders given to them by management. The shock to management was doubtless great, but it didn't substantially alter management's view about the importance of hierarchy or the wisdom of that same management in making decisions and passing them on to workers. To that extent, the existence of an informal system was viewed not as a potential aid to commercial achievement and accomplishment but as an impediment to the implementation of the always wise and knowledgeable orders and decisions given by management.

Perhaps the high point of interest in group processes within the organizational framework occurred in what might be called the group dynamics movement. Much of the previous work on groups already mentioned (Bales, 1950; Zander, 1982) led organizations to undertake development within the group field, focusing on helping "organizational teams" work together. This development continues to be important, although the nature of "team emphasis" has changed over time.

A number of organizations used "t-groups" (team groups) to help these teams function. Kotter, Schlesinger, and Sathe (1986) have a detailed case of an organization adopting t-group activity. However, the very conceptualization of these efforts focused on interpersonal interaction. Hence, they excluded information-processing requisites as part of the skills groups need. While t-groups doubtless helped individual members in the group get along better with other members, and developed an increased awareness and sensitivity among all group members of how they impacted upon the group, this lack of outcome focus was harmful. It created a sense of marginality for committees, meetings, and other decision groups.

This background goes a way toward explaining why committees and meetings have such a bad reputation in American society. By "bad reputation," we refer to their characterization as inept, incompetent, and, on occasion, as vehicles used by managers who wish to stall action. In reviewing dozens of cartoons depicting meetings and committee activities, the constancy is one of lack of performance, lack of accomplishment; and on those few occasions when accomplishment does occur, the result is somehow all wrong. This entire genre is symbolized quite well by the joke that goes, "The camel is a horse assembled by a committee."

In sum, then, emphasis on group activity has been low-key. Of course, such a result is to be expected in a nation that celebrates individualism as much as American society does. Nonetheless, the interactional rather than the decisional focus of much of the development of group theory has left group activity on the "soft" side of organizational life, a position that does not give it the clout it deserves.

All of these streams of thought have been important in their own way and continue to contribute today. However, to them an important additional stream was added. The decision-making aspect of groups had been almost completely ignored, or, if not ignored, subordinated into anachronistic and predictable by-products of group process. One day, someone had a profound insight: "Committees make decisions." The host of the jokes about committees and meetings indeed referred to their decision-making aspect, despite the multiple importance and conflicting functions of committees to the social fabric. As detailed in the 1979 introduction to this volume, the study of committees as information-processing systems, the output of which is a decision stream, had until the 1970s eluded scholars as well as practitioners. Even groups—like boards of directors—set up explicitly to make decisions were seen as social/psychological ensembles to be understood in that way and from those perspectives. Questions about the clarity of the mandate, the extent to which individuals understood what decision making was and how to do it, and whether such groups had the information and people they needed to make an effective decision were simply not asked.

The New Importance of Group Decision Making

It is difficult to pinpoint exactly when a new perspective arrives on the scene. Over time, scholars and practitioners bump into limitations of the old perspective, but frequently attribute some of their problems to their own difficulties and lack of knowledge rather than to faults in the paradigm itself. Partly, of course, an absence of focus on group decision making occurred because there was an absence of focus on decision making itself. The advent of computer-based information systems ushered in a full set of questions about how information is processed, assembled, synthesized, and, indeed, how decisions drawing on this information are, in fact, made. Two seminal pieces marked a pivotal fulcrum in the development of our understanding of the decision-making process. A major insight came from the work of March and Simon in their development of "satisfactory" decision-making approaches as opposed to "optimal" decision-making approaches (1958). Optimality, deriving as it did from theories of organizational rationality, simply assumed that individual decision makers reviewed all the alternatives and picked the best or most optimal one. March and Simon pointed out that, as a practical matter, this procedure was in fact impossible. One would never have the time to review all of the options, and their combinations and permutations, and then select that which was absolutely and unequivocably "the best." Leaving aside the mathematics of combinations and permutations, rationality also assumes that the world stands still while you're doing all of this adding and subtracting. Further complexity is thus added if one assumes a moving and changing environment, a developing context. Hence, optimality, even if it could be achieved, is only for "time one." By the time one gets to "time two," what's optimal may be quite different. Hence, one may often use an alternative model described by March and Simon as "satisficing," or picking a good-enough needle from the haystack to accomplish your purposes rather than looking for the perfect needle.

March and Simon did not actually detail what would be required for "satisficing" in an operational context, but in the early 1970s Michael Cohen, James G. March, and Johan Olsen, in their famous paper, "A Garbage Can Model of Organizational Choice," took a look at those processes (1972). Cohen, March, and Olsen argued that all organizations have four streams (we might also say roles) in them at all times. One stream involves "problem knowers," those individuals who are aware of the difficulties the organization faces, and the stresses the organization endures. They may not, however, know how to do anything about those problems.

A second stream present in organizations is "solution givers." These are individuals in systems who are able to provide solutions to problems if they know what the problems are. It's not at all clear, however, that solution givers have the raw material—problems—on which to apply their solutions. Although problem-knowing and solution-giving systems are often present in organizations, they may not interact with each other to any significant degree.

A third group is "resource controllers." Essentially, these are people who control the allocation of personnel and money within the organizational context. Even if one knows a problem, and has a solution for it, without access to the people or money to apply to the problem, neither will do much good.

The fourth group is what Cohen, March, and Olsen euphemistically refer to as "decision makers looking for work." Decision making, that central function of organizational life, is often ephemeral and unclear with respect to the opportunities and occasions for it to occur. One does not necessarily come in, sit down at one's desk, and say, "All right, let's decide something." It is in this sense that Cohen, March, and Olsen are suggesting that decision makers can seek occasions when decisions can be made. However, they also imply that decisions are in themselves somewhat ephemeral. What decisions actually do is bring together problems, solutions, and resources, and orchestrate their interaction. What Cohen, March, and Olsen suggest is that all of these systems, functions, roles, or people, need to be in the same room at the same time for effective organizational decision making to occur. If they are, then it is likely that a high-quality decision will be made. If, on the other hand, one assembles problem knowers and a few resource controllers without any solution givers or decision makers, then the process is arbitrarily truncated. Similarly, if one has a meeting made up entirely of problem knowers, then the famous "complaint" session is likely to be engendered. The "garbage can" portion of their title comes from their conclusion that in most organizations these four streams come together essentially randomly, as if tossed into a garbage can.

From the point of view of this volume, committees need to contain all four elements or dimensions, and if they do not, will indeed be inept. Cohen, March, and Olsen's characterization of a "garbage can model" reflects a conclusion already arrived at by the humorist who described committee decision making as inept. The humorist had the insight but didn't know it. Cohen, March, and Olsen gave it academic respectability and, even more than that, explained why ineptitude appears to be such an appropriate characterization of decision-making groups.

Information processing and decision making, therefore, are central human activities. These activities are performed by individuals, of course, but they are also conducted by groups. Indeed, if properly run, groups will make higher-quality decisions than individuals. Why should this be so? There are several features about individual decision making that create inherent limits to it.

This has to do with information processing. The reader may wish to try a small example that the authors often use to illustrate this point. Consider, before reading the answer below, an array of numbers from 0 to 100. Take a moment to count the number of times the digit 9 occurs within that array. Write the answer down in pencil in some convenient place. As a next step, check your work. The correct answer is XX (we put it in Roman numerals in order to temporarily discombobulate those whose eyes drop down quickly to find the answer). The most common answers to this problem are as follows: 10, 11, and 19. Most individuals begin by going up the right-hand column and counting ten 9s. A significant fraction start at that point, completely forgetting the fact that there are 9s in 90, 91, 92, et cetera. Those who get 11 for an answer typically go up the right-hand column, loop over and pick up the two nines in 99, and forget to go back down the 90s array. This answer is a particularly interesting one, since the student has looped into the second column but somehow fails to appreciate its significance. The third answer—19—is achieved by those individuals who count the right-hand column and then add nine more, forgetting the implications of the double-digit nine in the number 99.

This simple exercise reveals several important insights about individualized decision making. First, we often get into loops involving selective perception, in which that which is clear is nonetheless not seen. For a variety of individual psychological reasons (involving the psychology of perception), questions one asks oneself are often not answered objectively. Readers who actually perform the suggested exercise of checking their work may well have found what the authors found when taking this exercise—we "reviewed for proof only." In our own attempt, we came up with 11 as an answer. We were asked to "check our work." Knowing that we had just discovered 11 as an answer, and being convinced that 11 was right, we reviewed the array of numbers with an eye toward verifying that there were, in fact, 11. Since that's what we started out looking for, that's what we in fact found.

Getting the wrong answer through selective perception and failing to be open to usual checks because of the "review for proof only" mechanism lead to a third problem in individualized decision making—we become committed to our answer. The authors undertook this particular exercise at a luncheon meeting with a colleague. The colleague asked us how certain we were, and we, being very certain, agreed to bet lunch. Naturally, we lost. However, the fact that we engaged in a bet at all indicates the high level of commitment we had to our own—and wrong—answer.

Groups, if properly run, are able to avoid these difficulties. Through the process of asking questions back and forth among committee members, the obvious is much less often overlooked, and flaws in the approach of a particular individual are much more quickly revealed. A similar exercise performed in a committee of three almost invariably comes up with the right answer as frequently as individuals come up with the wrong one.

Groups also foster a certain competition for within-group respect that occasionally acts as an antidote to overcommitment to a particular line of reasoning. One wants to be right, but one also wants to be respected. Hence, counterbalancing emotional forces exist in groups, forces that can temper the potential overcommitment to a particular line of thinking on the part of an individual.

It is not necessary to point out that groups collectively have a much greater range of knowledge than can be possessed by an individual person. Particularly in today's complex problem-solving context, where decisions often require multiple forms of input, the very purpose of a committee is to assemble representation from these different knowledgeable domains (a point completely separate from assembling the problem, solution, resource, and decision-making vectors in an organization).

Groups, then, have two key skills. One already mentioned is that they are more likely than individuals to avoid getting the wrong answer. The questioning and interaction within groups allow errors to emerge more quickly because the back-and-forth discussion brings to the surface badly put-together decisions.

The groups have something else to offer as well—*they can add to a decision and improve its quality. Most decisions, unlike our example of the 9s, do not have a correct or incorrect answer. Rather, they have fields of ambiguity in which a "decision" is a crystallized course of action in a sea of multiple uncertainties.* Escaping error does not necessarily mean that quality has been achieved. Therefore, groups can be used to add elements to a decision that have great potential for increasing quality.

An important caveat in the previous discussion is the phrase "if properly run." Many committees, decision-making groups, and task forces are not properly run. We know this from our own experience, and the variety of problems that can result from groups that are improperly run. One deserves special attention—that which Irving Janis called "*group-think*" (1971). Groupthink is the condition that arises when an individual, often a powerful individual in a group—positionally or interpersonally—takes a strong and firm position on a particular issue, and asks what the others think. Typically, under these kinds of conditions, the other committee members will simply agree. It's too interpersonally costly to oppose the boss, or an individual of overwhelming interpersonal strength. *Groupthink occurs, then, when false agreement is achieved through interpersonal or positional dominance.* Most typically, the minute the meeting breaks up and the members leave, the "true meeting" will occur, with individuals often complaining about the unrealistic nature of the proposal. However, none of these objections were voiced during the meeting itself. Indeed, an executive consultant with whom we're familiar finds groupthink in its variations so common that this consultant has developed a phrase called "the meeting is the real meeting" (McCarthy, 1989). What McCarthy is trying to say to groups with whom he works is that this pattern of having a "false" regular meeting followed by a "true" irregular or ad hoc meeting, with the offending individual absent, really avoids dealing with organizational issues in any significant form.

Since 1979, therefore, there has been a virtual revolution in the emphasis on group decision making. Our 1979 volume took a group decision making (rather than group interaction) point of view. However, it is appropriate to strengthen and expand our original point within this second edition, and to consider some of the trends that have developed since that time.

For one thing, there have been a number of new books exemplifying the decision-making trend. One of them, *Meetings: How to Make Them Work for You* (Tropman, 1985), is a volume that explores, in a preliminary way, some of the techniques presented here. Other volumes, such as Dunsing's *You and I Have Got to Stop Meeting This Way* (1978) and Tropman's *Effective Meetings* (1980), as well as Doyle and Strauss's *How to Make Meetings Work* (1977), bespeak an interest in committees and meetings that was not present before. Indeed, the very use of the term "meeting" signifies this trend. A transitional volume called *Making Groups Effective* (Zander, 1982) is the attempt on the part of an individual who has spent a career doing group dynamics research to focus upon the issue of "for what" are groups to be assembled. Zander does not use the term "meeting," but he does talk about effective decision making within the context of his volume. Many other authors, however, have switched terms or picked up the term "meeting" in order to emphasize the decision-making aspect. Emphasis on group decision making has also come through a fresh emphasis on the board of directors. Many new books on boards emphasize the decision-making aspect. It is actually hard to avoid, since boards are specifically assembled—perhaps more than any other group—to make decisions.

However, a range of new studies and "how-to" books has not been the only development. There has been an upswing of discussion in the public press about effective meetings. Meetings and committees have become a public topic rather than something that one didn't particularly like to discuss. Articles on meetings in daily papers such as the *Ann Arbor News* bespeak local interest, while a long article in the *Wall Street Journal* testifies to nationwide concern. *Psychology Today* (May 1989) ran an in-depth piece on running effective meetings, and doubtless other examples will have already come to the attention of the reader. The important point here is that boards, committees, and meetings have emerged from meaninglessness in the 1970s to receive recognition as aspects of the life of human-service agencies, corporations, and government bureaus. They always were, of course, important aspects of life in those organizations, involving as they did millions if not billions of person-hours of effort. However, much like an unrecognized nutritional deficiency, people saw and felt the poor results but never felt that anything could be done about them. That attitude has changed in the past ten years. Throughout the land, individuals are now feeling that meetings and committees are something to be managed and developed. The 3M Corporation, in fact, has set up the Meeting Management Institute, designed to assist corporations in improving their meeting effectiveness (as well as to provide small grants for meeting research and occasional newsletters).

The Reasons for Change

Why has such a change toward accepting meetings as important occurred? There are several reasons that need to be touched upon.

First, it is clearer now than ever that American society—and, indeed, perhaps world society—is an information society. The society-wide emphasis on information systems of all sorts, which comes as a result of this recognition, must include committees and other "human" information-processing systems. There is, of course, an emphasis on machine processing of information through such new areas as artificial intelligence. Indeed, it may well be that, as the wag puts it, "Artificial intelligence is better than no intelligence at all." Still, the potential for glitches and hitches, as the film *War Games* suggested—in which a "supersmart" military computer began to fool itself into thinking America was being attacked, and prepared to launch missiles against an invisible enemy—reinforces our conviction that a group of human decision makers, sitting collectively, must be the final arbiters in the case of fateful decisions.

A second development is the recognition on the part of a number of corporations and individuals that organizational *processes* are things to be managed, just like facilities and people (Kotter, Schlesinger, and Sathe, 1986). One organization with which the authors are familiar has installed a "committee clock" in its meeting rooms. When an organizational committee gets together, the various hourly rates of the individuals on the committee are punched in. After an hour, the clock reveals the amount of money that has been used up in the particular meeting in question. As organizations—human-service agencies, government bureaus, and corporate suites—face cutbacks, reductions, and strictures on their financial resources, an interest develops in looking at all organizational activities as possible sources for savings. Here's where process management really comes in. Ten social-work therapists who normally would receive $50 an hour consume $500 for every hour they get together to talk about cases. Committee meeting time is not "free time," it's paid for. The only difference is that organizations had never fully realized the cash implications for those hundreds of hours of meetings that everyone put in. One consultant on effective committee meetings puts it this way: "If you follow my suggestions, you can get as little done as you do now in half the time."

Process management for efficiency—getting the same result in less time—is of fundamental importance. However, it is not sufficient. *Organizational analysts speak as well of "working hard and working smart," or "the difference between doing things right [efficiency] and doing the right thing [effectiveness]."* An efficient committee meeting that quickly takes a position on the wrong issues is not exactly what effective decision makers have in mind. Thus, effectiveness in committee activity means not only paying less attention to the unimportant items, but being able to identify what the items are on which attention should be focused, and concentrating explicitly on those items. Stating it that way does not make it seem terribly difficult, except that, as most readers know, the group that actually accomplishes this task is a rare bird indeed. Resource constrictions, though, focus attention both on efficiency and on effectiveness.

Other types of changes have been occurring in society as well, which have heightened the importance of committee functioning. As John Naisbett (1982) has pointed out, one of the important changes that is affecting our society is a movement from representation to participation. Individuals no longer want to "delegate" as much of their decision making to others, as perhaps was true in the past. Rather, an enhanced interest in "being at the table" is present in almost every area. This interest is both generative of and reflective of changes in organizational culture that are sweeping through agency and corporate suites. New management orientations focus on involving the workers in decision making on issues that affect them. This ideology is nothing new to the social-work community, of course, although we have not necessarily trained our staffs in the decision-making aspects of the participation process: we have shared feelings more than information. Thus, while participatory activity is nothing new in social agencies, participatory decision making has a bit of a new ring to it.

In any event, if individuals are going to participate in decisions that affect them, in whatever sector, then special attention needs to be paid both at the individual and the organizational level as to how this participation is to be orchestrated. If it is not carefully structured, participation will become as it has become in some other instances—a false promise.

One aspect of participation that has received lots of national attention, especially in the administration of President George Bush, is the renewed public emphasis on volunteerism and volunteering as a way of contributing to the public weal and providing significant new resources for dealing with social problems. Along with the emphasis on volunteer participation, however, comes a correlative demand to make the invested time worthwhile. There has been an increased interest in the provision of education and training for group involvement of volunteers in decision-making roles. The United Way of America maintains an academy—the National Academy of Volunteerism—specifically to train professionals and volunteers in the wide range of roles that they are undertaking, including effective and efficient committee management. Growth in volunteer involvement will be related to the participants' sense of satisfaction and contribution—especially as they serve on committees and boards of directors. This will require more attention to the committee process by both staff and volunteers. The United Way is especially interested in training professionals to work with volunteers, and in training volunteers in the expectations that they may legitimately have of staff, and in the way in which they need to go about their own business of volunteering.

Throughout this society, the emphasis on quality and excellence is everywhere. At one level, it is possible to view this emphasis as a trite, "verbal" attempt to paper over obvious deficiencies in our services and products. But any view that accuses the "quality/excellence" movement as simplistic is in and of itself simplistic. There are doubtless trite aspects to this emphasis, but there is also little question that the American economic machine is not performing well precisely in the quality/excellence area. Human-service organizations such as hospitals are undertaking human-resources development programs emphasizing total quality. Large corporate giants, such as the Ford Motor Company, have mottoes such as "Quality is Job #1." Part of any quality-management effort must deal with effective decision making. Without effective decisions, quality becomes vacuous, and excellence disappears.

As the above discussion suggests, the first edition, *The Essentials of*

Committee Management, was among those early volumes that heralded the new information processing and decision management trend, an emphasis to accelerate in the coming decades. It's an early work, however, and was not as rich or detailed in action implications and action steps as it might be. The new chapters to this volume seek to remedy this insufficiency. In many instances, completely new material, unavailable at the earlier writing, is added. In others, greater refinement of focus is given. For example, some attention was paid (page 91, first edition) to the steps in agenda formulation in the first volume. Research and experience have allowed more significant and graphic representation of "the agenda bell," which is discussed in Chapter 28.

Preparing a new edition of an older work is always a bittersweet process. While we were pleased to find we were at the beginning of a trend that was developed more fully by other authors, we were disappointed that we had not more fully recognized the components of this trend and more fully detailed useful action steps for readers. Nonetheless, through written and oral communication, readers have indicated how much that volume has helped them in the process of their own work. We hope that this revised and expanded edition will retain the vitality and centrality of the original volume while, at the same time, adding significant information and suggestions for action.

The bibliography of this volume has been significantly expanded exactly along these lines. Hence, a considerable amount of material focusing on effective decision making in groups and committees is heavily represented in the new material.

PREFACE TO THE
FIRST EDITION

In the United States we probably have more committees than we have people. It is a rare instance when a social, economic, or political action is taken, in either the public or private sector, without first being considered and acted on by a committee. Indeed, America is run by committees.

In scientific studies of power structures and key influentials, one important fact has usually been ignored. In today's complex, diversified, and interlinked society, the committee, or group of decision makers, has achieved a silent suzerainty and private prominence. Regardless of how influential an individual might be in terms of his or her personal characteristics—wealth, organizational position, education, or whatever—the major decisions that a person makes in most spheres of human affairs will at some point go to a committee. The committee will not in all cases have final authority. Sometimes it will "advise," sometimes it will "react," sometimes it will "ratify," sometimes it will "suggest policy options."

Certainly committees play a variety of roles. However, it is our assumption, and the assumption on which this volume is based, that a decision of any importance in contemporary American society will at many points in consideration, from the initial phase to final implementation, be weighed and shaped, if not decided, by a committee. Thus, regardless of whether one looks at decisions from the "issue" perspective and seeks to see who is influential, or looks at "important people" and seeks to find out where they get their way, the committee is more than likely to play a prominent and previously unacknowledged role.

The use of committees as instruments to achieve personal and organizational goals has increased dramatically in recent years. As the complexity of our society continues to increase, we can rest assured that the popularity and authority of committees will grow commensurately. It is interesting to note that despite our great reliance on committees to accomplish a wide variety of tasks, somehow they have escaped any kind of systematic operational examination. As with sexual behavior, Americans seem to believe that they are all instant experts about committee behavior. However, we are all familiar with the widespread dissatisfaction surrounding the effectiveness of committees. Complaints about numerous and lengthy meetings, poorly managed meetings, and poorly attended meetings are common.

This book was therefore conceived with two major purposes in mind: The first is to assist individuals in increasing their effectiveness as participants in the committee process. The second, and one that will be served through the accomplishment of the first, is an improvement in the quality of decisions made by committees, whether a given committee's decision is related to providing advice, as in an advisory committee; or seeking to implement a policy, as in an administrative committee; or approving financial proposals, as in a finance committee. These purposes, we hope, will be achieved as a result of a fairly complete discussion about committee roles, the mechanics and dynamics of the committee process, the various types and purposes of committees, and the common problems that beset their operation. It is our thesis that the effectiveness of committees will increase proportionately with the increased understanding of committees by their members.

We will be satisfied, however, if this book serves to focus attention on committees as social and political forums and increases objective analysis of them as such. Thus, if we fail to achieve our major purposes, at least we will be pointing the way for their achievement by others, or by a later edition of this volume.

Committees in America

Our society might almost be said to romanticize committees. They are formed at the drop of a hat. There is no way to estimate the number of committees existing in the country at any given time. Whatever the number, it is astronomical. Each reader can simply count the number of memberships he or she has on various committees and achieve some idea of the number of possible committees in the country as a whole. It is important, as we begin this rather practical volume, to indicate some reasons why America, perhaps in particular, is so enamored of committees.

One reason is our belief in participatory democracy. Though far from fully realized in practice, the national ideal is that the general citizenry is entitled to a voice in the decisional process. As a practical matter, one of the

ways this voice is made operational is through the organization of representative committees.

A second reason for the prominence of committees lies in a weakness
in our political system. "One man one vote" reflects, in effect, the extensity
of preferences over any issue. It does not and cannot reflect the intensity of
preference, the depth of feeling on a particular point. The preference of the
person for whom an issue is of casual interest and the preference of the
person for whom that issue is of burning importance are recorded equally.
The committee process has a "leavening" effect on how issues are resolved
in America. Various points of view, representing intensive feelings and extensive concerns, are brought to bear on most issues by diversely organized
committees.

Thirdly, committees are important because of the pluralism in American society. The fact that there are people of many different backgrounds
and orientations in this country enriches our social and political climate. As
a practical matter, however, this pluralism requires extensive efforts at socialization as well as some method by which the different perspectives can be
brought to the attention of the larger community. In this sense, the committee
tee serves to inform while extending communications and understanding
among the many groups with an interest in particular issues.

Participation, intensity, and pluralism provide the backdrop for a fourth
reason committees are important in America—representation. Americans
have always "gotten together" to discuss issues. Well over a century ago,
Alexis de Tocqueville noted this tendency in our national character. This
practice flows from our concept that people should be represented in decisions that concern them even though they may not always prevail. In fact,
there is a feeling that people who do not in some way participate in a decision
are not compelled to obey or be bound by it. The committee, therefore, becomes one of the ways in which various "interests" are "represented" in the
decisional process. We might add that the concept of representation in the
committee process, in which one speaks for others as well as oneself, is perhaps the most difficult problem, and one to which we shall turn later in the
volume.

These four reasons for committee activity are somewhat unique to
America. Other nations and societies may not have similar reasons for committee development. However, there are at least two reasons that are trans-
societal. These have to do with complexity and power.

The fifth reason, then, is societal complexity; as social life becomes
more complex, the number of committees increases. The rule proposed by
Garrett Hardin applies here: "You can never do just one thing." All events
and all decisions have implications for many other events and decisions and
are affected by many more events and decisions. For this reason, committees
are formed as small "crystallized" points in the social process, as modules

where some of the relevant information about matters that will pertain to a particular decision can be brought to bear. Hence, the more complex the system—whether that system is a society or a business or a community—the greater will be the reliance on committees.

The sixth reason is perhaps the personal component of the fourth one. In a complex and diversified society, "power" tends to be diffused, informally if not formally. As any issue comes up, it is necessary to bring together not only those who have relevant information on a specific subject but also those who have relevant power for the accomplishment of the goals in question. Since those who have information and those who have power are not always (or even frequently) the same persons, it becomes necessary to consider both the knowledge and the influence of potential members during the process of committee creation.

The Functions of Committees

These various reasons for the importance of committees imply functions that committees are expected to serve. Yet insofar as these reasons do reflect functions, they often operate at cross-purposes. One reason committees frequently perform so poorly is that they are asked to perform competing and (to at least some extent) mutually exclusive functions. If a committee is to have knowledgeable people on it, then it may not have powerful people. Hence, it may make a good decision that cannot be implemented. On the other hand, if it has powerful people who are not well-informed, then it may make a bad decision that is immediately implemented, with regrettable results. If it has some of both, the different perspectives and statuses of the two groups are likely to seriously complicate the process.

Similarly, committee makeup on grounds of *participation* may differ from that on grounds of *intensity of preference, pluralism,* or *representation.* The development of a decision on the basis of any one of these dimensions may lead to challenges based upon different values and points of view. Hence, a decision made on the basis of equality may be challenged on the grounds that it did not fairly represent intensity; one made on the basis of intensity may be challenged because it was not representative, and so on. Committees that serve one function or purpose, then, may fail to serve another, or may serve it badly.

Therefore, it seems that committees with diverse and multiple functions usually experience the greatest difficulty in reaching their objectives. Often, argument about procedures, and perhaps even about substantive matters, is in reality reflective of the "poorness of fit" among these several functions. Frequently, such strains will become most evident during the formation process of the committee, and this point is addressed in more detail later. Yet, throughout committee activity there are manifestations of the problems created by the inability of the committee to meet and perform a variety of functions simultaneously.

And should the reader feel that the problems of multiple functions exhaust the sources of strain on committee activity, let us hasten to dissolve such a notion. Most of the strains within committee work flow from the very specific, very practical problems presented in day-to-day operations, such as confusion of mission and role, acting as a completely different type of committee than is specified in the mandate, and failure to take appropriate action—not to mention all the practical difficulties of getting people together for a meeting at the same time and in the same place. Indeed, the entire remaining material in this volume concerns these strains and provides at least some ways to cope with them. But we would be remiss if we did not also indicate that committees are an important element in the functioning of the social system as such, and that some of the problems they face relate to the many ways in which the committees meet certain generalized social needs.

Smooth Committee Functioning

With these general and specific strains facing committees, what then holds them together? We believe there are five main elements that, if properly articulated, serve to promote committee integration and accomplishment. These same elements, when not properly developed and articulated, can hamper staff and impede committee operation and hence interrupt committee accomplishment.

Perhaps the most useful way to introduce these elements is through the metaphor of an orchestra. For an orchestra to appear on a stage and play, five things are needed: players, a musical score, a conductor, practice before the event, and logistical support. Without any one of these, the orchestra could not perform. And although there are differences in the artistic meaning of the requirements—a conductor is thought to be more important than logistical support—an orchestra whose players arrive without instruments is as unable to play as an orchestra that arrives without a conductor.

Each of these elements is an important part of the committee process. The players, of course, are the members, and the conductor is the chairperson. Each has a generalized understanding of the role to be played; each role is often modified by the score. The score, for a committee, is the purpose or mandate, which tells the committee what it is to do. Committees, however, like orchestras, take certain liberties in interpreting the score, depending on the context, the chairperson, and the members. A more specific version of the committee score is the agenda for meetings, which tells the members what they are to be doing at a specific session. The chairperson and the members, like the conductor and the orchestra members, usually have a conception of the overall "way the thing should go," and this conception provides a framework for the group to go about its business.

Practice sessions, too, are important. For an orchestra, the few hours of public performance are the culmination of many hours of intensive work. The same, though it may not seem so, is true for the committee. Each meeting of the committee is similar to the public performance of the orchestra, a crystallized moment in the ongoing life of the group. The players, singly and in groups, have practiced their parts. The manager has readied the hall, seen to tickets, lighting, et cetera. All these preparations come together in the public performance. Similarly, the committee members have informed themselves of their charge, read the material sent to them, developed their own thoughts on the items on the agenda, and so on. The chairperson has been working on particular topics for the meeting and overseeing the preparation of the logistical items—rooms, refreshments, parking—that are necessary for a successful performance. Perhaps the chair or an associate chair has been meeting with subcommittees regarding specific reports. Then the time of the meeting arrives; the chairperson and the members gather in the room, the gavel falls, and the meeting begins.

We believe that what happens in committee meetings, as in orchestra performances, depends largely on what has gone before. If the five elements have been properly developed and articulated, the meeting should prove successful. If little or no preparation has taken place, then the committee will perform poorly, much like an unrehearsed orchestra.

We do not intend to downgrade the meeting situation itself. And indeed, there are many books on "how to run better meetings." Our point is, rather, to place greater stress on the activities that go on outside the formal meeting. The committee process is an ongoing one, in which meetings represent important and formal centers of decisional activity in the group's life; these centers, however, require work and preparation. And achieving each goal in proper sequence and balance is what results in the effective operation of a committee.

Committee Process and Personality

Other writers have offered conceptions of the "meeting situation" that emphasize the personalities of the members, with suggestions on how to handle "Type A" and "Type B." Such approaches are useful. However, the perspective taken in this volume stresses looking at the committee process as a totality, rather than just the meeting. Our goal is to de-emphasize the importance of personality as the crucial determinant of committee behavior. Let us be more explicit and argue directly our belief that, generally, personality is a marginal modifier, rather than a dominant determiner, of committee activity. The emphasis on personality can be actually dysfunctional in that it serves to turn our attention away from some of the root causes of committee mal-performance.

Perhaps this point could be made more crisply by referring again to the analogy to an orchestra. Members of the orchestra have different personalities, and to some extent these are expressed in the music, but there is, after all, the score. Similarly, the conductor's interpretation is affected by personality, within the limits of the basic piece. Thus, the personality of the conductor may modify the presentation of a score, but it does not rewrite the music.

In the committee process, we expect that people will behave differently in basic ways, on different issues, at different times, and in different places. Generally, we manage to get along with these changing moods and personality orientations. In other areas of our lives, the same proposition holds: we do manage to develop productive relationships, even though the personalities of the people with whom we are working are often troublesome and difficult.

This view, though, should be put in its proper perspective. Personalities are important in committee functioning. The personalities of committee members can make much difference in the speed and pleasantness with which work gets done; in most committee situations, there are key persons who make a significant difference in the outcome of the meeting. Our point is that, during the lifetime of a committee, thorough preparation and competent role performance serve to smooth and standardize the public presentation of individual members in committee meetings. If a chairperson or member or staff person knows what to do and does it, then some of the unique features of his or her own personality will not be manifest. It is our considered opinion that many so-called personality problems in committee work are attributable to the simple fact that members and other committee people do not know what is expected of them.

Conclusion

The committee has become one of the key decision-making tools in modern American society. Millions of American citizens play an assortment of roles on innumerable committees—large ones, small ones, public ones, commercial ones, important ones, and trivial ones. Yet in spite of the prominence and importance of committees, very little scholarly or popular attention has been directed at them. In scholarly terms, we have little knowledge of the committee as a social form, although there are some materials on small-group process. In popular terms, there is little or no material on what to do and how to do it in the committee context.

It is our hope that this volume will serve the latter of these purposes—providing a practical guide for a wide range of committee participants. In some places—this introduction being one—some theoretical points are mentioned. But our purpose is ultimately practical. This large purpose has two specific goals: The first is to improve the enjoyment and sense of accomplishment that individual participants garner from their own committee participation; the second, and perhaps less attainable, is to improve the quality of the committee output and decisions. As participation is clarified and roles are clearly delineated, as preparation for meetings is improved, then the committee output will be enhanced, and the record of success will heighten the members' sense of accomplishment.

These, then, are the principles of effective committee process:

1. Clarification and understanding of the committee's purpose are basic and essential to the performance of its tasks. A committee must know why it exists and what it is supposed to accomplish.
2. The leadership of the chairperson is the single most important ingredient in successful committee activity.
3. The selection of committee members must be thoughtfully and carefully done, using as a guideline the purpose to be achieved by the committee's activity.
4. The staff person should support and not supplant the leadership of the chairperson and the work of individual committee members.
5. The quality of committee operation is related to the adequacy of the planning and preparation for all aspects and phases of the process.
6. The progress and movement of a committee meeting are directly related to the adequacy of preparation that preceded the meeting and the follow-through after it.
7. Participation is the keystone for productive and effective committee operation.
8. Leadership and not manipulation must be the approach of all who participate, and especially of all who have strategic roles or assignments in committee process.
9. There must be balance between thorough preparation for and control of the committee meeting—in the interest of covering a maximum amount of work in a minimum amount of time—and adequate discussion and the creation of the feeling of committee members that they are helpful participants and not just "window dressing" or "rubber stamps."
10. A sense of progress, movement, and accomplishment is essential for committee members' morale and satisfaction.
11. Committee members—and other individuals or organizations with a legitimate interest—must be kept informed of committee activity; and plans, proposals, or positions should be cleared before final action is taken.

THE NATURE OF

COMMITTEE ROLES

The basic key to the quality of committee participation is the spelling out and understanding of the roles and responsibilities to be assumed both while the committee is in session and between meetings. This is particularly true for the chairperson and the committee staff. It is a lack of such understanding that causes operational problems for most committees. On the other hand, awareness and acceptance of one's role and responsibilities can vastly improve the individual's performance and therefore the performance of the committee.

Proper role performance requires that the chairperson act like a chairperson and perform those duties that a leader should perform. Similarly, members serving in other capacities have particular tasks associated with their roles. Great confusion develops if an influential member begins to "steal" the leadership of a committee from a weak chairperson; or a secretary fails to take adequate minutes; or a staff person acts like a committee member. It cannot be overemphasized, therefore, that the central aspects of good committee activity are proper understanding, and proper carrying out, of committee roles. The interpretation of these roles and their requirements is the purpose of Part I of this volume.

We have identified three role-sets in committee operation—the role of the chair, the role of the officers, and the role of other members. These three types of roles are present in nearly every committee. Many committees also have someone playing a fourth role—that of staff person.[1] These four roles are the key ones to be performed. In this section we will discuss the chief role requisites of each and some of the problems that affect performance.

Proper role performance may be hampered by several factors. One such factor is ignorance. There needs to be (and this volume can perhaps help in this direction) a book of "committee etiquette." Even when one participant has clear knowledge of what needs to be done, the general orientation and preparation of the committee may be of such low quality that other members impede the better-prepared member from playing an appropriate role. At this point, it should be noted that role performance is not cast in a single or fixed mold. There are various ways in which roles can be performed. This fact calls for judgment and skill on the part of the individual participant.

Committee members are often called on to perform roles that alter their usual power or prominence in relation to other participants. For example, sometimes a person is asked to chair a committee that includes members from whom he or she is seeking social recognition or economic favors. This reversal of the usual structure of dominance makes for a tough task. This is especially true when, as often occurs, the "boss-now-member" subtly or openly assumes that his or her overall influence should be respected in the committee as well, and acts with more certainty and authority than is normal or proper for an individual member.

Role inversion of this sort is one of the kinds of role conflict individual members often observe and may experience. Another relates to tension between professional and work roles and committee roles. How far, for example, does one push one's own knowledge as an expert? Perhaps a committee needs to take a broader perspective. Can one escape the impact of personal social or economic status? These questions are illustrative of the difficult considerations that need to be kept in mind as we think about role performance in the committee.

From the committee point of view, as opposed to the perspective of the individual member, there are also factors that create problematic performance of requisite roles. Committee participants, for ex-

---

1. Because of some special complexities, the executive-board relationship is discussed separately in Chapter 5. In our terms, the executive is the "staff" and the board is the "committee."

ample, come to a meeting with different levels of motivation for the particular task at hand and with different levels of willingness to work. They come with a variety of committee experiences and different degrees of ability to participate. On any given committee, some of the members are likely to be present as part of their job and to be receiving some direct or indirect employment-related benefits. Others are there as "volunteers" and are completely contributing their own time, often at an economic cost or loss. Such membership mixtures create different bases of calculation and evaluation for deciding upon, and carrying out, various committee assignments.

In his volume, *The Presentation of Self in Everyday Life,* sociologist Erving Goffman took what he called a dramaturgical perspective in analyzing human interaction. Using Shakespeare's line "All the world's a stage" as a basis for one type of analytic approach, he looked at human interaction as if it were theater. Without going quite that far, we think some of that perspective would be useful in considering this section especially and subsequent sections as well. At a number of points in the discussions that follow, the reader will note metaphoric terms reflecting this approach.[2]

2. Additional material on specific demands and specific situations can be found throughout the chapters in Part IV on committee functions and types, and specifically in Chapter 20, on public and voluntary committees, and Chapter 21, on elected and appointed committees.

CHAPTER 1

The Chairperson

Introduction

The success or failure of a committee usually depends directly on the quality of the performance of its chairperson. This is particularly true in the numerous situations where committees do not have professional staff available to them. The chairperson sets the tone for a committee. The ultimate quality of the endeavor will reflect the chairperson's attitudes regarding the importance of the committee's mission. The pace of the committee's work will reflect the chairperson's commitment to the task. The participation of committee members will reflect the chairperson's comprehension of the task and knowledge and utilization of members' talents and interests. The chairperson must be able to lead and push, set limits, increase participation, and resolve differences. All these tasks must be accomplished in a dignified manner.

Conversely, many are the sad committee members and staff people who have sought to be "helpful" or to circumvent an incompetent leader, only to find that the chair retained enough prestige and authority to nullify their efforts. Generally, as long as a chair remains in the post, one must work with that person in order to achieve committee goals. Hence, the selection of a chairperson is a crucial act in the life of any committee, and this moderator needs to be aware of the full dimensions of the role he or she must play.

Acceptance of the Chair

The role and responsibilities of a chairperson are at least partially determined before the committee is formed. An organization or group of interested individuals has a task in mind and approaches a person to ask if he or she will chair a committee to undertake the task.[1] This request is a crucial one, and the response is equally crucial. The following items are important in considering the request and response. Generally, one who is asked to chair a committee should ask for enough time to weigh the pros and cons of acceptance or refusal.

Conditions for Acceptance

Sometimes, one is inclined to accept under certain conditions and disinclined to accept under others. Insofar as possible, these conditions should be spelled out during the preliminary discussions. Often, someone will accept a chair if certain resources can be made available for the committee or if the committee's meeting schedule and term of the assignment are compatible with other obligations. The scope of the charge to the committee is of particular importance. Will the committee have the latitude to avoid or include particular issues? These points should be clarified and preferably put in writing, either by the candidate or by the person extending the invitation. In America today, there are legions of chairpersons who, upon assuming the chair, have found that the terms of a verbal agreement, especially in regard to resources and staff, have become confused and are points of conflict.

Clarification of Mandate

The candidate should, before acceptance of the chair, seek to clarify the formal mandate to the committee. Whenever possible, the mandate should be in writing. Often a potential chairperson will be given only a sketchy and tentative mandate, with a promise of clarification and confirmation later. Such situations should be avoided. If the mandate is not clarified when someone is asked to serve, the committee charge may become clouded by personal and political misunderstandings. Any limitations imposed upon a committee should be identified and discussed before the post is accepted.

Specification of Membership

Although there may be limitations to the ability of the chairperson candidate to influence either the specificity of the mandate or the selection of the committee, both matters should be discussed. Often that person will

---

1. Chairpersons are selected in several ways—and it makes a difference in how they act. We have detailed the main approaches later in this chapter.

specify as a condition of acceptance that committee membership is to include or exclude certain individuals or organizational representatives.

This is not simply a question of dictating the committee assignment or membership, but rather a question of participation in the process of clarifying issues and establishing an effective work group. When chairpersons insist upon and avail themselves of the opportunity for such influence, it should enhance their effectiveness.

Evaluation of Issues and Participants

Before final acceptance of a position as chairperson, the candidate should do some of what can best be called "political reconnaissance" to gather information about the organization and its record of accomplishments, as well as the experience and interests of the people with whom he or she might be serving. One needs to know the nature of the issues—how politicized they are, what the important elements are, and so on. As this information is developed, one may become aware of "hidden agendas" on the part of those who have asked the candidate to serve, other directors, or particular groups in the broader community. One should not hesitate to inquire among friends and colleagues to improve understanding of the assignment and its implications, and of the time and effort that will be necessary to do a good job.

Time Assessment

Chairing a committee, irrespective of its assignment, takes time. A prospective chairperson should carefully analyze the time factor in two ways: (1) how much time the assignment will require, and (2) how much time can be set aside for this purpose. In evaluating the amount of time required, one must consider such factors as the scope of the charge, the availability and quality of staff, the skills and interests of prospective and/or present committee members, and the availability and quality of relevant information and materials. Of all the factors related to time requirements, undoubtedly the most crucial is that of availability and competence of staff. If competent staff with good interpersonal skills are available, they can facilitate the work of a committee and sharply reduce the demands on a chairperson.

In deciding how much time one should invest in a particular committee, as a chairperson or member, consideration should be given to the following factors: How concerned are you about the assignment? How does the committee assignment relate to other interests and responsibilities you have at home or at work? What are the rewards for accepting this responsibility? Will it improve the quality of life for some members of your community? Will it increase your knowledge about a substantive area? Will it heighten your visibility? Will it assist you professionally? Will it expand your contacts and influence? These factors should be given careful consideration before accepting a committee assignment that may take a significant amount of time. Unfortunately, such factors are rarely granted due consideration. And, in most cases, when one fails to carefully consider such assignments, the results are frustration, conflict, uncompleted assignments, or sloppy products.

Duties and Roles

Once a chairperson has accepted the position, he or she has accepted as well a set of organizational duties and roles (or role requisites). It is in the performance of each of these roles, as well as their integration, that problems usually occur.

Chairperson as Leader

Perhaps the least-understood aspect of the duty and role of the chair is that of leader. The chair clearly has more authority in the committee process, formally and by general agreement, than the members. On the other hand, the chair should not be in complete control, by any means. As leader, he or she is responsible and accountable for committee activity. In addition to *accountability*, there are two other aspects of the chair's job as leader that are important and need to be identified. These are the matters of *committee tone* and *issue conceptualization.*

The committee leader is highly influential in setting the tone of the committee. Very much like the professor in a class, the chairperson can create a seriousness of purpose, or he or she can approach matters in a cavalier fashion. Committee members are surprisingly sensitive to the attitude of the chairperson on this point. They quickly sense it when the chairperson is uncommitted or unsure of purpose, and they place their energies elsewhere.

Lastly, the chairperson is a conceptualizer, not only of the broad realms of committee goals and objectives, but also of the narrower meeting situations where a fresh idea, coming from the chair, can bring together two contesting points of view. Sometimes these ideas are substantive, finding a new basis for agreement previously unrecognized. Sometimes they are procedural—for example, moving an issue into a subcommittee, or providing for a new group to consider it, so that other business can proceed. It is to ensure the political integrity of these suggestions that the chair should seek to remain in a neutral posture. When the chair becomes an advocate of a particular position, then suggestions for dispute resolution will often be seen as simply one way of achieving the chair's objective.

Generally, the chairperson is not a direct partisan. Sometimes this occurs, and, when it does, special care must be taken to see that the interests of the other group are properly represented in the committee process—a hard task indeed! It is suggested that the chair be yielded at this point to minimize the awkwardness of the situation.

Each of these roles implies, and indeed requires, a reciprocal relationship with the membership. The chair needs to lead the group, yet it must recognize that, to some extent, the group must lead itself. Part of being a leader is to be a facilitator, too.

Chair as Administrator

The role played by the chair during meetings has a counterpart when the committee is not in session: we call that role the administrator's role. As the administrator of the committee, the chair either supervises staff, if the committee has staff, or performs or assigns a variety of tasks that should take place between meetings. Such activities, which will be considered in greater detail later in this volume, include, for example, seeing that reports are ready, handling the mechanics of meeting arrangements, conferring with individual members on points of particular interest to them, meeting with subcommittees, and obtaining information that the committee has requested. Some of these tasks, like any other set of administrative tasks, do not seem very glamorous. Indeed, they are often viewed as so demeaning that they are not undertaken. Yet these tasks are crucial to smooth and adequate meeting sessions; they must be performed if the committee is to function effectively. They fall ultimately on the chair as the leader of the committee and the one who is responsible for the committee activity. He or she can certainly obtain help, either from staff persons or committee members, but if the chair does not see that they are done, they will not be done, to the detriment of the meeting.

Chair as Meeting Presider

Perhaps the most publicly recognized part of the role of chair is to preside during the meetings—the duties that occur, as it were, from gavel to gavel. The role of presider is often performed poorly, in part because people do not understand how to carry out this role well or because between-meeting tasks have not been performed and one is left to preside without the proper preparation. More detail on this latter point is developed in Parts II and III. Suffice it to say here that the person presiding at a meeting is charged with beginning and ending the meeting on time, with ensuring that the agenda items are considered properly and fully, and with making sure that the meeting process is orderly and equitable and that various viewpoints are represented in discussion. The chairperson needs to be both proactive and reactive to the meeting process: proactive in taking the initiative in making suggestions for action, and reactive in the sense that these suggestions respond to the ongoing process and help to crystallize viewpoints. If the meetings are quite formal, then some set of procedural rules, such as *Robert's Rules of Order,* should be used, and it is the chair's responsibility to know and fairly implement them.

Chair as Representative

Each committee has someone who represents the committee in matters of "external relations" with other committees and the broader community. Such representation may involve reporting on committee business and progress before various groups, acting on behalf of the committee in ceremonial roles, and being the representative of the committee at sessions of other committees—in such matters as negotiations, strategy sessions, and the like. The chairperson should realize that, in the eyes of others, he or she personifies the committee. Everything about the chair—appearance, demeanor, presentation of self—provides signals about the committee. If the chairperson appears sloppy and gives a sloppy report, listeners will conclude, however rightly, that the committee process for which he or she is responsible is also sloppy, and this judgment may seriously affect the success of the report. In the reporting aspect of this role, care must be taken to report accurately and thoroughly and to avoid personal points of view. If one is asked to speculate and does so, it should be clearly indicated that the point of view presented is personal and not that of the committee. If one is negotiating on behalf of the committee, care should be taken to agree or to commit the committee only in those areas in which prior agreement with that group permits; in other areas, even the chairperson needs to obtain committee ratification. It is not unusual for a committee to modify the terms presented by the negotiator. Sometimes here, as with other roles and duties, the chair delegates to a committee member or to a staff person the responsibility for carrying out certain specific portions and aspects of negotiations.

One external assignment, however, that can almost never be delegated is the relationship with the media—press, radio, and TV. Media people will deliberately seek out the chair, or the associate chair, because they believe that person can speak authoritatively. One must keep in mind in making press statements that the refinements often are eliminated, so simple, direct statements are desirable. Wherever possible, written statements should be provided to the media to maximize accuracy and to facilitate coverage. In instances when one does not have adequate information for dealing with delicate matters, then a "No comment!" is in order.

Issues and Problems

The roles and duties of a chairperson become, here and throughout the book, a case of theme and variations. A number of issues and problems can arise that cause no major change in the magnitude or variety of the chair's roles and duties but do create the need for thought on the chair's part about how to deal with them. Some of these issues and problems are common enough, and pose dilemmas with such regularity that we can alert the reader to them.

Method of Selection

Perhaps the most important item for a chair to keep in mind is how he or she was selected in the first place, and what implications the mode of selection has for the role performance. There are several common methods of selecting chairpersons. Sometimes the chair is already designated, by law or bylaw, and the committee is elected. Sometimes the chair is designated automatically by seniority among the elected persons. Sometimes the member with the highest number of votes is automatically selected. Chairpersons can be elected by the committee, or they can be appointed by the authority that appointed all members. Each of these common methods of selection— (1) legal, (2) seniority, (3) highest vote getter, (4) committee election, and (5) appointment—creates issues and problems for the chair.

Legal. Where the chair is legally appointed, there is little choice about the role. It comes with an office. Whether the committee is appointed or elected, the chairperson is responsible both to the committee and to other constituencies related to that office. The responsibilities of the person selected in this manner are complicated by the fact that the committee members may be appointed by others, or elected. The chair has all the responsibilities attendant to the chair but can expect some differences between his or her objectives and those of other committee members, due to the fact that the chair and the committee often have different and polarized constituencies.

Seniority. The chairperson who is selected by means of seniority of service (in legislative bodies, for example) is frequently there because of a keen interest in the matter covered by the committee. In such a system, it is not unusual to see the important decisions being made by the chair and other senior people, while the newer people "wait their turn." Senior people may have greater knowledge and resources available to them. Chairpersons here should see to it that all members have an opportunity to participate. If permissible, one might appoint a less-senior person as co-chair to bring about better balance in the committee leadership.

High Vote Getter. In elected committees, the chair may go to the one who received the highest number of votes for committee membership. In these cases, the chairperson often assumes that his or her views should prevail. And, indeed, there is some merit to that point of view. Yet as chairperson, one must remember the responsibilities of that role as well as the responsibilities to the constituents who did the electing. The chair cannot (or should not) use the role to suppress the views of other representatives while advancing his or her own.

Committee Election. A situation that creates a close relationship between the committee and the chair occurs when the committee elects its own chairperson. In this situation, unlike any other, the most important constituency of the chair is the committee itself. There is less strain between the role as chair and other elements of the system to which some allegiance might be felt. The chair does, however, continue to have the constituency he or she had as a member. This situation may create some problems because the chair's effectiveness in representing the original constituency may be reduced.

There are two problems that the committee-elected chairperson must recognize, however. One is related to the majority of the committee who voted for the winning candidate, and the other to the minority of opposition. The elected person must be sure to act as chair. Often those who voted for the new chairperson will feel the chair should use the position of the office to further their interests or should show partiality to them by granting key subcommittee appointments, recognition to speak, subtle support of their positions, et cetera. They may even assume they have more rights to be absent, not work, comment at random, and so on, than others do. Feeling grateful, many chairs fail to deal effectively with these partisan problems. When that failure occurs, the committee is out of hand.

Conversely, the chairperson must show the minority opposition that, now that the issue has been decided, he or she will act evenhandedly, seeking cooperation and support from those who were in opposition and seeing to it that they enjoy their fair share of committee privileges. Many chairs have converted opposition into friendly support because of proper handling of committee business after the election is over.

Appointment. Some chairpersons are appointed or designated by the same authority that appoints the committee. In such a case, political, social, or economic factors may outweigh competence in the appointment of a chairperson. Although this situation can develop under any of the forms, it is most common in the appointment mode.

In such a situation, the chair must realize that there may well be others who, from a technical point of view, are more qualified. In that event, it may be prudent to appoint a vice-chairperson who has, perhaps, greater responsibility than usual in working with the committee. Such an appointment broadens the base of the chair, increases the potential of the committee, and avoids another possible conflict—the tug of loyalties for the chair between the appointing authority and the committee itself. Chairs can often become trapped between the differing expectations of these two groups. A vice-chair can both act as ballast and provide additional knowledge and skills.

Accountability

One of the great problems a committee must face is that of accountability—and the chairperson is at the center of this problem.

Constituency. One aspect of this issue is the question, To whom is the committee accountable? In most cases, committees have multiple and loosely defined constituencies. It is part of the chair's job both to define the various constituencies and to shape their expectations and hopes to conform to the reality of the committee assignment and resources. Defining the constituencies and interpreting their wishes to the committee form part of the chair's role. However, the committee, even when it understands fully the expectations placed upon it, may not wish or be able to honor those expectations. Such a situation should be openly stated and discussed with the interested parties.

Mission and role. One of the reasons the committee may violate constituency expectations lies in the fact that most committees have multiple missions and roles, as well as multiple constituencies. The expectations of a constituency may violate one of the missions, or charges, of the committee. For example, a committee may have been appointed to make a "show" of activity. Upon looking into the issue, however, the committee may be moved to advocate changes. There may, in fact, be disagreement over what matters. A committee, for example, may wish to produce a high-quality, critical report, while some of the constituencies might like a less-critical report to maintain the status quo.

Reputation

An important but subtle factor in the operation of any committee is the effect of its work and products on the reputation of the chairperson in particular and members in general. The desire to maintain and enhance one's reputation is one of the main forces motivating committee activity, and the possibility of loss of reputation is one of the important mechanisms of accountability.

As leader, the chair is the person responsible for the accomplishment of the committee. This means that the chair gets the credit for committee progress or the blame for the lack thereof. When credit is to be given, this role is not an unpleasant one; where blame is to be assigned, the problems become acute. It is at this juncture that many chairpersons are especially adroit at indicating the ways in which others have failed to meet their responsibilities. Such shifting (rather than actual passing) of the buck is unacceptable, however common. The chairperson has the most difficult of duties: the acceptance of responsibility for matters over which he or she has far from complete control. It is, nonetheless, one of the risks of the job.

Role Flexibility

Perhaps as difficult as performing the roles and carrying out the duties of the chair is the necessity of avoiding those roles and duties when one is serving in other capacities on other committees. In the course of events, most of us are members of more committees than we chair. This overall ensemble of roles means that each of us needs to play the role we are assigned in a particular situation. Role shifting is especially hard when moving from chair in one committee, with prestige, rights and resources, to member in another, where one must grant deference to someone else. It is similar, in a way, to a star playing a bit part in one movie while at the same time playing a headliner at some other location. This problem is compounded when the chairperson-as-member feels that the current chair is doing a poor job. There is usually an impulse to "take over" and "do the job right." This tendency is a dangerous one and should be resisted. Those who are chairs elsewhere should be careful, in those committees where they are only members, to play the proper role. They will, in the usual case, earn more respect than if they attempt to assume leadership or otherwise behave inappropriately.

Conclusion

In this chapter, some of the basic roles and duties of the chairperson have been presented. The chair, and the performance of the role of chair, is certainly the most crucial role in the committee—similar, as we mentioned, to that of the conductor in a symphony. We have pointed out only some of the most obvious formalities here, and there are infinite numbers of subtleties of which one needs understanding. Yet, if the chair can carry out these basic roles and duties, he or she will have a running start toward the goal of effective leadership.

CHAPTER 2
Officers

Introduction

The number of officers and the functions they perform will vary with the size and purposes of the committee. Smaller and less formal committees often do not require more than one or two officers. In these groups, functions generally conducted by officers are handled as special roles for members. (See Chapter 3.) Occasional roles—such as the taking of minutes for a single meeting, or a short-term assignment as fund raiser—also qualify as special responsibilities for members rather than officership.

As committees become larger, more complex, and more formal in their operation, however, officers become a necessity. The officers usually represent the secondary leadership of the committee. Some of the officer roles in committee operations are those of vice-chairperson, treasurer, financial secretary, secretary, parliamentarian, sergeant at arms, and chairs of such standing subcommittees as bylaws, nominations, and membership. These officers should be elected or appointed for specific terms of office.

The performance of the officer role and its significance for a successful committee operation are discussed in the following pages.

Duties and Roles

As with all other committee assignments, full understanding before acceptance of the officer role is very important. Unlike the chairperson, however, the officer does not have an assortment of roles to manage. There are basically only two: the officer role and the member role. Typically, the officer role is better specified than that of the chair. However, confusion occurs, even though the range of the role is limited, because of the way in which that role is played and the multiple purposes it serves.

Acceptance of the Officership

Careful thought should be given before acceptance of an officership, because, contrary to popular opinion, such a position does demand leadership skills as well as extra time and effort. While the roles of officers are certainly less demanding than those of the chair, they do involve many specific duties, the performance of which has an effect on the operation of the committee. As an example, if the treasurer fails to prepare a financial report, a committee may be unable to decide about purchasing some equipment or staging a particular event.

It must be emphasized that one should also assess one's skills in relation to particular officer roles, since these roles tend to involve special interests or the application of specific skills. One should not accept the job of treasurer, for example, unless he or she knows something about finances or is able and prepared to acquire the requisite skills.

The Officer Role

Officers, by virtue of their position, often chair subcommittees of the larger committee. In that event, much of what we have said about the chair applies to them in that role. There are, however, additional specific duties relating to officerships.

The Vice-Chairperson. Many committees have a vice-chair (associate, deputy, assistant, et cetera). The duties of such a person, other than those specifically mandated under the governing rules of the committee, tend to depend upon the wishes of the chair. If the chair does not designate some specific assignments for the deputy, it may be possible for that person to suggest, for his or her own special focus, an area of perhaps secondary interest to the chair but of importance to the committee. If such an arrangement cannot be worked out between the chairperson and the deputy, the role may become quite similar to that of a regular member. However, the vice-chair presides when the chair is absent.

The Secretary. The chief duty of the secretary is to be the historian/archivist of the committee, a role that is first one of record keeping and may, but does not necessarily, involve actually writing the records.[1] Committees

---

1. This type of secretary should not be confused with the position of executive secretary, which is a staff designation and carries a very different set of responsibilities.

need records of past actions and decisions. Members and the chair may not have complete accounts. The secretary is the one who should see to it that a file is kept that has all material pertaining to the committee. It is a good idea to have two copies, stored in different places.

This record-keeping role is often not understood to its fullest extent, and people elected to the post of secretary may think their job is simply to take minutes. Secretaries often do take minutes and often they are called recording secretaries; sometimes they also communicate with the "outside world" and perform the role of corresponding secretary. However, in some committees, the responsibilities for minute taking are passed around the group, or the staff person takes the minutes. Therefore, we see the role of the secretary as primarily one of records management and secondarily one of records producer.[2]

The Treasurer. Although the essential job of the treasurer remains much the same in all contexts, its scope and responsibility vary a good bit. It is a key slot in all cases and, where the amounts of money handled are substantial, a crucial one as well. Since almost all questions of importance involve the committee's resources, the treasurer needs to be aware not only of the details of the accounts and what the encumbrances are likely to be but also of the policy implications of spending patterns and rates as well. If finances are simple, then record keeping is easy to handle. If the finances are complicated, then the treasurer may need to obtain the advice of a controller or bookkeeper to supplement his or her own skills. What is sought is an easy-to-understand format that presents (1) income, (2) outgo, (3) the relation of these to a budget, usually on a monthly basis. The committee can then see whether the expenditure pattern is consistent with its own program priorities.

Two items are of importance here for the treasurer: the regular reports to the committee and the yearly budget in relation to which the monthly reports can be assessed. The treasurer often plays a key role in planning the budget. If the committee is a board of an organization, then the treasurer may chair a finance subcommittee that has the responsibility of considering the financial health of the corporation.

In recent years, the role of the treasurer (or other financial officer) has taken on added importance as the government has increased its oversight of profit and nonprofit (charitable) organizations and committees. Comprehensive and high-quality regular reports and third-party audits are becoming absolutely essential for most groups. Only the most informal committees and task groups are free from this obligation.

---

2. The minutes, and how they are to be taken, and who takes them, form one of the most sensitive points in committee life.

Issues and Problems

Because the officer structure is handled so differently in different commit-tees, and because there are wide variations in the expectations for various officer roles, two issues of critical importance are discussed here.

Purpose of the Officer Corps

Officers may be selected not only for recognized competence in per-forming specific tasks but also for a variety of personal and institutional rea-sons, including the desire to have various points of view represented in the decision-making group, pressures to have certain representation (by race, by sex, by age, by region, et cetera) in the officer corps, and so on. These various factors often serve to reduce the effectiveness of the committee as a whole and make task performance difficult for any incumbent selected for reasons other than competence to perform the role. A committee member may, for example, be doing an effective job of representing a constituency, one of the purposes for which he or she was elected, but an unsatisfactory job as trea-surer, his or her specific assignment. Consequently, committees may have to modify the number and responsibilities of officers in keeping with the inter-ests and talents of the office-holders. As an example, it may be prudent to appoint or elect an assistant treasurer with the requisite skills to support the member in the example.

This multiplicity of function extends to the nature of the roles the of-ficers play in relation to the chair and the membership. Some officers as secondary leaders find themselves mediating between the chair and the membership, while others function as advocates for particular groups. It be-comes very difficult for an officer to be both an advocate and a mediator, adding to the inherent role strain.

The Chair and the Officers

Implicit here is the need for the officers to understand the way the chair wants them to function and to come to some modus operandi that takes into account both the chair's view and their own. Chairpersons who have difficulty delegating responsibility create tensions for officers who seek clearly defined and specified areas in which to function. Conversely, chairs who assume that officers are going to carry out specific tasks will be disap-pointed when an officer assumes that the role is merely ceremonial and does not carry out assignments.

In many committees, the officer roles are steps to the role of chairper-son. If this is the case, then the purpose of the officer corps is, in part, to train potential chairpersons. This purpose informs and dictates some of the tasks the officers undertake, tasks that may deviate somewhat from a narrower conception of their role.

Conclusion

Officer roles are hard roles. They often serve multiple purposes, and there is frequently confusion and misunderstanding among the parties—the chair, the officers themselves, and the membership—with respect to the nature and types of duties to be performed and the relative priority to be accorded to specific tasks within an appropriate distribution of tasks. Perhaps most important for persons occupying these roles is to maintain an open process of clarification of expectations and assignments and thus hope to avoid misunderstanding.

CHAPTER 3
The Committee Member

Introduction

The committee member is the backbone of the committee process. He or she is the basic element of an effective committee. One may read about classic member types such as the "overparticipator," "strong, silent Sam," or "voluble Veronica," but as we indicated earlier, personality seems less important in most committees than well-defined and thoughtful participation in the committee process.

Many members are simply unclear about what it is they are expected to do, a problem surely complicated by the fact that the core of expectations and responsibilities varies to some extent from committee to committee.

Duties and Roles

In the broadest terms, the member has the same duties as the chair, though he or she does not play the same roles. The member should consider the purpose and character of the committee before agreeing to participate, and be willing to accept responsibility to prepare for meetings and participate appropriately. *Appropriate participation* refers not only to the need to both comment and be silent but also to achieving a proper balance between one's own interests and the mixed interests of other members. Finally, the member must be ready to perform, on occasion, a series of special duties and roles.

Membership Acceptance

The request to serve on a committee usually comes from the sponsoring body or the chairperson. If one has already been appointed, it is important that the new member become familiar with the sponsoring group, the mandate and/or past work of the committee, and its membership. Careful investigation initially may save considerable embarrassment later; it is easier and better to avoid getting onto a committee than to resign. One might wish to talk to other potential members or to people who are already members. One should be in general agreement with the selection of other members, since considerable time will be spent with them in committee work.

Newly organized committees are often more time-consuming for the member than established ones, since it takes time to clarify policies and procedures and for members to become acquainted. However, it seems, too, that new committees can be more receptive, for exactly these reasons, to the ideas and influences of the member.

One should consider the situation from the viewpoint of conflicts with other responsibilities. One source of conflict, of course, is time. As was mentioned in the case of the chairperson, a member should not accept a committee appointment unless he or she has time to fulfill the role. It is unfair to the chair and to the other committee persons if one retains formal membership yet is not able to function. There are other sources of conflict as well. The potential member may find himself or herself philosophically out of harmony with the operation and decisions of the committee. Some conflict over representation, a point discussed later in this chapter, may be experienced. And, despite the argument we make that personality is less important than commonly supposed, one may find that there are members on the committee with whom one simply cannot work harmoniously, or that differences among members are so excessive that the personal price of participation outweighs any potential benefits.

Meeting Preparation

Once a candidate has accepted membership on a committee, then he or she is obligated to prepare for meetings and to make the necessary arrangements for committee participation.

Schedule Time. The member should make it a responsibility to schedule adequate time to attend the meetings. Many members become careless about planning the time for meetings and are therefore continually suffering from schedule conflicts. Such a member may recognize himself or herself, and is recognized by others, as frequently complaining about not being aware of a meeting, not getting the notice, et cetera. One also needs to make some time available for special committee activity outside the actual meeting time. There may be special duties, the preparation of materials, conferences, and the like. The member who claims to be too busy to assist with such functions should resign.

Read Background Materials. Materials often sent out in advance of the meeting include the agenda, financial reports, and other program materials that should be carefully reviewed by the members. It is a basic responsibility of the members to read this material and to be prepared to discuss it at the meeting. When the committee is in session, it is unproductive, inconsiderate, and annoying for members to seek information covered in materials distributed by mail or discussed at meetings they have missed. Another key reason why the review of material is important is that, if a committee member wishes to influence the outcome of a particular issue, he or she needs the facts covered in the material. We have all seen situations in which members protested they had not noticed item X, or had not understood its implications, and asked for a postponement of action on the item. In many cases, they were taken by surprise because they had not read the material. As a member, one cannot expect to achieve and retain respect and influence unless one does the necessary homework.

Submit Written Comments. Additionally, the material or the items for the meeting may be such that a member would like to make a more extensive and formal comment than can be made through verbal participation at the meeting. Detailed technical information may be needed to elaborate a point. Often such information is not readily available or would take too long to present. It is helpful and proper for a member to prepare written memos in such instances. Should one wish to submit such a memo, it is courteous to inform the chairperson in advance.

Comments submitted in memo form should be distributed to the members in advance of the meeting. It is very distracting for committee members to attempt to read extensive material as the meeting is going on.

Meeting Participation

One of the basic responsibilities of a member of a committee is to make a contribution at the committee meetings. It is surprising how often members either make no contribution to facilitate the work of the committee or behave in such a manner as to actually retard the committee's progress. Many times this situation occurs because people do not understand and observe the simple rules of meeting participation.

Participate Appropriately. Each member needs to be sensitive to his or her own level of participation. This level, of course, will vary somewhat with meeting topics and member mood. Nonetheless, some members regularly underparticipate—and never comment; some members overparticipate—and always comment. There are members who are always bringing up business not germane to the topic being discussed, others who regularly cite

reasons for not acting on issues, some who seize every opportunity to deni-
grate the ideas of others, and so on. Constant self-appraisal is important on
the part of the member to assure participation in an open and moderate
manner that will optimize the smooth functioning of the committee. Too
much participation often results in diminished influence, and so, of course,
does too little participation. Within a small-group context, the silent member
is generally viewed as a negative and hostile member, simply as a result of
the silence. Such a member has little effect on the decision-making process.

Aid in Committee Process. The aim of the committee process is to
make good decisions. The member should attempt to assist the committee
in two ways: by helping the committee make each decision as quickly and
fairly as possible, and by assuring that the best possible decision is made.
Members, like the chairperson, will sense when the discussion of an issue
begins to deteriorate. That point may be the one at which a decision can and
should be made. Alternatively, it may be that a suggestion to table the matter
until the next meeting, to appoint a subcommittee to provide additional information, or some other action, would be appropriate. The member should
try to be sensitive to the "drama" or "theater" of the committee process and
to take advantage of key moments to make suggestions that will move the
process along. This action is, of course, difficult to take if the issue under
discussion happens to be one in which particular members have a special
interest. In that case, such members may not act in the best interests of the
committee; they want their own judgment to prevail. In such situations, other
members should feel free to intervene on behalf of the committee's best interests. Members must understand that good committee process is not all up
to the chair.

Apart from making procedural suggestions that aid in issue resolution,
members need to be helpful in making substantive suggestions that aid in
achieving decisions of highest quality. Such suggestions often involve providing additional information or obtaining the opinion of those to be affected
by the decision. It may mean rejecting a compromise when such a solution
is clearly not in the best interests of the committee or the larger community.
On the other hand, a decision delayed is not always a decision of high quality; sometimes delay is simply a way of attempting to avoid making a difficult
decision.

Perhaps the best illustration of the kind of contribution we have in
mind comes from the rather well-known incident in the Cuban missile crisis,
in which the special-action committee formed by President Kennedy had
two messages from Premier Khrushchev—an earlier, more favorable one,
and a later, less favorable one. Robert F. Kennedy, then attorney general,
made the suggestion that the second message be ignored. This brilliant con-

ceptual stroke permitted agreement to be reached.[1] This is the kind of contribution that yields high-quality decisions.

Special Assignments and Responsibilities

One of the duties of a member is to perform his or her share of special assignments and responsibilities. Sometimes the special duty is ongoing, such as holding an office other than the chair or chairing a standing committee. At other times, the member accepts assignments of a shorter term—perhaps as head of a special-purpose subcommittee or representative of the committee at some special function.

In the event that the member holds an office, he or she has special responsibilities for attendance and the performance of roles. Officers, of course, have regular reporting and informational responsibilities at meetings, as indicated in the previous chapter. Nothing is more annoying to a committee than to have an officer who does not attend or is unprepared. The committee may require particular information and input from an officer in the course of deliberations; without it, decisions often have to be delayed.

Members may also undertake other special duties for the committee. Such duties may consist of serving on subcommittees, assisting with the preparation and distribution of reports, or acting as a subcommittee of one to investigate and report on particular issues.[2] These are tasks every member should be willing to perform in roughly the same proportion as other members. However, committees usually have unbalanced participation. Competent members interested in the improved functioning of the committee will always be doing more than the deadwood. Often the chair needs to provide active leadership in making assignments rather than relying on volunteers to perform the work of the committee. Despite such intervention, there will be those who are unwilling either to work or to leave, and the contribution of members will remain uneven. Nevertheless, balanced participation in the committee process should be a priority objective.

When a member accepts a special assignment, it is his or her responsibility to carry it out with dispatch. We are only too familiar with the

---

1. The explanation for the two messages may never be fully known. In "The Missiles of October," a television special dealing with the incident, the interpretation was made that the two messages resulted from tensions in the central committee of the USSR. Khrushchev sent one message without informing the committee, and they, hearing of this, sent another, in his name, but with their content! An interesting bit of committee process.

2. We might note here that the single-person subcommittee is one of the most useful and least used techniques. When the chair wants information presented or key issues of a topic placed into perspective, it is frequently the case that a single person can perform this role more expeditiously than two or more.

joiner and the perennial volunteer who make themselves available for every task, who reject no request, but who complete no task and fulfill no request. It appears to be a sort of passive resistance—an inability to say no and an inability to produce results. The same rule that applies to committee membership as a whole also applies to special services and tasks: *If you can't complete the assignment, don't accept it.*

There are, of course, times when an assignment gets out of hand, when it is just not possible to complete the required task in the assigned time. In that event, one should discuss the matter with the chair in terms of alternative courses of action. One should be sure of two points here, however—first, that the delay is due to the nature of the task rather than to foot dragging; and second, that the difficulties are in the task assigned rather than in the personal conceptions of the task developed by the subcommittee.

This possibility—the complication and diversion of subcommittee assignments—is one of the good reasons why the chair and the subcommittee, or at least the subcommittee chairperson, should meet regularly. A continual monitoring is important to assure that the definition of the task and the course of action being taken around that definition are appropriate to the mandate of the full committee.

Provide General Feedback

One role a committee member plays, and one that can be misused quite easily, is that of providing general feedback to the committee about the way it and its activities are being perceived by special constituencies and the larger community. This information is vital if the committee is to properly modulate its behavior in relation to other community groups. And there is no assumption here that any member is especially representing community A or community B. Rather, it is simply a case of each member endeavoring to keep the committee as well-informed as possible.

In the process, however, individual members have the obligation to reflect accurately the context within which information is provided to the committee. Members should not report only information that is favorable to the postures they support, nor should they represent the feedback as more serious or more or less broad-ranging than they know it to be. Other committee members should be aware that certain members might mask their own views in quasi-accurate reports.

Responsibility, Loyalty, Discretion

By virtue of membership on the committee, each member shares responsibility for the actions of the committee. This responsibility obtains even in the painful event that the committee receives some public "heat" for actions that the particular member opposed within committee session.[3] In this situation, one is sorely tempted to disavow responsibility and to claim opposition to the action and thus freedom from blame. This diminishing of responsibility is justifiable only when a member has requested that his or her opposition be recorded or when one has resigned immediately after some objectionable action. When such a step is taken, there is a clean disassociation from the particular action, and one cannot be held responsible. Otherwise, members must try to explain the rationale for the committee's decisions.

Committee responsibility shades into the matter of committee loyalty. In the case of responsibility, we are referring to some specific action that has caused dissension in the wider community. In the case of loyalty, we are referring to the general disposition of an individual member toward the work of the committee. Some members are forever complaining about committee activities, other members, the chairperson, and committee decisions. It is almost as if they were not members of the committee. And, although they do not realize it, some of their own criticism of others does indeed rub off on them. It is not being suggested here that a member is not free to openly and candidly air a point of view on issues, policies, and procedures—within the committee. When in public, however, one should actively support the committee. A member who feels misled and is in disagreement with the committee's purposes or operation should resign immediately. Such a resignation may be discreet, or it may be made publicly to dramatize the problems.

Discretion is essential, not only in situations of loyalty but in all matters of committee business. What one reveals of committee business to others is usually a matter of judgment. Sometimes, especially in personnel and finance committees, items of delicacy and importance are discussed that have great personal significance to others. Matters of personal problems, promotions, salary, and competence may come into the discussion. Committees may also deal with plans for land, et cetera, information about which would be very advantageous to certain interests. In such situations, the chair should make it clear that the discussion is confidential and no information about the discussion is to be shared with others. The more difficult problems, in a sense, occur at the level of serious but less than completely confidential information. If a member has any uncertainty about such matters, he or she should ask the committee about the level of confidentiality of material to clarify the question for all.

The dilemma is that committees often want to provide their publics with some ongoing sense of what is happening, yet are not able to be candid

---

3. One exception here, and in some other aspects of the member's responsibility, is the elected committee made up of people of partisan identification.

and open. Hence, the committee may appear to be withholding information about its work from the community or from special elements of the community. Committee members who refuse to discuss any business are as problematic for the committee as those who discuss all the business. Both the "clam" and the "blabberer" need to use more judgment about what information they release and in what form. We wish we could specify the question of judgment more concretely in a way that would be helpful and nontautological—but the course of discretion really comes down to using one's head and considering the well-being of the committee and the community before talking.

It is often the case that the very times when people want to know "what's going on" are also the times when the member feels least able to tell them. That is why, on a general basis, the committee member should give thought in advance to the nature of the discussion to be had with outsiders about committee business, especially in regard to sensitive issues. Such forethought pays great dividends, especially if the press is clamoring for a statement as the committee leaves the committee room. And although the situations most of us encounter are seldom dramatic, many members and chairpersons become very "uptight" when a reporter calls or a TV newsperson asks for an interview. Such feelings can be minimized by anticipating such situations and preparing oneself.

Discretion applies not only to comments made to outsiders but to comments by members inside the meeting. Despite the position we have taken here, a member would be well-advised to assume that there will be at least one member on every committee who will be indiscreet. Even in the most confidential situations, memos and remarks are likely to be leaked, especially if they are on sensitive issues. Thus, comments, oral or written, especially personal ones, should be made carefully. Internal and external discretion go a long way toward making committee work proceed smoothly.

Issues and Problems

The member role is a difficult one. There are many conflicting pressures, loyalties, and constituencies. Some of these conflicts are more regular than others.

Representation

The member must ascertain who or what is being represented. Is it the member only? Does he or she have a constituency through election by or membership in some other group? Is he or she being asked to be a liaison between this committee and some other committee? Does he or she typify a particular group or point of view that is important in the community? More attention will be given to this point later, in the chapter on elected versus appointed committees. Suffice it to say now that the individual member may be "representing" multiple constituencies. Some of these linkages may involve formal arrangements, in that the member assumed this position as an official representative of a constituency and is expected to report back to it at regular intervals. Although the practice is not too common, a member is sometimes instructed by his or her constituency as to what position to take and how to vote. At other times linkages with constituencies are informal and require only the most casual reports from the member.

In any case, the matter of representation is consistently an issue. Generally, this problem seems to be solved if members take the position that they are independent. They profess to listen to their constituencies but are not obligated to be controlled by them, unless formally instructed otherwise, and act on the basis of their own best judgment.

Multiple Memberships and Roles

Committee activity is complicated by the fact that each member plays multiple roles and has multiple duties, within the committee itself and between that committee and other committees. In the committee itself, the member role may be made more difficult if one also seeks to fill a role as representative of a particular interest or point of view. Indeed, some chairpersons will seek to neutralize the cutting edge of a member's view by placing that member in a role that requires neutrality.

Many members, of course, serve on several committees simultaneously. Often their roles and duties in these several committees are different: a member in one committee may be a chairperson in another committee, a staff person in a third committee, and a secretary in still a fourth committee. Various types of confusion can result from these multiple roles, as well as from one's social and economic relationships with other members or interested parties. As we noted in Chapter 1, a common problem is the psychological difficulty of making swift role changes, such as going from a meeting in which one is chairperson to another in which one is a member. If such a member behaves at the second meeting as if he or she were the chairperson, carrying out a previous pattern of activity, the behavior is inappropriate. To make matters worse, this behavior is often unrecognized by the member in question. Other types of inappropriate behavior resulting from fuzzy role separation may be more obvious. One should be alert and, as indicated before, should continuously monitor one's own committee behavior.

A third type of multiple role confusion occurs when a member has several different constituencies, each clamoring to dominate his or her behavior. Constituencies are often split over goals, with situations arising in which the goals are mutually exclusive. Additionally, even when constituencies agree upon goals and purposes, they will frequently disagree on strategies for goal achievement. As an example, some African American groups endorse hiring quotas as a viable strategy to achieve equal employment opportunities, while others reject the concept.

Role Parameters

The difficulties that members encounter in the management of multiple roles raise another difficult problem with which all members must cope. What are the effective parameters on membership? While one cannot resign after every defeat, neither can one stay on under any and all conditions. Should a member block movement on one issue that otherwise would be deemed good as a "trade" for committee support on some other matter of importance? How long should one push a point when it is clear that the committee is not interested in pursuing that particular line, yet the member feels that it is of utmost importance?

There are no guidelines here. Readers have doubtless all experienced (with frustration) the member who is always threatening to quit if this or that does not happen—sort of the committee version of a suicide threat. Yet occasionally issues do develop in which the member wants to make clear how strongly he or she feels. Only a general sensitivity to these problems can be recommended here, along with the more specific suggestion that such serious reactions must not occur too frequently.

The Inadequate Chairperson

One of the situations difficult for the member, especially for one who takes committee activity seriously, is that involving an inadequate chairperson. The best efforts of the member will usually come to naught if the chair is not handling the committee properly. Unfortunately, this is a situation in which little can be changed until it is time for a new chairperson to be elected or appointed. It does suggest that members pay special attention to the "elevation" of someone to the chair.

In such a situation, assistance to the chair is possible. One might suggest that an associate chair be developed, and specifically plan for that person to assist the chairperson. Sometimes the assignment of a staff person may be helpful. Sometimes a member or members can perform more tasks and facilitate the committee process. One should not assume, however, that simply because someone is performing poorly in a role, he or she does not enjoy that role and secure a measure of psychic nutrition from it. On the contrary, one might speculate that the poorer the role performance the more committed an incumbent is to remaining in position (since it is likely to be that person's only opportunity!). To remove such a person is generally difficult;

climbing Mount Everest is likely to be speedier. We recommend, rather, working with the committee and the chair, as difficult a process as that is, to enhance committee functioning with an eye toward achieving a more able replacement.

Conclusion

Proper role performance by committee members is one of the keys to successful committee work. Yet too often members give no thought to the nature of their responsibilities, what conflicts might exist within the performance of those responsibilities, or how they are carrying out those responsibilities. This chapter has outlined several key areas to which members should pay attention and outlined as well some of the ways in which role performance might be improved. Despite the very best efforts of members, much continues to depend upon the chair, and, if the committee has one, the staff person. Yet the members' activities are crucial, as anyone who has ever chaired a meeting knows, to the smooth or fractious functioning of a committee.

CHAPTER 4

The Staff Person

Introduction

If the committee has a staff person, that individual, like the chairperson, has a major responsibility for the effective functioning of the committee. A staff person is one who is employed to assist the committee in its work. A large and well-financed committee may have a staff person paid directly from committee funds who has no other work responsibilities. His or her office is the office of the committee. When the work of the committee ends, the staff person seeks other paid employment. More common is the situation where a committee staff person works for an agency—a planning agency, a community organization agency, a labor union, an industrial or business firm. In such cases, the parent agency assigns one of its employees to be a staff person for a committee as one part of his or her regular job. Sometimes such committees are internal to the organization and a part of its regular functioning. Planning and community organization agencies are in the business of forming committees, and part of their function as an organization is to staff these committees. Business firms may need staff for internal committees, or they may assign an employee to serve as a staff person for some community-type committee as a good-will gesture to the community.

However the arrangement develops, and we will mention some of the more difficult peculiarities later, the result is a committee with a staff person. It is important to have a job description for a staff person and important that the person employed for the position possess the necessary qualifications to perform effectively. The chairperson must know how to use the services of such a person, and the committee must know what to expect in the way of leadership and assistance from a staff person. If these requirements are met, committee functioning will be vastly improved. If not, problems can be created that will hamper the successful functioning of the committee more than absence of staff assistance would have.

Duties and Roles

The duties and roles of the staff person are many and varied: resource person, consultant, technician, catalyst, enabler, leader, implementer, analyst, and tactician. In general, his or her role is to support and not supplant the roles of the chairperson and other committee members. The range of tasks a staff person will be called upon to perform depends upon how adequately the chair and other committee members perform, the scope and complexity of the committee assignment, the particular phase of the committee activity, the kinds of problems the committee encounters, et cetera. The staff person is a "balance weight" in terms of committee movement and quality of performance. He or she tries to help committee members—especially the chair—to carry out responsibilities, and, to the extent that they falter, tries to compensate for their shortcomings.

Many differently qualified persons are called upon to serve as committee staff. As previously mentioned, within the areas of planning and urban development, agencies assign their employees to committees, and such assignment is part of their work. Industry, too, has developed this pattern and assigned administrative aides to committees within the company or outside. The complexity of the staff role and the lack of preparation for it make it essential that staff and committee members alike understand the requirements detailed in the ensuing discussion.

Policy Loyalty

By *policy loyalty* we mean that a staff member cannot act in ways that are contrary to the letter or spirit of the committee's mission. There will be numerous occasions when a staff person, largely because of access to information, could sabotage the committee's efforts. Such actions as "leaks," premature disclosure of decisions, partial reporting, and selective collection of information are but a few of the techniques through which a staff person can lead the committee in his or her direction rather than help the group to make its own decision. And it sometimes takes time for even the most experienced and astute chairperson to realize what is happening.

This activity is improper. A staff person must be loyal to those whose mission and role he or she services. If such loyalty cannot be provided, one should decline the assignment, or resign. As staff person, advantage should not be taken of the position to covertly embellish or to accomplish personal policy preferences. This person can, as we will discuss, have opportunities available to make his or her policy preferences known. If serious policy differences do develop between the staff person and the general thrust of the committee, then discussion with the chair at the earliest possible time is essential.

Available Time

Frequently it is difficult to estimate the amount of staff time required by a committee. Unanticipated developments increase the most careful estimates. This underscores the necessity for a staff member to have a clear understanding with his or her administrative superiors and with the chairperson regarding the amount of staff time available for the committee project. Such communication helps to keep committee activity from overextending itself and also minimizes misunderstandings.

The amount of staff time available for a committee project often affects the quality of the committee's performance. Therefore, every effort should be made by staff to make realistic estimates of what is required.

Aide to the Chairperson

One of the most basic and important roles of the staff person is as an aide to the chairperson. Initially and regularly thereafter, the staff person should meet with the chair to develop a mutual understanding of the task and approaches, to clarify and coordinate each other's efforts, and to assure unity and support in carrying out the committee mission.

At the initial meeting, the staff person should help clarify the purpose of the committee and background factors leading to the committee's creation. Staff should also outline possible approaches to the assignment and the range of tasks to be undertaken, as well as the time that may be required on the part of the chairperson and other committee members. Staff members often have an opportunity to exercise some influence in the selection of committee members. If the committee has already been appointed, the staff person can share with the chair whatever information he or she has about the interests and talents of those who will serve on the committee.

In general, the objective of such an initial meeting or meetings is to begin to develop a mutual understanding about how responsibilities will be divided between the chair and staff person, and how the chair wants the committee to function.

Assistance to Committee Members

Staff should also be available to assist committee members. Members often need additional information or clarification of substantive matters, or they may want to get reactions to ideas they have or proposals they might make. When members carry special assignments or are a part of a subcommittee, the staff person should provide the same type of assistance he or she would provide to the chairperson.

Caution and good judgment must be exercised here because the requests of particular committee members often extend beyond the scope of committee activities and make excessive demands upon staff time. A safeguard is to clear questionable matters with the chairperson.

Support of the Committee Process

The committee process includes not only all mechanics and logistics related to the committee meeting but also all the dynamics of the process, i.e., the advance preparation, the meeting itself, and the follow-through. The staff person is crucial to every phase of the process. The duties range from the most menial and routine to the most delicate, sensitive, and complex.

The mechanics of a meeting include the notification of members, the adequacy and comfort of the meeting space, seating arrangements, supplies, props, materials for distribution, name tags, and parking. Such details are usually handled by several people. However, the staff person should monitor the operation and make certain that all these mechanics that add to the smooth functioning of the committee have been done adequately.

The importance of the agenda and the thought given to its preparation cannot be overemphasized. The staff person is usually in a key position to prepare a tentative agenda for review by the chairperson. Consideration must be given to—

1. any directives that evolved from a previous meeting;
2. readiness and timeliness for submission of reports;
3. strategy relative to discussion or action on a particular item;
4. time available relative to the items that need attention;
5. estimated amount of time various items will require;
6. availability of committee members who occupy special roles in relation to items that may be discussed;
7. the arrangement of the items on the agenda.

After the agenda has been set in cooperation with the chair, the staff person must make certain the agenda and necessary supporting material are mailed or delivered to members in ample time for thoughtful review. Whenever possible, an agenda should be distributed one week in advance of the meeting.

The committee meeting itself is the crucible in which various elements come into contact with each other—where the participants try to intensify interests, or reduce conflicting interests, or develop consensus. Here is where the staff person's knowledge and skill in group dynamics come into play. But the role must be that of assisting and complementing the chairperson, who should play the key role in this process. The chair should provide direct leadership, while the staff person gives indirect leadership. The staff person should not be a vigorous participant, but rather one who facilitates participation by committee members. He or she should help to make certain that information is adequately and accurately presented and help to articulate ways of approaching issues that will assist the committee to make decisions.

An important input at committee meetings is the presentation of progress and informational reports. This is sometimes done by committee members, but often staff must assist members in the preparation of the reports and, in their absence, present the reports. One must be careful not to have pride of authorship in these reports to the extent of becoming defensive when committee members begin to suggest changes.

The keeping of a record of the meeting is usually a responsibility of the staff person. Even where there is a secretary, the staff person might be requested to prepare a rough draft for the secretary's review, or requested by the secretary to review the minutes. This means the staff person must be certain to have a record of the main points of view presented and an understanding of any recommendations or directives for action. Minutes of meetings are a very important part of any organization's records and should receive careful attention from the staff person.

Finally, there are always details, suggestions, or actions during the meeting that require follow-through. Sometimes the chairperson assigns tasks to committee members, but more often these tasks fall to the staff person. In any event, the staff person should monitor the follow-through to make sure assignments are completed.

Fact Finding, Analysis, Synthesis, and Presentation

The quality of a committee's performance is often related to the adequacy of the available information related to the problem or issue under consideration, and to how well this information is understood. The task of gathering, analyzing, and synthesizing a vast array of information and finally presenting it, in both written and oral reports, is usually carried by the staff person. Knowledge, skill, and experience all come into play at this point. The staff person must know (1) what data to collect, where and how to get it; (2) how to analyze and synthesize it so as to provide sound, objective insight into the question; and (3) how to present it in a clear, understandable, and concise manner that will facilitate the committee's work.

The supplying of information pervades the entire committee process.

It can range from brief memos to very elaborate reports; it can be just for the chairperson or for subcommittees, or it can be for the committee as a whole. It is a role that committee chair and members expect a staff person to perform and in which staff members have the opportunity to make one of their most significant contributions.

Issues and Problems

The role of the staff person is a difficult one for many reasons. It involves managing many diverse relationships. It is, without question, very demanding in terms of time and effort. In the following paragraphs, we shall cite some key areas of repeated difficulty that complicate the role of a staff person.

Maintaining a Balanced Role

The key to successful performance of staff roles and duties is balance, and three types of balance are often troublesome: (1) between staff and chair, (2) among staff, chair, and the committee, and (3) among multiple staff roles.

Staff and Chair. The division of labor we mentioned earlier is often difficult to maintain in the face of day-to-day operating problems. Ultimately it is a question of judgment. On the one hand, the staff wants and needs a certain freedom to carry out assignments and duties. On the other hand, the chairperson has a right and need to know how things are progressing. While the staff person cannot check everything with the chair, staff should not go too far without clearance. A good working relationship will usually produce guidelines in this regard. Such guidelines must be developed and modified to fit different situations and different casts of characters.

Staff, Chair, and Committee. One of the most delicate tasks of the staff person is to follow the direction of the chair without jeopardizing the prerogatives of the committee. Such a situation can occur initially if the chair outlines an extensive program of work for the staff person that has not been approved, in broad outline, by the committee. Or it can occur if the staff person is directed by the chair not to pursue something the committee as a whole has decided to undertake. Sometimes a chairperson may seek to "use" a staff person in areas of disagreement with the committee. In such situations, the staff person must tactfully indicate when assignments need the approval of the committee as a whole and, if directed not to undertake an assignment, should make certain that the chair reports that the assignment was disregarded at the direction of the chair. One should keep in mind that, while direction is given to the staff by the chair, the responsibility is to the committee as a whole. There is no simple way of escaping such situations, but one should be aware that they can arise. As with most other problems, they are more difficult to deal with the more involved one becomes. The chair should, of course, keep its own interests and the interests of the committee in view and in balance. This is equally true for the staff person. Generally, however, the staff person accepts the direction of the chair with minimum comment and "hassle."

Multiple Staff Roles. Through all phases of committee work, the staff person must be mindful of the differences among acting *on behalf of* the committee, acting *for* the committee, and acting *as* the committee. Generally, a staff person should never presume to speak *as* a committee member or to behave in such a way that such an interpretation could be made. Aggressive staff on prime committees sometimes misuse their position to usurp the committee's rights and responsibilities by making predictions about committee action, providing interpretations about committee mood, making analyses of committee behavior, and even commenting on specific members, while outlining what they believe the agenda of the committee should be, et cetera. At the other extreme is the committee staff person who feels the need to check every action with the chairperson and make no comment about anything without such clearance.

Acting *on behalf of* the committee and acting *for* the committee differ slightly. When a staff person is acting on behalf of a committee, he or she is acting under explicit instructions to engage in some action. Usually these instructions will appear in the committee minutes. When a staff person is acting for the committee, he or she is acting without explicit instructions but under general permission or, preferably, under agreed-upon guidelines. The staff person should be careful, in acting for the committee, not to leave the impression of acting on behalf of the committee. Often staff exceed their authority in this way by using the prestige and influence of the committee as a means of securing cooperation from those they believe will otherwise be recalcitrant. Here, as elsewhere, it is a question of using good judgment, once one is aware of the potential pitfalls.

Participation in Meetings

Another difficult area for a staff person is the level and style of participation in the meeting itself. We have noted that the staff person has a crucial role to play at meetings, but the way this role is carried out is subject to a good deal of variability. Some committees seem to assume that the staff person is just like another committee member; others actually assume that he or she is more than a member and ranks as the custodian of committee purpose and mores. Still other committees expect that the staff person will say nothing except in response to a direct question. Again, questions of judgment are involved. We do caution against the extreme in which staff people take argumentative postures in relation to committee members. In the final analysis, the staff person is an assistant to, not a member of, the committee.

Part of the difficulty is that the staff person usually comes to know the committee business and activities more thoroughly than the members do. The committee may actually treat such a person as an executive director rather than an executive secretary (staff assistant). The difference between these two terms has diminished somewhat over the years, with executive becoming a noun and the designation of executive secretary falling into disuse. Yet the term *executive secretary* does indicate most of the features of the general role of the staff person and suggests an active, but reserved, demeanor. The executive director role, on the other hand, has distinctive differences, including more prestige, authority, and freedom to act.

Level of Tasks

As executive secretary or staff assistant to the committee, the staff person performs a wide range of duties, the more essential of which we have suggested in this chapter. The difficulty lies in the fact that some of the more important duties from the viewpoint of helping the committee to function are, in fact, relatively meaningless from the viewpoint of one's sense of self. Arriving early to be sure the room is open and the chairs arranged hardly seems a fulfilling activity or, in modern argot, "meaningful work." In itself, of course, it is not. The meaning derives from the importance of this task to the smooth functioning of the committee.

The problem is that some staff balk at these essential tasks and either neglect them or ask someone lower in the organizational hierarchy, usually clerical personnel, to perform them. The staff person should remember that calling members, arranging for refreshments, and moving chairs are not the most exciting jobs, and clerks will not find them any more fulfilling than the staff. Yet these tasks must be done well, and, while they may at some points be delegated, it is often more appropriate for the staff person to handle them personally.

Conclusion

In this chapter, we have tried to present the role requisites of the staff member assigned to assist the committee in carrying out its responsibilities. Additionally, we have sought to clarify what some of the elements of good staff work involve. Our view of the role of the staff person, it seems clear, would not be acceptable to more "aggressively" oriented staff. Generally, we believe that staff persons should seek to clarify, and then carry out, the wishes of the committee. Inevitably, a good staff person will have an effect on the committee's concept of its mission and role. This is as it should be. The committee expects the staff person to make this kind of contribution. However, we do not expect that the staff person will use this channel of influence to develop, under committee aegis, private and personal conceptions of mission and role.

This perhaps sounds a little like the committed public servant with a "passion for anonymity" waiting for the "politics" to be finished so the "administration" can begin. We hope the substance of the text does not support this view. We argue for an active and involved staff, a staff sensitive to both the opportunities and the constraints that organizations, committees, and assignments present.

CHAPTER 5

The Executive and the Board

Introduction

One staff role is very common and yet so filled with uncertainties and questions that a separate chapter seems warranted. The role is that of the executive (executive director, executive vice-president)—in particular, the executive as he or she works with a board of directors or trustees.

In organizational literature, there is a good deal of material on "administrative" roles and on the role of the "boss." Much of this literature ignores the fact that the ultimate boss, the "chief executive," in many cases has a board of directors to whom he or she is responsible and must report with regularity. The board is the legally responsible unit of the organization. Although it may meet only occasionally, it is responsible for setting the key policy course for the organization. Unless there is a clear understanding and agreement about the roles and responsibilities of the board and the staff, there will inevitably be friction and undue delays in the transaction of business. Basic policy differences between a board and its executive occasionally occur. However, it is our contention that the vast majority of differences between a board and its executive result from role confusion. Too often executives attempt to make or manipulate policy, and too often boards attempt to administer an organization's policies.

Duties and Roles

The executive has all the responsibilities to a board that a staff person has to a committee, with some differences in tone and emphasis. First of all, the executive is assumed by the board to have a high professional stature in both

41

administrative and substantive areas. Secondly, the executive has somewhat greater freedom in handling issues that come to the board. He or she is responsible for alerting the board to potential problems and policy issues before they become crises. Thirdly, the executive is both entitled and expected to make a case for those things he or she believes are proper on the basis of professional knowledge and values. In this sense, the executive is much more of a "resident expert" in the board meeting than the staff member is in a general committee meeting. Fourthly, the executive is responsible for "working with" the board, for assisting the board to act appropriately in the ongoing life of the organization. This often involves drawing upon the specialized knowledge and experience of board members in specific situations. An executive has a responsibility to increase the understanding of board members about the organization's purposes and programs and role in the larger community. This requires a good working knowledge of the members, their talents and special interests. Lastly, the executive is responsible, along with the chairperson of the board, for the development of a working relationship between the executive corps and the board as a whole.

Professional Presentation

Each executive is not only a process manager, as is true of all staff persons, but also a substantive specialist in a program area of relevance to the organization, e.g., public health, urban planning, public welfare. The board of directors expects that the executive will provide policy leadership in the appropriate substantive area. If the organization is a business firm, then the board expects the executive to know the business, to be alert to developing trends, and to make suggestions and proposals to the board in line with his or her assessment of these trends. As professionals, most executives have access to professional publications, conferences, national meetings, and the like, which should serve to keep them abreast of current professional developments. An executive should have adequate professional contacts to provide the organization with a broadly based information network.

The executive is expected not only to be an informed professional, but, in some areas, to be or become a leading professional. Agencies and firms benefit from executives who are considered leaders in their fields. Some of the executive's time—and it is always difficult to determine the proper proportion—is spent in what might be called purely professional activities. Such activities have payoff for the organization through improved programs and the establishment of new and innovative projects in the firm or agency itself.

Alerting the Board to Policy Issues

By their nature, boards are usually external in their focus. Board members tend to think of the agency in terms of how it affects the larger community and how issues important in the larger community affect the organization. They are less alert to professional issues, or issues developing internally. Unless a board is "directed," it rarely spends much time thinking about the internal problems of the agency. Even the best board member, even the best president, simply does not have the intimate knowledge of events as they impinge on the daily life of the organization that the executive possesses. They have the advantage of a broader perspective.

It is therefore helpful to the board members if the executive presents problems and policy issues for their consideration in the formative phase rather than the crisis phase. It is always difficult to make decisions in a crisis. The executive needs to anticipate those matters that are likely to require the board's attention and action and bring them to the board at the earliest possible time. Sometimes it is best for the executive to set up a regular review schedule for standard policies. One rule of thumb is that, within a seven-year cycle, all major policies should be reviewed. Sometimes this review means that the same policy is retained; sometimes minor changes are made; often chaotic surgery is required—but the routine review at least provides the chance for thoughtful scrutiny.

At other times, the review is not so routine. As relevant matters come up in the larger environment, it is the responsibility of the executive to be alert to them, bring together what information he can, and present it to the board. It is preferable if such matters can be reviewed in a written memo that is distributed to the board, unless the matter is so very sensitive or complex that the executive decides to organize a formal presentation at a board meeting.

An executive can alert a board to probable or impending problems in a number of informal ways. The executive can call to the attention of the board articles in news media or professional journals; he or she can, with the permission of the chair, invite experts to make presentations on particular topics at board meetings. Sometimes such experts are staff, or board members. Sometimes representatives of other organizations with competence bearing on a particular subject may be invited to meet with the board. In some cases the executive has a technical advisory committee in addition to the board, and items may come to the board through the chairperson of that committee, and so on. It is simply important for the executive to realize that, in this role, unlike other staff roles the executive may be playing or have played, he or she has much more responsibility to be proactive with respect to salient issues.

Making a Case

As the preceding chapter makes clear, it is our opinion that the behavior of the staff person in the meeting situation should be circumspect and reserved. Staff may occasionally offer some helpful suggestion, and more experienced staff may venture an opinion, but this opinion should not be pressed to any degree. This relationship changes markedly in the executive/board relationship. The executive has more latitude in pressing points, and indeed should press them. One reason he or she is the agency's top person is professional competence. Hence, when making a policy recommendation for consideration and action by the board, the executive has every reason to assume that his or her judgment will be treated with respect even if not supported in every instance.

For favorable action to occur, in addition to enjoying the respect of the board for personal competence and judgment, an executive must exercise discretion. To maintain credibility, he or she must restrict policy recommendations to the important issues. Too many executives, or staff for that matter, become involved in debates over issues that are not crucial or even important. Then it's almost like the boy who cried wolf: when they have a recommendation they do consider vital, the board may treat it lightly.

With the condition that recommendations are occasional and nontrivial, the executive can press a point more vigorously, and at greater length, than can the regular staff person. The executive may not always win the point, and only a judgment in the situation can dictate whether additional argument, compromise, a motion to table, or a loss is then the appropriate course of action. Strong and well-informed boards will expect executives to take stands on key issues, just as they will expect their executives to accept the final board decision. When policy differences between a board and its executive become frequent and serious and mutual respect deteriorates, resignation or discharge must be considered.

Working with the Board

There is, overall, a strong sense in which the executive "works with" the board, as a partner and colleague in advancing the interests of the organization, with almost the full rights and privileges of membership. What the executive does not have in the fullness of membership, he or she has in additional information and the ability to actively lead the organization on a particular course of action, often with only minimal checks and balances. However, it must always be kept in mind that the partnership is, ultimately, asymmetrical. The board is first among equals. In the final analysis, it is the board that has the authority to hire and fire and to make promotions and give raises to the executive.

Deserving of additional comment is the fact that an action taken by an executive can in effect commit the organization and the board to a course of action that has not been thoroughly discussed or approved. This is often a source of difficulty between the executive and the board. Because of day-to-day involvement in affairs and events, the executive is often called upon to indicate the board's position regarding a community problem, or to say whether or not the organization can do something. The executive's relationship with the board should be such that he or she can accurately interpret the board's position. Some issues, such as problems regarding the implementation of policy, are properly the executive's responsibility. Other issues clearly require board consideration and action. There is a large middle or gray area, however, in which it is unclear how far the executive can go before board approval is required. The executive should avoid having too many situations develop in which he or she is in essence asking the board to ratify decisions already made.

Potential problems can be minimized or prevented if the executive has done adequate homework in bringing up potential issues for board discussion before actual decisions are made. In that way he or she can get the "feel" of the board's position on an issue. And it is rare that matters of great importance develop overnight. In the event they do, the executive should confer with the chairperson and the executive committee for guidance.

Board Development and Education

Every executive accepts as part of his or her responsibility the area of staff development and education. Staff are provided with a variety of programs to encourage the development of skills and to enhance their usefulness and commitment to the agency's purposes and program. Executives often forget, however, that similar efforts need to go on at the board level. While the executive does not appoint the board, he or she can be on the alert for people who would make good board members and might seek to involve such people in other committees and services of the organization in order to give them some exposure to the agency and assess whether the initial impressions about them are correct. And indeed, organizations should have, and the executive should create, an "infrastructure" of positions and committees through which volunteers can gain experience and work their way to the board. We call this process board development, in the sense that the executive is developing a pool of people from which board members can be chosen. It is surprising how many organizations have a completely inadequate procedure for recruiting new members to the board.

A second phase of the process, already implicit in the initial phase, is the education of members of the board. Each member should be aware of the mission and role of the agency, its resources, and the problems it is fac-

ing. Some may regard this process as "socialization" or (even worse!) cooptation. Perhaps in a sense it is just that. These words, however, need not be
negative. Every board member, to fully participate, must be knowledgeable
about the purposes and program of the organization. Such knowledge never
implies that all will speak with a single mind. Should that happen, it is likely
that the board needs the infusion of some new people, and it may be that
current members have served too many repeating terms. The executive
should seek the opportunity, through special orientation and regular meetings, informal lunches, tours, and social gatherings, to fully acquaint the
board members with the organization. The executive should seek to discover
(and may, if the development process has worked, already know) the special
interests and skills of all members so that each one may be productively uti-
lized with respect to board roles and projects.

One part of the education process is to inform board members
with respect to the range of demands they can appropriately make on the executive and the staff of the organization. Without such information, some
members will make demands for instant service or for a variety of special
favors and arrangements that are inappropriate and create organizational
stress. Usually a member will see through observation the general range of activities permissible. However, it is often necessary to deal explicitly with this
matter.

Dealing with Board Sensitivities

One of the most difficult tasks of the executive, and one that is almost
always recognized and never mentioned, is the management of board sensitivities. Board members are, in the main, not paid for their services. (Some
boards, particularly those of corporations, are provided honorariums and/or
expense accounts.) In most cases, what board members get out of board
membership is not fiscal income but the psychic income of prestige and deference as well as "contacts" and a form of training. The executive must be
aware that board members deserve deferential treatment, even when they
lose or when the executive disagrees with their views. This may be simply a
matter of style, but it is important. If the board develops the idea that the
executive is not treating it properly, i.e., with sufficient deference, the board
may react by opposing proposals and programs the executive advances.

This matter of style becomes especially important for the executive
who has had the job for a long period of time, because, as we note later, the
board may change, and with board changes may come new practices and
procedures that the executive does not welcome. Subtly, the executive may
come to believe that he or she, rather than the board, possesses the ultimate
authority of the agency.

The management of board sensitivities goes beyond interpersonal relationships and attitudes, as important as they may be, into some concrete areas. There are three areas that have in our observation been areas of frequent confusion and unpleasantness.

Letterhead. Care should be taken in the preparation of the stationery to represent all the board members. It is useful to include their terms of office. Trivial as it may seem, the letterhead is one way in which one's association with the board is publicized, and thus it brings a measure of recognition to the member. Often the board members' names are listed prominently, with the executive's name in smaller type. Care should be taken to print each member's name as he or she wants it (Dr., Mr., Ms., et cetera). Each member may be provided a small supply of stationery for personal use on authorized agency business.

Accommodations. Boards see themselves as an important part of their respective organizations and expect to be treated in keeping with that assumption. As a practical matter, this means that the setting for board meetings should be comfortable and nicely appointed. Holding board meetings in a messy, unkempt area communicates the wrong message to the board, a message that the board is not viewed with respect. No board likes to be thought of in that way. Hence, special efforts need to be made in arranging the site of the meeting and in seeing that all necessary materials are available.

Reimbursements. When expenses of board members are reimbursable, such obligations must be paid promptly by the organization. Often executives think that because the amounts are so small, relatively speaking, this is not important. As a matter of respect, however, it is.

The Executive, the Board, and the Staff

While the executive meets with the board regularly and has in addition many meetings with individuals on the board, the rest of the executive corps—the deputy director and other key staff—and the staff as a whole may never see the board. Similarly, the board may never have the opportunity to meet and talk with staff. While there is no ideal format for board/staff interaction, one of the responsibilities of the executive is to work with the chairperson or president to guarantee and develop such opportunities. Staff members can be invited to describe their work and to make reports at board meetings, or selected on a rotating basis to attend meetings as observers; or board members may be encouraged to observe staff activities. Whatever the format, it is important to work out some pattern so that the executive is not the only staff person who ever sees, or is seen by, the board. The importance of communication between board and staff will be discussed later in this chapter.

Issues and Problems

Being an executive is a difficult role, not only because of the administrative problems one must face, but because the delicate relationships with the board require constant attention, and these relationships are never firmly established. The board's expectations and demands shift. Perhaps one measure of the differences here lies in the fact that sometimes executives are called "executive secretary" and sometimes "executive director," the former, as we have pointed out, implying a much more subordinate role to the board than the latter. Often these titles simply indicate different historical positions taken by boards with respect to the executive and do not make a great deal of difference in the administrative assignments of the executive. Yet, as can be readily understood, the range and scope and responsibility, by title at least, are quite different in the two cases. The difficulty for the executive lies in the fact that boards often expect the executive to play both aggressive and submissive versions of the role, and, withal, hold the executive accountable. Because of the role confusion created by such circumstances, there is a trend in nonprofit and public organizations to follow the industrial model of labeling the executive "executive vice-president" or "president," to denote the post as the chief administrative position.

Who Rules?

The dilemma facing the executive is that, although the board is officially responsible for the organization and the board is the executive's boss, the board and the community at large tend to hold the executive responsible for the progress or decline of the organization. Executives often feel trapped between what is expected of them and their lack of freedom to act in ways they see as commensurate with those expectations. And, not infrequently, "power plays" occur between the board and the executive because the executive has usurped the board's authority or because the board needs or wants to show the executive "who is boss."

This situation is simply one of the difficult aspects of the executive's role. Often boards change in composition. Often they have as members some people who are uninterested or incompetent. The executive naturally feels resentful if such a board ties his or her hands. On the other hand, some executives act as if their boards do not exist and seem to assume that all decisions should come from the executive corps.

There is no pat solution to these difficulties. Good judgment on the part of both the board and the executive is important. Proper use of the process of "clearance" helps (see the next section), as does continual conference between executive and chair.

Administration versus Policy

The generally accepted modus operandi for dealing with the issue of "who rules" is the division of labor between the determination of policy and its implementation. Policy decisions are the prerogative of the board. The executive has the authority to make administrative decisions within an agency's policy framework. This solution would perhaps work better if there were a clear line between policy and administration. Unfortunately, this is not always the case. The board frequently becomes interested in things that the executive defines as "administrative," while the executive will on occasion make some decisions that the board feels are properly "policy" decisions. And naturally, each sector tends to be somewhat self-serving in its designation of issues. Boards tend to call "policy" those things they are interested in considering. Administrators tend to call "administration" those things they wish to decide. And, at times, the administrator will use this designation politically, in the sense of designating an issue as being administrative so that a prompt decision can be made, and made in the direction he favors. Conversely, if an executive does not wish to handle an issue, or feels that a decision should be delayed, he or she may call it a policy issue and, as such, refer it to the attention of the board.

The difficulty in this situation is that many issues have both administrative and policy aspects. Either aspect can be highlighted. Some issues, of course, have, on balance, more of an administrative character than a policy one or vice versa, yet clarity here is often elusive. Hence, it is a continual problem with which the executive must struggle.

To further compound the problem for the executive, it is usually he or she who has to make the decision about which issue is which, since the executive is the person on the scene when issues come up. This strategic location gives the administrator/executive great discretion and power about allocating issues to either sector, and his or her judgment here is one of the key areas in which the board, and others, evaluate performance.

The Clearing Process

In part because of the difficulties attendant to making a distinction between administration and policy, there has developed informally a process called *clearing*, in which the executive in most cases (or the board in some cases) "checks out" an intended action with the other unit. Most often, it is the executive who clears with the chairperson. Thus, the decision is not left totally to the executive; he or she can get some sense of how the board might react in this or that eventuality. The clearing process embodies the dual aspects that make life difficult for the executive—who is both colleague and subordinate. But it provides a mechanism that lets the executive get the advice or consent of the board without always appearing, or being, completely subordinate.

Clearing also helps promote a climate in which the executive can, in effect, participate in the decision on a more collegial basis. If an item is cleared with the chair or executive committee, it is not guaranteed that the full board will approve it; yet it is unlikely that whatever has been worked out in that context between the executive and some key members of the board will be opposed by the whole board. Indeed, one of the purposes of the clearing process is for the executive and the chairperson to alert each other to potential difficulties inherent in a situation. Thus, if during a discussion about a particular matter the chairperson feels that the issue is "hot" and needs fuller discussion, he or she in effect tells the executive that clearing is not appropriate here, and the item requires the discussion of the full board.

Between Staff and Board

One of the difficult dilemmas an executive faces is his or her position between the staff, on the one hand, and the board, on the other. Sometimes the issues involved here are very predictable—for example, the staff want additional personnel to improve services, while the board sees a need to economize. Sometimes the issues become very idiosyncratic. In either case, the position is a difficult one, and the executive is likely to be criticized, often sharply, by both groups. One simply has to understand that occupying an executive position makes this type of criticism inescapable. There is not a great deal the executive can do to avoid the feeling by each that he or she favors the other.

Overall, however, such problems can be minimized if the executive has developed the policies and practices of mutual information sharing and has built a sound relationship between staff and board. While adequate information may not eliminate friction, it is often the case that a lack of information or communication between the board and staff heightens tensions. Keeping that channel of information as open as possible is helpful. As suggested earlier, arranging board meetings that feature staff and inviting the board into the organization to observe actual activities should prove helpful.

A Changing Board

One of the difficulties faced by many executives is the occasionally abrupt realization that, in the final analysis, they are employees of the board. This realization is most likely to occur when a new board is constituted or when new members are added to an existing board. The new people may create a situation in which procedures and practices that have been previously accepted are now being questioned. Frequently problems occur at this juncture because the new board people are not trained for this new role. All too often they simply "come on," and it is assumed that they know everything about committees and boards in general, as well as all the important matters specific to the particular board they have just joined. A little board training and education will go a long way for them and will also serve to acquaint the executive with their needs and orientations.

Conclusion

The role of the executive is a difficult one, involving much judgment about process and procedures in uncharted waters. The small amount of material we have included here is of only the most preliminary sort; it does not capture the multivariate complexity of the executive's role, the many echelons on which he or she must work, and the many additional contradictions that are inherent in the role. It is a role, as we indicated, like a staff role; on the other hand, it is much more complex than a regular staff role. There are greater and more numerous difficulties in leading an organization in a situation in which the executive, as a professional leader, must continually relate to the board members as volunteer leaders who are ultimately responsible for the organization. That responsibility does not necessarily mean they know the proper way to go. They rely on the professionalism of the executive to help them in this regard, but there may be many nonrational factors that make it difficult for board and executive to agree and move ahead.

THE MECHANICS
OF COMMITTEE
PROCESS

Our perspective in this volume rests on the assumption that what happens in a meeting is determined largely by the quality of the plans and preparations made for that meeting. Committee activity is oftentimes thought to be simply that which occurs during the committee meeting itself. That activity is indeed important, and we will pick up that aspect in Part III of this book. Yet to overemphasize the meeting ignores the importance of the preliminary work. Subcommittee meetings, the preparation of reports, the "homework" of individual members, the dozens of arrangements are all essential to a smoothly functioning meeting, even though they may not be appreciated by those present.

Successful meetings, then, do not occur automatically—they are a planned part of the entire fabric of the committee process. And what is involved in this planning? In our view, three items are of continuing importance. First, for a meeting to be successful, the committee members must attend. And as all of us with committee experience know too well, prompt and regular attendance is a problem. Second, the meeting location and setting must be accessible and comfortable and must have the necessary services (adequate rooms, audiovisual hookups, good lighting, et cetera). Third, the committee members need to have the material to be discussed at the meeting well in advance of the meeting date, so that they will have had the opportunity to consider it and react to it before the session.

As the title of this part of the volume indicates, these details are mechanical. They are not terribly earthshaking, yet they make a major difference in the quality of participation. There are literally hundreds of these, not all of which could be covered in these chapters, and so the discussion will focus on those which, in the authors' experience, have proved most important. It is hoped that the committee chairperson, members, and staff will think through those mechanical details relevant to their own activities and roles.

Throughout the next two sections, we have attempted to clarify some of the issues involved through the use of vignettes, or small bits of illustrative dialogue. These, in the main, come from the firsthand experience of the authors.

CHAPTER 6

Getting People to Attend Meetings

Introduction

Attendance is one of the key problems of committees. If a meeting is poorly attended, those who do come may be disappointed or angry. On the other hand, if important decisions are made, those who did not attend may be frustrated or hostile. And sometimes the validity of decisions made when only a few members are present can be called into question. Perhaps the best way to ensure attendance is to have an active committee with a clear sense of purpose. Laggard committees do not involve even their own members.

> Mr. Z. had attended only three meetings out of the ten sessions held so far. When he was contacted about this matter, he said, "Sure, I think the task force is important. But I've got lots to do and nothing ever happens at those meetings. At least half of the time, whenever we get started, is spent on gossip and personal stuff."

One cannot, of course, always have meetings that interest each member. But members do invest time and energy in attending, and the integrity of that investment must be protected. Certain mechanical details that are useful to keep in mind are discussed in the following sections.

Notices

The staff person or the chair should provide ample notice of the meeting time and place. It is best if a monthly or annual schedule can be developed so that members can reserve the time on their calendars. Then meeting no-

55

tices including the agenda for the upcoming meeting can serve as reminders. Notices should also be accompanied by other materials relevant to the meeting, such as financial reports, subcommittee reports, and the like.

The notices should reach all members well in advance of the meeting. Generally speaking, notices, agendas, and relevant materials should be in the hands of committee members one week in advance of the meeting, as we have indicated previously. If the agenda is accompanied by a considerable amount of materials to be read, it should go out even earlier. If necessary, the notice may be mailed early with the other material to follow, but in ample time for careful consideration.

> As the meeting got underway, Laura T. asked if she could make a comment. "I heard about today's session from Sally," she explained, "and if we had not run into each other, I would not have known about it at all." The chairman said that notices had not been sent out until two days before, because of secretarial pressures. "I wonder," commented Sam Z., "if we could not try to agree on the next meeting date at the close of each meeting. Then everyone would know."

Once notices have been sent, a second contact by phone is appropriate just before the meeting. This procedure follows the "two-media" rule of contact: Use two different media to contact the membership—letter and phone, advertising and letter, et cetera. The enclosure of a return card indicating whether or not the person will attend is useful. Experience indicates that when attendance cards are returned, the probability of a member actually attending a meeting is significantly increased.

Community Calendars

The scheduling of meetings is always difficult. Yet some committee people make matters worse by scheduling meetings in conflict with other major meetings or special events.

> Fritz P. answered the phone. It was Mrs. Cohen. "Fritz," she announced, "you have scheduled the next meeting of Community Neighbors on Yom Kippur." "Wow," Fritz replied. "I'm sorry, but we can't change it now. The Deputy Mayor is coming to talk about renewal plans." "Do what you want, Fritz," said Mrs. Cohen with an edge in her voice. "Some of us will not be at the meeting, and it may be unwise to approve the plans."

One advantage of a tentative advance schedule is that such conflicts can be pointed out while there is still flexibility. The committee staff person or chair would do well to check a proposed schedule against a community calendar or a listing of holidays, special events, and other meetings. In most mid-size and large communities, a central agency (public library, YMCA, Chamber of Commerce) has been designated to list all available information about religious holidays, special events such as concerts, committee meeting schedules, and school schedules. Such a community calendar serves to prevent or minimize conflicting timetables.

In communities without such a community calendar, every effort should be made to establish one immediately, as a means of promoting cooperation among community groups. Further, where possible it is advantageous to persuade a local paper to publish each week a list of community meetings and activities.

In instances when community events have been taken into consideration and it still appears impossible to develop a schedule of meetings that satisfies all members of the committee, alternate meeting times may be arranged (e.g., some daytime meetings and some evening meetings) to maximize participation.

Following the Agenda

An agenda serves three purposes: (1) It alerts members to the issues they will be discussing, giving them time to think about these issues and read and discuss any relevant material. (2) It provides a guide to the meeting itself. And (3) it alerts committee participants to those items that might need to be followed-up. If the agenda is received by members in sufficient time for them to prepare for the meeting, it can serve all three purposes. When it is merely passed out as the meeting begins, it is still of some assistance, but effective participation is reduced by a significant measure if members do not have the agenda in advance.

The committee itself can always modify an agenda, but this is not likely to happen if the agenda is thoughtfully prepared and contains current items as well as those items that need to be cycled back for committee approval, review, or information. Members and others have an investment in the agenda—they have prepared reports, read reports, and discussed items of particular interest to them. They are prepared for those items. If the agenda is changed, their preparation may have been wasted insofar as this particular meeting is concerned. If agenda changes become common, then the members will be less likely to prepare, since they judge that the committee norm is to add or delete particular issues or items.

> Ed P. was angry. The chair had just pointed out that he had not read the material for today. "Mr. Chairman," Ed responded, "it is true I have not read the material contained in the MacDonald Report. Yet I must say that over the past ten meetings this committee has never once stuck to its original agenda. In those times I have been prepared, but we always talked about things that came

up at the last minute. It simply never occurred to me that we would, this time, actually follow the agenda." The chairman looked a little embarrassed.

Further, it should be noted that the addition of a major item to the agenda during a meeting is patently unfair to absent members. Except in unusual emergencies, new items should not be added to an agenda and acted upon at a single meeting. The items should be tabled until members can be notified and given the opportunity to present their respective points of view, and until necessary information can be developed.

Punctuality

There are two interrelated aspects to punctuality: when the meeting begins and when people arrive. We indicated earlier that the chair has the responsibility to begin meetings promptly. That habit being established, it is likely that most members will arrive on time. Those who arrive late tend to delay the process of the meeting. Hence, promptness is an important responsibility of both members and chair.

Sometimes a member will use late arrival as a type of "theater of the committee," designed to secure attention.

> The meeting was twenty minutes under way when Ed arrived. He did not slip quietly into the room, but strode in, apologized for being late, and, as he sat down, asked, "Well, where are we?"

At other times, the chair may be involved in other business, so that time slips by without his or her notice, and members are left sitting there waiting for things to begin.

> The committee was gathered around the table, waiting for the meeting to start. Fred, the chairman, was talking to Fritz, the staff person. One of the newer members, Edith, noticed that it was already fifteen past the hour when things were supposed to start. She had another meeting the next hour and was anxious to get down to business. She whispered to the member next to her, "Shouldn't we be getting started?" "We should," was the reply, "but we won't. Fred will fiddle with that stuff for half an hour. He does it all the time." Edith resolved to bring this matter up when the meeting began.

The other side of promptness is ending on time. When a meeting begins late, then members' other commitments begin to intrude, and they start to leave early. We say "early" with respect only to the committee process. A meeting that was scheduled from 2:00 to 3:00 and does not begin till 2:30 is very unlikely to finish its business by the scheduled time. At least some of the members will have other appointments and will have to leave, which means that they will forfeit some of their ability to be influential with respect to the matters under discussion. If they stay in order to maintain that influence, they will be late for their next appointments. This can have a chain effect and inconvenience several other people. It also explains much irritation expressed indirectly as items are discussed.

We believe that a meeting should end at the designated time, regardless of when it starts. No one is thus penalized for having other appointments. And the practice acts as a mechanism for shaping committee behavior, because people will realize that meetings must begin promptly if they are to accomplish their goals.

Interaction

A committee meeting is not a social gathering. Yet one cannot ignore the social graces, as it were, and there must be some attention given to informal interaction. The chair should be sensitive, as should the members, to certain amenities. Someone (usually the chair) should arrive a little early to welcome the members. New members and visitors should be introduced. There have been times in our experience when strangers sat for some time in the wrong meeting because no one took responsibility for introductions. The "host" function is especially important if the committee is relatively large and if it meets infrequently. Some members may never know, or may forget, the identity of some of the other members.

> As she walked down the hall to the meeting, Susan thought of how good she felt about this board. Mrs. J., the chairwoman, was always there to greet people and say a pleasant word. Susan felt this got the meeting off to a good start. It certainly made her feel like a valuable member of the board. Mrs. J. made it a point to introduce members to each other and say little interesting things that facilitated conversation.

Identification tags, name placecards, or personalized folders not only serve purposes of identification but also help to create a feeling of identity and importance. These devices may be too formal for a small committee but can be useful with larger groups.

Conclusion

Attendance is a sine qua non of committee life. If no one comes, there is no meeting. Encouraging attendance is an important function of all members. There are clearly many factors that affect attendance, but some of the most significant relate to the very small details that are or are not accomplished prior to and during the meeting. Notices, meeting schedules, and agenda are important pieces of information to get to members before the meeting. Dealing with substantive items, preserving the integrity of members' prior effort by following the agenda, beginning and ending on time, and paying some attention to the social interaction of the group will yield large dividends in attendance for any type of committee or board.

CHAPTER 7

Planning and Preparing the Meeting Space

Introduction

The physical setting in which the meeting is held can go a long way toward encouraging attendance and making the meeting go smoothly. An attractive and comfortable setting, even a prestigious one, that is easy to get to and fun to be at creates a very positive atmosphere. A place that is hard to reach, or is generally unattractive, can create a negative feeling about the meeting. National conference planners are perhaps the most sensitive to this point. To induce attendance, they select a location members would like to visit because of the social amenities (San Francisco, Boston) or a place that is geographically central (St. Louis, Chicago, Kansas City). Thought is given as well to parking and transportation, to meals and room layout, and to accessibility for any members who may be handicapped. Unfortunately, many of these considerations, important as they are, are not given much systematic thought for local committee meetings.

> Harry and Sandra were complaining as they drove home from the meeting. "Sandra," said Harry, "remind me never to come to one of these meetings again." "I know what you mean," said Sandra. "It took us one hour to find a place to park, there was no place to have lunch, and no place even to get a cup of coffee." "And the room," added Harry, "was a nightmare. I thought Mrs. Letty was going to fall off that folding chair. It kept making those terrible creaking noises." "Well," commented Sandra, "it's simply exhausting to go through all of that for such a meeting."

Refreshments

Depending on the time of day and the type and length of meeting, refreshments may be necessary or desirable. Refreshments often may be simply coffee, although sometimes meals need to be arranged. The need for food and the type of food required create one limitation on the meeting space.

> "Why," said Miss P., "can't our group meet at the central library downtown?" "Well," responded the chairperson, "we could. However, they have no coffee there, and they do not permit refreshments to be brought into any of the rooms. And the neighborhood has changed around there. I do not think we would want to eat in the local restaurants in the area." "Oh," said Miss P.

One rule of thumb we have found useful is that the amount of refreshment that should be available is inverse to the distance people come to the meeting and the length of the meeting. A brief staff meeting does not require refreshments. If people are coming from the local area, coffee may be provided. If people are traveling longer distances, then a meal, or meals, are necessary. When we say necessary, we are not implying that the convener pays for the meal, but rather that the meeting space must be located so that people can conveniently go and eat or a meal can be brought in. The cost of a meal has an influence on participation; some members may not be able to afford this expense and will decline to attend rather than suffer any possible embarrassment. It should also be remembered that having a meal served during a meeting can significantly reduce the amount of business accomplished.

Refreshments are important in relation to the flow of time during the meeting. If the committee breaks for lunch, for example, and no thought has been given to how this meal is to be arranged, the members may not be able to eat and return to the meeting on time. If they go out for coffee, this disrupts the meeting. If coffee is to be brought to the meeting, and a break is scheduled for a certain time, then the coffee should arrive on time. If it is due at 10:00 and does not come until 11:15, members may become edgy, and the eventual break may run right into the lunch hour.

> As the meeting was about to start, Irv looked around. "Where is everyone?" he asked the few who were present. "They have gone out for some coffee," answered Sol. It was twenty minutes before everyone returned. Then the coffee smelled so good that two more members slipped out to get some.

Overall, the meeting planner needs to understand that meals are, in a sense, "props" for a "theater of the committee." They are important, but secondary to the work of the committee. They must be in the right place at the right time, and inconspicuously so, if the committee's work is to be accomplished. If that happens, the informal interaction that food fosters and the ability to get work done over meals are both greatly enhanced. If arrangements are not appropriate, the food itself often complicates or disrupts the work of the committee.

Physical Arrangements

The physical setting of the meeting is an important element of committee mechanics. After all, the members will be spending a fair amount of time there. Heat, light, ventilation, acoustics, electrical outlets for any necessary appliances (e.g., projectors) are of great importance. Furthermore, the participants themselves must also share in the responsibility for creating a pleasant environment.

> The chairman, Mr. T., had the habit of smoking cigars during meetings. He was simply not sensitive to the pungent, irritating odor. Finally, on a day when the group met in a room very poorly ventilated, Mr. L. commented, "At the risk of being offensive, and I hope I am not, would you mind not smoking that second cigar?" Before Mr. T. could reply, everyone around the committee table was nodding vigorously.

The meeting table needs to be adequate, and there must be sufficient seats for all the members and any guests.[1] This point might seem too obvious even to mention. But too often this detail is ignored, and time has to be taken during the meeting to obtain and arrange the necessary tables and chairs. In one case in our experience, the meeting room could not be used because someone had borrowed all the furniture, so there were no tables or chairs. (If your committee borrows equipment, return it!)

An important part of physical arrangements that go beyond tables and chairs is provision of the small pieces of equipment needed for work. Such items as pads, pencils, maps, blackboards, and other paraphernalia are often helpful in making a meeting go smoothly. The smoother one can make the meeting process, the more productive the meeting will be—especially if there is only a certain amount of time for it.

The matter of reports and memos that need to be considered by the committee will be discussed in more detail in the next chapter. It is important to note here, however, that material to be passed out at the meeting should be on hand and ready for use. We have all experienced the situation in which someone comes with material "hot off the press" that has not been collated.

---

1. Most, but not all, meetings are held around a table. If no table is used, there should be some provision for clipboards to write on and a place to set papers, drinks, et cetera.

Page after page is passed out, and confusion reigns as everyone tries to assemble a complete copy.

> Matthew was exhausted. Copies of the final report, all hundred pages, had been brought in by the secretary. He and the committee had spent the better part of an hour assembling the copies, and the job was nowhere near done. "Matthew," said one of the members, "we are not even going to finish pulling these pages together, much less look at and approve the report. We will have to have another meeting after we have had a chance to look over this draft." Matt sighed. Nothing was going right. His count indicated that several of the pages had not been reproduced, so not even one complete copy was available, and one page of the summary was so blurred it could not be read.

Conclusion

The degree of committee accomplishment depends directly on the extent to which many of the mechanical details of meeting arrangements are properly managed. If these details are handled well, the chances are enhanced that the meeting and the committee process will go smoothly. If they are handled poorly, they become at best an irritant to members and at worst an obstruction to committee action.

CHAPTER 8

Compiling and
Distributing Reports

Introduction

We have emphasized throughout that much of the work of the committee takes place outside the meeting. One particularly important preliminary activity is the compiling and distributing of materials needed for discussion during the meeting. Most frequently these materials take the form of a report.[1] Endless amounts of time are wasted in committee sessions because people insist on discussion of material that requires preparation—but the preparation has not been undertaken.

> Mrs. P. began the discussion by referring to the change in the clientele of the agency over the past year. Erving S. asked her how she knew that the clients were now likely to be younger and of ethnic origin. She replied that anyone could tell that by just walking around. Erving S. commented, "I think that we should not discuss this matter in great detail today, but ask the executive to look into some of these matters and bring back some comparative information." Mrs. P. agreed, but it was clear her feelings were hurt.

The key element in prior preparation is quality—how well the job is done, how accurately the information is presented. Beyond quality, however, or in addition to it, are a variety of details to which one needs to be sensitive.

---

1. For a detailed discussion of report and memo preparation, see John E. Tropman and Ann R. Alvarez, "Writing For Effect," in F. M. Cox et al., eds., *Tactics and Techniques of Community Organization* (Itasca, Ill.: F. E. Peacock, 1977).

Quality of the Report

The basis of sound committee action is good information. If the information provided to the committee is inadequate, then the decisions are likely to be of low quality. No one can guarantee, of course, that if the information is adequate, the decisions will be good, but the chances of higher-quality decisions are greatly enhanced.

It is therefore paradoxical that many committees seem to operate with almost no information on the matters before them. It is this point that can make the assignment of staff so crucial. Someone must collect, analyze, synthesize, and prepare for presentation the information pertinent to the committee's tasks. In the absence of staff, it is unlikely that the committee members and/or chair will have the time or resources to prepare adequate reports. Committees may need information on a wide range of topics—finance, legal, personnel, client and product information, sales and forecasting data, or whatever is pertinent to the committee's assignment. Where staff is not available or can provide only limited assistance, committees often assign specific subjects to small subcommittees with the intent of bringing some of the expertise available on the committee to bear on those subjects.

There is often within the membership considerable and diverse expertise with respect to the field of interest under consideration, but often this expertise is not exactly on the problem at hand. The challenge, in such a situation, is to refine and focus the expertise, often through a subcommittee. Many times some additional information is needed. Thus, there are two matters of concern—getting the necessary information, and refining and specifying the information available in order to address the particular problem under consideration.

> Mrs. Z was lost. The committee had been discussing the "fee-for-service policy" of the Helping Arms Children's Agency for the past two hours. In the past the agency had charged no fee. Now it was under consideration. Yet she could not follow the discussion. "Excuse me," she interjected. "Perhaps others are feeling the same way I am: lost. Could we ask our executive to summarize the information he has into some recommendations?" The executive replied, "I can, of course. But that would just delay a decision until next meeting." "I feel," said Mrs. Z softly, "that on a matter as important as this, I need to have all the issues and facts before me. I may be dumb, but I can't keep all the proposals and justifications in my head." Other people on the board nodded.

The chair needs to be constantly sensitive to the committee's informational needs and make preparation for them to be met in an informed, informative way.

Report Graphics

Apart from the substantive content of a report prepared for committee consideration, there are certain graphic details that are important—that give it a professional character. These details are often ignored, so it is not inappropriate to emphasize here that many an excellent report has been rejected because it looked "messy" and was poorly put together. In such a case, the content may have been excellent, but the impression it made was all wrong.

Type

Reports can be made very attractive by a judicious diversity of size and style of type for the various parts. For example, the recommendations might be printed in italics, the main headings in a second style of type, and the rest of the text in a third. At one time, this variety could have been provided only by a printing firm, but today even a small office is likely to have small computers with printers that will allow the report maker to use a variety of fonts in putting together a report. Larger and smaller sizes of type can be used to highlight specific points of interest. A variety of type styles can make a report very interesting and attractive. On the cautionary side, however, report makers should be careful not to overdo the variety. In that case, a report can have a bewildering array of type styles and faces, sizes, and presentations that make the report difficult to read. Desktop publishing kits and programs allow even the smallest organization access to an impressive array of technical alternatives in report preparation.

Format

Whether or not different type styles are used, the report writer can create different work formats on the page. Indentations, underlining, numbering and lettering the main points, leaving more than the usual space between points—all are components that add to the attractiveness and readability of the report.

Organization

Some thought must be given to the organization of the total document, and this attention is necessary even if the document is only one or two pages long. More extensive documents, of course, will present more complex problems in organization. When a report has several sections, the use of color coding often is helpful to add dash as well as to indicate different sections. If a report has five sections, for example, each of the five can be on paper of a different color. Such color coding makes for easy identification, provided one remembers that later additions must be in the selected colors.

It also is sometimes useful to number the pages of each chapter separately, using a decimal system to designate chapters and pages. The first pages of the first chapter are then 1.1, 1.2, 1.3, and the second chapter begins with pages 2.1, 2.2, 2.3. This system permits additions to be made to any section without changing the subsequent pagination. A variant of this system, especially useful in documents such as bylaws, manuals of procedure, and the like, is to number each paragraph. Then one can be explicit about which of the paragraphs is to be deleted or revised. If the document is one that is likely to be revised with some regularity, it is best to put each paragraph (or topic) on a separate sheet of paper. In that pattern, the old page can be removed and the new page inserted.

Binding

Once all these other matters have been considered and the decision made, it is necessary to put the report together. Attractiveness is enhanced by using one of the many different types of commercial covers available. Often, too, loose-leaf assembly facilitates both reading and replacement of specific sections.

Reproduction

Throughout the preparation of materials, attention needs to be given to the matter of copies, and some estimates of the number of copies necessary will have to be developed. If a large number is needed, offset printing can be relatively inexpensive and looks attractive. For more limited numbers, less-expensive methods of duplicating or photocopying a report may be desirable. Some thought might also be given to the intended distribution of documents from a cost perspective. If the report is to be widely distributed, the per-copy cost of reproduction and mailing should influence decisions regarding the format and choice of materials.

Record Keeping

Any report, whether a one-page memo or a multi page tome, is likely to go through several revisions before a final version is achieved. The staff person should keep a file and log of all drafts and, if possible, develop a coding system that identifies each document. With a code number entered in the log and on the lower left-hand corner of each sheet, it is easy to retrieve a specific version if needed. As part of the log, each version should have clearly indicated the level of draft (1st, 2nd, 3rd) and the date. These items should, similarly, be on each page. Much confusion will be prevented if these procedures are followed.

Types of Reports

There are many types of reports. Two of the most common are summary reports and annual reports.

Summary Reports

When committees have heavy agendas, it often proves useful to pre-pare summaries identifying the highlights of lengthy reports. Such summar-ies may be prepared by staff members or committee members. Copies of the full report should be available for interested committee members. Summar-ies also are advisable within the full committee report. Our rule of thumb is that for every five pages of report, there should be one-half page of summary. Often these are in the form of "Summary and Recommendations" and are placed first.

Annual Reports

Nearly every committee should issue some report of its activities to its constituencies once a year. Such a report is often presented and discussed at a meeting to which the public is invited. We should like to emphasize that the process through which a committee goes in preparing the report is likely to be useful to it, whether anyone looks at the report or not. But in most cases, people do look to see what the committee has been doing over the year. The report provides an opportunity to make suggestions about altera-tions in directions.

Action on Reports

Not all reports and materials need action in the sense of committee accept-ance or rejection. Yet many do, and this necessity sometimes poses a prob-lem. Typically, unless the circumstances are unusual, committees do not like to reject reports, but often a committee is unclear exactly what options it has. The following procedures are possible.

Discussion Only

If it appears that a report is going to be controversial and a variety of positions may be taken by individual committee members, the report can be scheduled "for discussion only," and so labeled in the agenda. Such a tactic means that no action is intended until a future date. Discussion can occur on the merits, without any pressure to reach consensus at that particular time.

Receipt of the Report

Often a committee does not wish to act in either a positive or a negative way with respect to a particular report. In such a case, the official action can be simply the receipt of the report.

Acceptance of the Report

The word "accept" has a more positive connotation than receive but is still within the neutral range.

Approval in Principle

One of the more useful devices to help committees move forward is the "approval in principle" mechanism. Committee progress is often impeded by disagreement over specific language in a report submitted for approval. In such cases, it is often useful to take the posture that the document is before the group for approval or rejection in principle. Such an approach means that the wording is not at issue—but the main ideas and thrusts of the document are. (These main points should be singled out if this has not already been done.) Such a separation between the thrust of the ideas and the language in which those ideas are specifically expressed facilitates discussion and progress.

Approval of the Report

If the committee wishes, it can approve the report. This action usually takes place after discussion of the report and its implications and indicates the support of the committee for the report and its recommendations.

Conclusion

Preparing material for committee discussion and action is a complicated task. Of first importance, of course, are the quality of the material itself and the scholarship and intelligence that any document, however small, should reflect. The form in which the material is presented can also be crucial, however. While no amount of processing skill can improve a basically bad document, the absence of such skill can seriously harm a good one. For this reason, committee personnel should be knowledgeable about ways of preparing documents and getting them to members, the ways in which documents can be packaged, and the types of actions one might ask the committee to take with respect to a report.

These matters of procedure are, as we have said before, matters of detail. Yet they are details too often overlooked to the detriment of good ideas. From the committee perspective, members have a right to receive materials that are well organized and readable and to have the discussion about those materials proceed with some focus and dispatch. The right procedures can help serve both goals. It should also be emphasized again that such procedures must be decided on before the material is prepared for distribution. Otherwise it will be too late.

THE DYNAMICS
OF COMMITTEE
PROCESS

Any separation between mechanics and dynamics is likely to be somewhat artificial. Nonetheless, there is a distinction between the more mechanical functions, discussed in Part II, and the dynamic behavior that leads to particular decisions by a committee. It is to this latter aspect that we now turn our attention.

By committee dynamics we mean the reciprocal processes of influence that occur in committee transactions. Chairpersons, members, and staff behave as they do in part as a response to how they see and hear—or think they see and hear—others behaving. The mechanical aspects of committee process become, in a process view, props that facilitate or obstruct the achievement of a decision, in terms of time and quality. For example, a report in the hands of a committee can provide new information that causes committee members to be less willing than they were before to make a decision on a particular issue. Alternatively, the additional information can assist a committee to make a decision by providing needed clarity.

It is perhaps overly dramatic, but a view of the committee as a theater of decision helps to convey our point. Events that happen before the meeting influence and shape events of the meeting. Behavior and impressions in the first meeting contribute to attitudes in later meetings. We are dealing here, in part, with impressions, with assumptions, with expectations, with prognostications, any and all of which may be in error. This condition reflects a felt need by members to add structure, both intellectual and programmatic, to a situation that is inherently fluid. Committee members often *do not* know where they will end up in a particular decision episode. Part of the reason for the committee process in the first place is to discover crucial information on a particular topic, consider that information from various perspectives, and make a decision on the basis of all information available. Uncertainty is virtually inherent in the committee process. It is one of the most difficult, and yet one of the most rewarding, aspects of committee work. It is the job of the chair, staff, and members to shape this uncertainty into definitive actions and decisions. For this reason, the dynamics of committee life are important. The alert and informed committee participant can make the most of this flexibility to influence the committee's behavior and decisions.

This shaping and molding occurs in various ways. Both the chairperson and the members may use the committee charge as a means of providing direction. The staff person and other nonmembers of the committee, including outside consultants, are important in the process. The chair is particularly important. But members, too, may chart progress, using time as a key variable and working with the committee against the clock. Written materials and reports provide benchmarks or key points to codify the developing process.

The committee process is one of development. Each member enters with some impressions about what should be done in a situation and some perspective on how this should be accomplished. As the committee moves along, perspectives begin to harmonize as individuals weigh their views within the context of the views and interests of others. The viewpoints of all members of the group tend to modify to some extent. Throughout, the chair and the members must see that this process has a direction, a focus, and a purpose. If it does not, the committee may come to be known as one of those groups that serve splendid refreshments but accomplish very little business.

The key factor in the committee process, in our judgment, is the dynamic element of time, the way events occur in time. Hence, the first meeting is especially consequential because it sets the stage for what comes later. Many impressions and messages are conveyed at the all-important first meeting, whether they are intended or not. Similarly, other significant elements in the temporal process are premeeting activities, the meeting itself, and postmeeting or follow-up activities. Each of these phases needs some special attention, and each provides certain opportunities and constraints.

CHAPTER 9

Premeeting Activity

Introduction

The cornerstone of committee work is preparation. A committee meets, at least ostensibly, to do work. In order for work to be accomplished, a clear picture of the day's work needs to be outlined (agenda), and any necessary materials (minutes, memos, reports) need to be prepared and placed in the hands of the members. It may often be appropriate for "premeeting meetings" to occur—meetings of a subcommittee or subgroups of members including the chair, staff and/or selected members.

> Seymour F., chairman of the Sewage Commission, met with his staff assistant. They went over all the details for the upcoming meeting of the commission. Mr. F. commented to his assistant, "You are doing a good job, but more attention is needed to getting material out in time, Frank. The commission members need an opportunity to think about the items in advance of the meetings."

Agenda Preparation

One of the most important premeeting activities is the construction of the agenda. It is also one to which many people give little attention. The agenda is for the meeting what the score is for the orchestra. It is the vehicle through which committee work is specified. The chair can use this tool to direct the committee, both in the longer-range strategic matters, including goals and scheduling, and in shorter-range tactical matters, such as moving discussion along.

"Why is it," asked Sally Z., "that in the PTA we always finish our agenda, while in the School Board meetings we never seem to finish?" "I don't know," her friend Margaret replied, "but it's the same in our church women's organization. We seem to go on and on."

Getting through an agenda is not an easy task. Many of the problems occur, however, because the agenda was not planned carefully in the first place.

Number of Items

The number of items on the agenda is crucial. There should be sufficient business to be conducted, yet only that number of items listed that can reasonably be completed within the time available for the meeting.

"I am delighted," announced Mrs. C., "with the fact that the Lawton PTA Board seems always to complete its agenda by the end of each meeting. It gives me a real sense of accomplishment."

In order to achieve this, the chairperson or staff person planning the agenda must make subjective estimates of the time required for each item. Naturally, these estimates will not always be on target, but experienced people will usually be able to make a good guess.

Arrangement of Items

In the dynamics of committee process, the timing of items—that is, the point during the meeting at which each item is introduced—is crucial. The details of agenda preparation are discussed in Chapter 27 on the fraction rules and Chapter 28 on the rules of the agenda bell. They are considered briefly here, but readers may wish to consult those chapters as well. We suggest the following arrangement:

1. Approval of minutes
2. Announcements (for information only)
3. Short, easy items
4. More difficult items
5. Most difficult item
6. Discussion only items
7. Adjournment

The items are arranged in order of increasing difficulty, with the most difficult item near the end of the agenda. Time permitting, an easy item may follow to accentuate the sense of accomplishment.

During the last part of Item 6 a member can bring to the attention of the committee new topics or particular concerns. Often such matters can be disposed of quickly. If they require detailed study, they may be tabled or carried over to future meetings.

In this way, the committee proceeds through its agenda, accomplishing what business it can; those items that it cannot complete do not serve as blocks to other work. When the most difficult item is located earlier on the agenda, discussion about it often takes up most or all of the meeting. It is often desirable to locate noncontroversial committee items at an early stage of the agenda. Accomplishment on increasingly difficult items permits a positive attitude toward the most difficult item when it comes up. This item may be "most difficult" because of its inherent complexity or because it is the most controversial.

Additionally, the chairperson can use the clock to move the meeting along. Committee members can spend a great deal of time on a simple item, giving that item much more discussion than it merits. If a more difficult item is in the middle of the agenda, the chair can use the committee's desire to get to that item, combined with limitations on the total amount of time available for the meeting, as a force for shaping and speeding up discussion on the less important items and still getting them decided.

Similarly, the clock is useful in shaping discussion on the most difficult item. If, after a period of time, agreement or a decision has not been reached, additional discussion may not be fruitful; rather, an action such as tabling may be appropriate. The presence of an item after the most difficult item can serve as the argument for stopping discussion of the most difficult item and moving along. In that event, the most difficult item can be brought up again at the next meeting, along with additional information that appears to be needed on the basis of the discussion. If the discussion has been rich and full and action seems promising, the item might be located at an earlier stage in the subsequent agenda.

Of course, many unforeseen elements intrude into the agenda, and so this system is workable only part of the time. It is helpful, however, to give thought to the flow of items and the relationship of that flow to the type of decision and the difficulty of decision.

Jim and Fred were having an afternoon cup of coffee and comparing committees. "I can't explain it," commented Fred, "but the Finance Committee is always arguing, and we never seem to come to any decisions. The topics we're considering get all mixed up." "That's odd," replied Jim. "In the Capital Funds

Committee we always move rather well, right through the agenda." "Drat," complained Fred, "we don't even get an agenda, much less move through it."

For Discussion Only

If items are arranged on the agenda in order of increasing complexity, consideration of the more difficult items does not prevent the committee from making decisions on the items with which it can deal more easily. There are also other procedures worth taking into account when dealing with a difficult and complex item. If the item is to be on the regular agenda, the chair can sometimes list it as "for discussion only," thus removing any pressure anyone might feel for making an immediate decision. A more relaxed discussion may create a situation in which a decision can be more speedily reached at the next meeting. Alternatively, if the item is unusually complex and difficult, a special meeting can be called with discussion of that item as its only agenda. In either way, a full discussion can emerge without pressure for a decision.

"You know," said Sally F., "I think we cleared a lot of air in that discussion." Fred, the vice-chairman, agreed. "Next week we may be able to come to a decision on the matter," he commented.

Agenda and Daily Schedule

Sometimes committees are very fractious and hard to manage. It may be difficult to enlist the members' cooperation and proper participation. In such situations, chairpersons, members, or staff members may wish to consider one of two techniques. First, there is the single-item agenda, which consists only of minutes and one item. The meeting can be brief, and the chair can use the single item as a mechanism to focus discussion. Secondly, the meeting can be scheduled at 11:00 A.M. or 4:00 P.M. so that the committee must work against lunch or dinner—a circumstance that tends to shape and focus participation and deter unnecessary conversation. When used together, these techniques can be a powerful way to shape committee behavior.

"Boy," said Jim P. "We are meeting three times a week now." "I know that is a lot," commented Harold J., "but with one hour, and one item, we have really quieted down the people who went on and on." "I sure agree that we are making decisions," replied Jim. "And they are good ones," said Harold. "The focus we can give each item means that there are better materials and comments brought to bear than otherwise."

Material for Agenda Items

Many agenda items require that material be available for committee members to study. This is always true of the minutes, of course, and is usually true of budgets, subcommittee reports, et cetera. It is of utmost importance that the relevant material be available for members to read before the meeting. It is the chairperson's responsibility to make certain that any material needed for each item on the agenda is ready. If the item is there and the material is not, the chair should amend the agenda at the beginning of the meeting and delete the item. This procedure always causes some problem and consumes time, as one member wants to know why the material is not ready, others may ask for a brief oral report, and so on.

Each item on the agenda should have a number, and this number should appear in the upper-right-hand corner of any materials in the members' packets that relate to that item. This avoids the paper shuffling that so often occurs as people look for the right exhibits. If the relevant material is not in writing but rather is an oral report from a committee member, the chair should make sure that (1) the report will be ready and (2) the person, or a substitute, will be present. The chair or staff person must check with the member before the meeting. It is also helpful if the person giving the oral report submits a copy of the remarks to the staff person or secretary. This will (1) assure accurate reporting in the minutes, (2) keep the speaker more sharply focused, and (3) provide better control over the time allowed for the report. Sometimes the chairperson or staff person will need to help with the preparation of the report in order to ensure its delivery.

Distributing the Packet

As has been emphasized, the packet of materials must reach each committee member in time to be studied before the meeting if discussion and decision are to occur properly, and this means that ordinarily the material should arrive a week in advance of the meeting. It is inefficient to have the material distributed at the meeting. We are all too familiar with the meeting that begins in a whirl of paper as multiple copies of different items are passed around and several members hastily read reports instead of participating in the business under discussion.

Mrs. Willis and Sam Harris were talking after the board meeting. "You know," commented Sam, "I think that meeting went very poorly. I just cannot keep track of all the material we get. Not only does stuff come in the mail, but more stuff is passed out at the meeting. It all looks the same to me. I sit there in a sea of budget reports, personnel committee reports, and copies of newspaper clippings." Mrs. Willis replied, "That material is needed, Sam. But I agree that there has to be some better way of organizing it and receiving it in time to digest it before the meeting."

Even when materials are mailed well in advance, there is likely to be at least one member who insists that copies were not received. Every effort should be made to check addresses and mailing procedures to ensure the receipt of materials by all members of the committee.

Each member's packet should contain, in this order, the following materials:

1. A notice of the meeting—date, time, and place
2. A copy of the agenda
3. A copy of the relevant material for each item on the agenda, numbered and in order, starting with the minutes

The notice should provide any information people need in order to reach the meeting site, including any peculiarities about the meeting room location and information on parking, if necessary. It is far too common an occurrence to have meetings disrupted by members storming in late, loudly proclaiming that there had been no place to park!

Conferences

The details of agenda preparation are one essential of preparing for the committee meeting itself. A second aspect is interpersonal—meeting with people in groups or conferring with individuals before the meeting begins. Conferences and subcommittee meetings become an important part of the dynamics of preparation. The chairperson and staff person are likely to be the ones on whom the burden of conferences falls most heavily. This burden is one of the responsibilities of those roles. Others on the committee, however, may also meet regularly. Several types of meetings are common.

Subcommittees

Subcommittees appointed by the chair will meet to do whatever work they have been assigned to do. They may be standing subcommittees, which are permanent or ongoing, or ad hoc subcommittees, which are appointed on a temporary basis to accomplish a particular task. The chairperson or staff person will sometimes meet with subcommittees to aid in their work, help to solve particular problems, and show interest.

Members

Members meet with other members on a variety of specific topics. Perhaps the most frequent form of such conferences is between the chairperson and a member. Sometimes the chairperson wants to obtain from that member additional, specialized input that is too technical, or too delicate, for a public or general meeting. Sometimes the chairperson may want to discuss problems in his or her relationship with the member that have occurred in meetings, or the chair may seek advice on committee progress. Sometimes the chair needs to share with a member the perception that he or she is not participating or is somewhat disrupting the committee process—one of the more difficult kinds of conferences, but occasionally necessary.

Relevant Nonmembers

As the work of the committee progresses, the chairperson and members will in the course of time need to meet with people who are not members of the committee. These meetings may be to obtain outside input on the committee's assignment or to gain information and feedback on committee performance. It may be necessary to obtain support or to clear some special aspect of the committee's work with other committees or organizations. The chairperson or staff person usually carries out such liaison activities. It may be necessary to attend meetings where the committee's work is discussed; such attendance falls within the purview of the chair. But regardless of what the specific focus is, a number of these special contacts will need to occur, and the chair should make itself, or a designate, available.

Staff

If the committee has a staff available to it, one of the most important conferences is between the chairperson and the committee staff person. Each has specific responsibilities. It is the responsibility of the chair to make the assignments and the responsibility of the staff person to perform the work assigned. Until they are very familiar with each other's strengths and weaknesses, it is wise to schedule rather regular meetings for mutual education. Nothing is more frustrating to a staff person than to have a chair who is mercurial, unspecific, and temporizing. In order for the staff person to do his or her part, the chair must do its part, and this is largely accomplished through conferences.

Of special sensitivity are the premeeting conferences between chairperson and staff person relative to agenda preparation and strategy. The chair and staff should make certain that their respective opinions on the various items are clear. Conflict between chair and staff person at the meetings is usually not helpful to the committee process. The role that staff should play in the meeting should be understood and planned.

Staff should also share with the chair any insights into the attitudes and positions of committee members and regarding what might be anticipated by way of effectiveness of opinions and strategies. Finally, the chair and staff should explore possible alternative ways of handling the issues that might surface at the meeting.

> Mr. Brown was talking to Al Sweet, the staff person for the M & O committee. "Al, our meeting went so smoothly today, and I want you to know that you deserve a lot of the credit." "Thank you," replied Al. "What do you think was especially important?" "Well," Bob Brown answered, "you and the chairman had obviously met and secured agreement between yourselves on many items. All the subcommittees reported on time, and I assume that you were working with them toward this purpose. And the information you brought us from persons around the country was very helpful."

Conclusion

Dynamically, the process of a meeting begins long before the gavel falls to open the session. Hundreds of details become involved, and they are dynamic details because they influence the ways in which committee participants act and think, which in turn affects the way the meeting will go. Indeed, the point of this chapter, and of this section, is to emphasize the interactive nature of the process, including the preparation. It is that to which the committee participant needs to be sensitive.

CHAPTER 10
Regular Meeting Sessions

Introduction

The earlier discussion of dynamics in the committee process was devoted mainly to premeeting activities. If these activities have been carefully attended to, there is a good chance the meeting will run smoothly and that the business before it will be accomplished. A good chance, however, is not a certainty. There are eventualities that can hamper committee functioning, and there are still tasks that need to be carried out by the participants to achieve closure—an informed, high-quality decision—on the items before them.

The Chair

It is at this point that the crucial aspect of meeting leadership becomes evident. Leadership implies a direction and the encouragement and assistance to reach that objective. As Chapter 1 indicates, this responsibility falls heavily on the chair. While others may take leadership roles in premeeting activities and may even serve as the intellectual or political "brains" of the committee, it is the chairperson who must provide the leadership when the meeting is in progress. Just as an orchestra will perform badly with a poor conductor, a committee will perform poorly with an inadequate chairperson. And once the performance has begun, it is difficult for anyone else to be of much assistance, just as it would be difficult for the first violin to compensate for the errors of the conductor.

Harry and Bill were talking over the meeting as they left. "You know, Harry," Bill said, "I can't explain it, but the meetings of this committee always seem to go well. I look forward to coming." "That's true," replied Harry, "and especially in comparison to some of the others we attend. The difference seems to be in the way John organizes and conducts the meetings."

It is during the committee sessions that the dynamic, interacting functioning of the various committee roles becomes most obvious. In the main, it is these aspects of the roles with which most of us are most familiar. And while this book has emphasized the work outside the meeting itself and will continue to do so, there are many important elements of "role playing" that become important within the moving, developing action of the meeting situation.

Perhaps the key responsibility of the chair during the meeting situation is to see that the committee moves through the agenda and comes to some decision on each item. He or she has previously thought through the agenda, so that the number and complexity of items are not excessive and the work probably can be handled during the time allotted for it. What remains now is the delicate process of managing the meeting so that the following results are achieved.

Adequate Discussion Time

Enough time should be provided for adequate discussion of each item, as determined by the complexity of the issue and the interest of the members in it. The chair, staff person, and members need to guard against situations in which the discussion is so short that key issues are not fully aired, or, on the other hand, continues on and on, perhaps with the goal of avoiding a difficult decision.

"Mr. Chairman," asked Arthur during the meeting, "may I request that this item on salaried employees be acted upon?" "Of course, Arthur," replied Victor, chairman of the Finance Committee, "but let's spend just a little more time thinking through this raise policy. Better a little time now than have to revise it later."

Appropriate Participation

Each item needs to have adequate discussion, in terms of both persons and substance. The chair needs to create opportunities to hear the opinions of those who have not commented and to find ways to "cool" those who have already made their position, as it were, "perfectly clear." The chair needs to be concerned, also, about the substance of the discussion. Sometimes discussion does not focus on issues that the chair knows to be present. Often extensive discussion fails to add new insights or information. It simply becomes repetitious. Interminable discussion is cancerous to the life of a committee.

If premeeting responsibilities have been attended to, the chair and some members have informed themselves on the item through conferences with people outside and inside the committee. Hence, they should recognize when the "true," or at least important, issues are being ignored. To avoid the essential aspects of an issue leaves the committee open to a continual return to that issue. Problems avoided on one agenda topic often crop up in another discussion. For these reasons, a good chairperson works to guide the committee process by seeking balanced participation, by reorienting the discussion, and by curbing some members, so that appropriate discussion can ensue. Good committee members and staff will try to follow this lead.

> As the meeting progressed, Lawrence, the chairman, noted that Monsignor O'Grady had not spoken. Lawrence was sure that if he did not get the monsignor to comment now, there would be trouble later. "Monsignor O'Grady," Lawrence asked at the next appropriate moment, "we know that the Catholic schools might be asked to take some of the children of parents who oppose busing. Have you had an opportunity to consider this matter?" It appeared as if the monsignor had been waiting for this. "I am glad you asked, Lawrence," he replied. "We have decided not to accept children under these conditions, and we will be issuing a statement to that effect in a few days."

Reaching a Decision[1]

One common fault of chairpersons, even those who perform other functions well, is that they often fail to obtain a decision on the issue under discussion. All issues, except those specifically noted on the agenda as "For Information/Discussion Only," require some kind of action. A decisive action is not necessarily approval or disapproval; it may be tabling, instructing a subcommittee to bring additional information, deferring, et cetera. For each item on the agenda, the chair should be able to answer the question, What did the committee do with this item? If the questions cannot be answered, the chair has not done its job.

Sometimes the chair will suggest a decision, such as tabling, if the committee seems to be floundering. Most often, however, the chair tries to

---

1. More detail on this topic—reaching a decision or decision crystallization—is found in Part IX, Achieving Decision Crystallization.

conceptualize and summarize the remarks of the members, with an eye to capturing the elements of a decision. The chair should seek to sense the direction in which the committee is moving and frame an acceptable action within that direction.

> There had been a great deal of discussion about the specific content of the policy statement on part-time help. Jim, the chairman, spoke to the group. "We have two possibilities here as I hear the comments. One is to circulate this document for further discussion. However, if you are satisfied with the essential spirit of the piece, then I can ask the subcommittee to polish it up within the bounds of the discussion here and bring it back for final review." The committee agreed to the second alternative.

Often this process will not be necessary; the committee will come to an obvious agreement, or some member will frame a decision action acceptable to the group.

Neutrality of the Chair

In acting as a meeting mover and decision framer, the chairperson should maintain a neutral posture. Too often chairs do not realize that assuming the chair means they are required to give up partisanship on most issues and seek to facilitate the committee decision. The only bias the chair should have is in support of committee action rather than inaction.

It is often difficult for a chairperson to act evenhandedly in the face of decisions with which he or she disagrees. And, indeed, if the disagreement is strong enough, the chairperson should resign. But he or she should not sabotage the committee process in order to obtain favored outcomes nor use the powers and prerogatives of the chair to sway or influence unduly the actions of the committee. The chair is entitled to an opinion and the opportunity of advancing it. If it is pressed strongly, however, the committee loses confidence that the chair is acting neutrally, even if there is not direct evidence for that opinion. If there is an occasional issue on which he or she wishes to make a substantive argument, the competent chair passes the gavel to someone else and becomes a member for purposes of the discussion.

This approach may seem to detract from the chairperson's leadership role, but leadership does not mean just furthering one's own point of view; rather, it involves facilitating the committee's progress.

> "You have got to hand it to Sid," commented Ira during the break. "I know that he is in favor of a more liberal admissions policy, but he handled that discussion as evenly and as fairly as if he had no preference at all." "Well," replied Jack, "isn't that why we elected him chairman?"

An Active Posture

The chair is an active role, not a passive one. Too often chairpersons act as though their concept of the job is to permit wholesale confusion and conflict to prevail in the name of participatory democracy and to periodically call for votes. Nothing could be further from our concept of the chair. In a neutral way, the chair should continually work during meetings to ensure that issues are fully discussed and to guarantee everyone the chance to participate. This should be accomplished in such a way that decisions are reached and the openness and integrity of the committee process is maintained. Neutrality, fairness, and the other attributes mentioned should not constitute a reason for inaction or for failure to engage fully in the committee process and seek to shape and direct it. Overall, that is the key to the role of the chair.

> Wilfred never ate during the bag lunch meetings of the Staff Analysis Group. Fritz once asked him why. "Well," replied Will, "as chairman, I have to see that things move along. I cannot do that and eat too. I eat later, so there is no problem at all."

What Do Members Do?

For the chairperson, there exists a set of relatively fixed expectations and responsibilities during the meeting situation, tasks that can be spelled out and observed. The tasks of the members are less clear. A member may, of course, be given specific assignments to carry out. Equally important, however, are his or her larger but more general meeting responsibilities that contribute to the dynamically moving aspects of the committee process.

Contribute to Committee

The first responsibility is to be prepared. This means not only reading all material forwarded in advance of the meeting but also giving thought to the topics to be considered and making appropriate explorations. A committee person cannot discharge a responsibility if he or she begins to think about the subject of the meeting only at the moment of arrival.

The member has the responsibility to participate appropriately in the process of the meeting. By *appropriate*, we mean to convey several dimensions of participation. Phrasing one's remarks so that they prevent or minimize conflict, and avoiding vagueness or sweeping generalities, helps the committee process. The degree of participation is another important dimension. Neither the member who is always silent nor the member who feels constrained to comment on every point is an asset to a committee. It is the mem-

ber's responsibility, sometimes necessarily helped by the chair, to monitor his
or her own behavior in this regard.

> When Mrs. Simmons began to talk, the others on the committee went to sleep.
> What poor Mrs. Simmons did not know is that the other committee members
> just could not stand to have her participate because once she started talking
> she talked at least fifteen or twenty minutes. It was virtually impossible to get
> her to be more moderate in her comments. It is safe to say that her influence
> was zero, if not actually negative.

The tone of participation should be varied as well. One should not
always make light, humorous remarks any more than one should always be
ponderous and philosophical. And the nature of participation may also vary.
Members who find it difficult to participate in the verbal give-and-take of a
lively discussion should consider making a contribution in writing prior to
the meeting. When a shy or reserved member examines the agenda and
notes an item of particular interest, it is appropriate to express this view in a
memo to the chairperson or committee members. Similarly, following the
meeting a member may, for the record, wish to submit a written opinion on
a particular issue, even if a decision was made.

Aid in Decision Process

The member must be constantly aware of being a part of a group of
people working on an issue. Although free to press personal views up to a
reasonable point, the member has also the responsibility of aiding the committee as a group in coming to a decision. This responsibility might require
a readiness to (1) accept some compromise solution to a problem when the
member's own view is acceptable only to some or only in part; (2) offer compromises when others are involved; or (3) offer actions, such as tabling or
voting acceptance or rejection, that move the group toward a decision. The
proper role here is similar to the one the chairperson takes. If an issue becomes confused and the chair is not actively leading the group, a member
may seek to synthesize comments and views. Such a summary may serve to
clarify the issue and identify commonalities along which resolution can occur. Or the member may formulate a proposal to sharpen the issue and focus
discussion. Once the exact range of attitudes is known, the proposal may be
modified in such a way as to obtain adequate support to reach a decision.

> Herman was a valued committee member in the firm because he pushed for
> decision. "Fellow members," he would say in one of his favorite phrases, "I

think we should adopt the proposal before us." Herman's remark frequently served to crystallize opinion. Even if the exact proposal was not adopted, the technique spurred members to make suggestions about changes and then act on a revision.

Decision and Agreement

There are two traps the member should be wary of slipping into. One is to assume that decision means agreement. It does not. It means only that a majority of members present at a duly constituted meeting agree on an action. There may be a significant number of members in disagreement. Indeed, the key purpose, functionally, of *Robert's Rules* is to permit decision in situations where there is a good deal of disagreement. One needs to be sensitive to the time at which the decision needs to be made and to the point at which the committee is able to reach a decision. Everyone might not agree; indeed, generally everyone will not. But decisions must be made. The member must recognize that decisions are a group action unless—and this procedure is quite common with reports—one files a minority report. Members who feel strongly opposed to a committee action often request that their vote be so recorded.

> The discussion had been going on for more than an hour. Two members of the Planning Committee would not agree. One of the minority said to the group, "Look, let's take a vote. My position will not be preferred, but you can't win them all, and I think enough of the time has been used here. I am not about to be persuaded to change my position. So I will just have to vote my conscience." The committee defeated the proposal he and a colleague favored.

Members should avoid being so "helpful" that they appear to be, or actually are, taking over the role of the chair. When the committee feels that an individual member is moving in this direction, it will often seek to cut him or her off. Indeed, the committee member needs to work in such a way as to facilitate the process, rather than simply confront and embarrass the chair.

Aid the Chair

A member should not take over the role of the chair, but should stand willing to aid in the performance of the chairperson's duties. The chair cannot run the meeting independently. The support of the group is needed, and this support is usually expressed through members' comments.

Support from members can be particularly welcome in such instances as when the chair needs to invoke rules to achieve germaneness in the discussion, or when members must be reminded that they must read some material for the upcoming meeting or were to have read something for the current meeting. Support for the chairperson's action here serves to cement businesslike norms for the committee's functioning and posture. Indeed, it is reasonable on occasion for a member to comment to a fellow member that his or her point is not germane, or to note that the member has dominated the discussion. These interventions are not pleasant, whether undertaken by the chair or a member, but they are sometimes necessary if the committee is to function effectively. Intervention by a member can not only be very helpful to the chair, but it can build committee cohesion, since there is always a latent tension between the pursuit of the committee's objectives, which is the responsibility of the chair, and the vested interests held by individual members. In some situations the strategically oriented member can even take a position stronger than the chair would take, allowing the chair to come in to "mediate" between two opposing members. The chairperson may offer a compromise that avoids polarizing the committee and/or placing severe controls on a particular member.

> Fred P. had been commenting for a few minutes on a proposal before the Budget Review Committee. It had become obvious that he had not read the proposal. Jack Johnson spoke, "I suggest that we put the proposal to a vote." "Wait," protested Fred, "I think we need to discuss a number of points in the proposal." "Many of your questions are answered in the text of the document, Fred," commented Jack, "and I am sure that you would not thus object to our moving ahead." The chair, Allen H., observed, "Well, let's take about five more minutes for discussion and then move to a decision." Fred looked a little chagrined and was very subdued for the remainder of the meeting.

How Does the Staff Person Act?

The staff person does most of the work outside the meeting. Once the meeting begins, it is the chair who takes the greater part of the responsibility. The main role of the staff person during the meeting is to assist, without undercutting, the chair. This requires knowledge, sensitivity, and flexibility. If the chair is doing an adequate job, the staff person may occasionally find himself or herself with nothing to do. But often the dynamics of a meeting are complex, and the staff person can observe things happening or become aware of things to suggest that might be overlooked by the chair. Also, if the chair is performing less than adequately, the staff person often complements the chair's role. To the extent that the staff person has special knowledge pertinent to the topic, arrangements should be made for its presentation.

Staff Performance

The staff person should sit next to the chairperson to facilitate their interaction. The staff person should be sensitive to and concerned with the image presented to the committee, which is related to such seemingly minor but subtle things as the seating arrangement as well as more obvious matters such as how he or she and the chair address each other and the manner of participation in the committee's deliberations. It must always be remembered that the staff person is not a committee member but rather a resource consultant and enabler. This places responsibility on the staff person to exercise restraint in injecting information and promoting or pursuing its discussion.

> The chairman of the Finance Committee was talking to Milo Smith, the new staff person to the committee. "Milo," the chairman commented, "my rule for a good staff person is the same as for children. They should be seen and not heard!" "That's nonsense," responded Milo. "I am as much a member of this committee as anyone." "Not really," replied the chairman. "As a staff person your work and activity goes on primarily outside the meeting. During the meeting itself, you generally should let me handle things. Staff are not members of committees; they are participants in the committee process." "That distinction is an interesting one," replied Milo. "I'll keep it in mind."

Relationship with Chair

If the chair asks the staff person a complicated question, then the staff person should try to write an answer. That procedure is simpler than giving a lengthy explanation in a whisper while the chair is trying to run the meeting as well.

> As the Finance Committee broke up, two of the members were talking in the coffee shop. "That Milo," said Jerome, "is unsettling. Did you notice that throughout the whole meeting he seemed to be whispering and talking to our chair?" "I know," replied Linda. "The thing is, I couldn't hear anything he said, but it just looked funny."

When the point of inquiry is of general interest, the chair may ask the staff person to explain or comment to the whole committee. Such comments should be as concise as possible. The staff person should not use the opportunity of the floor to add comments on tangentially related matters, nor make extended explanations. If it seems that the point cannot be clarified at that moment, then the staff person should offer to find the answer and communicate it by memo to the committee prior to or at the next meeting.

Restricted Participation

Generally, the staff person should refrain from making comments unless asked to speak by the chair or a member. And at those times the contribution should be factual and straightforward, not indicating favor or disfavor with elements of the meeting process. After the staff person is known well by the committee, and if he or she enjoys their respect, added liberties may be taken in the discussion. However, the point is a delicate one because committee members resent any staff person, even an experienced one, who acts in ways that suggest he or she is a member or is "overdirecting" the committee discussion. Staff members can express opinions but should never argue their opinions. Committee members can take the stance of pressing their point with other committee members, but they react negatively when it seems they have to convince the staff person, too.

About the middle of the meeting, Milo Smith was asked by H. T. Taylor for his reaction to the draft raise policy Taylor had proposed. "No one who knows personnel would propose such a policy," commented Milo. "To give everyone the same raise without any consideration of merit is stupid." The committee was silent for a moment. The chair then said, "Thank you, Milo; now let's vote." The Taylor proposal passed unanimously. Later the chair visited Milo's office. "Dammit, Milo, your comment was uncalled for," he snapped. "Not only is Taylor very experienced in personnel work, so your statement was audacious, but it was discourteous. Never tell anyone his point is stupid! The fact that everyone voted for it was a rebuke to you. And the policy did have many flaws that I hoped we could correct. You really blew it."

Expressing Opinion

In some cases the staff person may feel strongly on a particular point. In that event, and with the permission of the chair, he or she may communicate that feeling verbally or in memo form to the committee. In the latter case, the staff person may be asked to discuss the memo in a committee meeting. Such discussion should always be circumspect and respectful of other views and opinions. The staff member must still be aware that he or she is not a member of the committee.

The chairman of the Finance Committee announced to the group that there was an extra page in their salary analysis report. "Milo, our staff person, has completed an analysis of the salaries paid to similar staff here in town, in the state, and in the country, as far as he could get national figures. Based upon that work, I asked him to add his own recommendation as to the action he thought proper. His report is attached, with his recommendation." Harold Taylor commented, "I hate to admit it, but the job is a good one, and the recommendations make sense to me. I move we adopt Smith's proposal." There was a second followed by some discussion and minor modification, and the proposal passed. Milo felt good.

What Does the Staff Person Do?

While the demeanor of the staff is circumspect and low-key during the meeting, one should not assume that staff has nothing to do. Indeed, there are many tasks to be performed, and much of the success of the meeting requires that the staff perform those tasks well—but within, as we have suggested, a somewhat different framework from that of a member.

Assists with Mechanics and Dynamics of Committee Process

While the chair or committee members will assume responsibility for many aspects of the committee mechanics and dynamics, the staff should be the "back-up" monitoring the process and making certain that everything possible is done to further the effectiveness of the committee.

The details of premeeting preparations, ranging from follow-up telephone calls to the physical arrangements for the meeting, are likely to take more time than committee members can give. If they are to be done, it often falls upon the staff person to do them.

Once the meeting is under way, the staff's major responsibility, as we have said, is to assist the chairperson. This assistance covers every role and responsibility of the chairperson, but with the staff person injecting himself or herself only when there is reason to believe the chair could use assistance. The staff person must not appear to be taking over the chairperson's role. There is such a thing as being too helpful.

Staff in its role as technical consultant may also be called upon to interpret data, comment upon reports, or provide a perspective of trends or developments pertinent to the committee's assignment. The image and status of the staff person will be greatly affected by the competence with which these tasks are discharged. Adequate preparation and anticipation of information that might be needed or requested should be the goals of the staff person.

Milo Smith noticed that the meeting was very sluggish. The point of contention seemed to be the experience of other agencies in space rental, and exactly what, per square foot, was a proper charge for commercial space. Milo spoke up. "With respect to the matter of rental, why don't you let me look into what other organizations pay at various locations and talk to the bank. Then we can have some firm figures." The chair said, "That's very nice, Milo. We will pick this up at the next meeting, then."

Data Collection, Analysis, and Synthesis

Among primary responsibilities of staff are likely to be the collection, analysis, synthesis, and presentation of information for the committee's use and the preparation of the committee's final report.

These tasks sometimes are carried partially or entirely by committee members. But more often, if staff is available, it does most of the work. Committees expect staff to be professionally and technically competent in collecting, interpreting, and presenting information pertinent to the committee assignment.

> The chair turned to Milo Smith. "Milo, last week you said that you were going to look into the matter of space rental. Do you have any report?" Milo replied, "I do. I am sorry that I was not able to send it out before today's meeting, but there was some information from the United Way I wanted to get on a national basis, as well as the information on space costs here in town." He passed out two printed pages, "As you can see, the material is easily summarized here in these charts. Most of the people are paying about the same as we are for space that is not premium. To get a better location, or more services, we would have to pay considerably more." There was some discussion of the report and what it would mean for the organization. "What do you suggest we do now, Milo?" "Why don't a couple of you accompany me to look over a few sites; the preferred locations can be identified today. Then we can report back." "An excellent idea," said the chair.

Taking Minutes

Unless decision is made otherwise, it is usually the responsibility of the staff person to take the minutes of the meeting. Minutes are the official record of the meeting and therefore highly important. Generally, staff should prepare the minutes as soon as possible after the meeting and then clear them with the chair or secretary for accuracy and "sense of the meeting."

Writing minutes can be complicated. Sometimes it is possible to "tease" clarification out of the meeting process that was only latent in the actual meeting. Recorders often attempt to convey in the minutes a little more order than was, perhaps, actually present in the meeting itself. This process is both delicate and tricky. The staff person needs clarification from the chair as to how the minutes should be taken. Some prefer very full minutes; others prefer that only the essence of the discussion on any specific point be recorded. In preparing minutes of the latter kind, the staff person must take great care to record the central points with a minimum of his or her own material and to present conclusions only when decisive action was taken.

Milo Smith and his chairman were meeting to talk about the minutes. In the past, the members had taken the minutes, and this job was now being given to Milo since he had been assigned as staff person. "Milo," said the chair, "what I want is essential minutes, in the sense that the key items of decision are recorded." "But," replied Milo, "there are likely to be many differences of view. Should I get them all in?" "Up to a point," said the chair, "but not in terms of names; just in terms of substance. I want each item on our agenda to be clearly indicated in the minutes in terms of what we did." "I thought that minutes had to have what each person said," commented Milo. "Perhaps in courts and formal legal proceedings," said the chair. "For our purposes, just the key decisions and a crystallization of the substance of the discussion will be fine."

The minutes also should reflect tasks that remain to be accomplished before and during future meetings, by reporting postponement of topics, assignments given during the meeting to subcommittees or staff, et cetera. Submitting the draft minutes to the chair provides a good check on accuracy and completeness. And the committee will always have to approve them at the next meeting. (For more details, see Chapter 29.)

Postmeeting Follow-up

The follow-up on assignments evolving from the meeting will often be carried out by the chair or other committee members. But again, the staff person must monitor the process to be certain that such tasks are undertaken, and he or she will sometimes assist in carrying out the assignments.

As Milo walked out of the meeting, he mused to himself, "Boy, that was a heavy meeting. It's a good thing I made a list of the things that people agreed to do so that I can keep track."

Conclusion

Regular meeting sessions include the many interacting elements we have illustrated in this chapter. The patterns of staff role, member role, and chairperson role each become shaped by the actions of the others in the meeting situation itself. This process is, of course, what is supposed to happen in committee. What is needed, however, is for the players in the committee "theater" to have some idea of their roles and how these conceptions work out within the dynamic setting of the meeting.

CHAPTER 11

The First Meeting

Introduction

The first meeting of a committee is of critical importance in setting the tone, pace, and seriousness of subsequent proceedings. As we previously mentioned, the members are watching to see how the other members and the chair are going to act. Since all members are likely to be waiting for all other members, the chair should exercise leadership at this moment—an opportunity that is often foregone. From the start, the chair should perform all the tasks specified as the responsibility of anyone who is in that role.

For members and staff, similar considerations apply. The opportunity to make the committee one of the few to which members devote their more detailed attention is present in the initial sessions and then passes.

> "Boy," said Sam, leaving the first meeting of the Affirmative Action Task Force, "was that a dud. If our company plans its recruiting program like that meeting was planned, it's no wonder we haven't acquired more minorities." "You are right," said José. "I am not going to waste my time with that group."

Of course, first impressions are sometimes incorrect—people we do not initially like and groups that seem very exciting can both turn out to be just the opposite. And this can happen with committees.

The first meeting of a group will be a new experience for participants in at least one of two possible ways. If the members do not generally know each other, then there is social newness in the situation. Newly formed groups are likely to be receptive to the establishment of a schedule and a set of activities that will help them to become better acquainted. The meeting planners must take into account the need for such orientation and information. A second type of new experience occurs when the members know each other but have never before worked together as a committee or on a particular assignment. In such a situation, introductions are less necessary than more subtle messages about the nature of the committee process. The chairperson, whom many people may have seen in other roles, needs to articulate his or her style; the various members need to make clear their respective positions. Much goes on in the initial meeting, or series of meetings, that many committee members are unaware of. Only later do they feel vaguely that "things got off to a bad start" or that the committee's work has gone unusually well from the beginning.

> "I wonder," commented Chris, "how Ken is going to do as chairman?" Chris and Norm were walking down to the first meeting of the Budget Priorities Task Force. Norm replied, "He has been an excellent staff person for groups outside the organization; we will just have to see how he handles the role of chairman."

Because of the different kinds of newness the committee can experience at its first meeting, as well as the special opportunities for directions to be set and habits to be formed, the initial meetings of any committee deserve special consideration. Basically, these considerations are of two general types—procedural and substantive.

Procedural Considerations

Whether the committee is new socially or new in terms of tasks and roles, as it assembles, its members will expect to be informed about committee procedures and to contribute to them. They will want to learn proposed meeting schedules and to know who else is in the group. Committee members will, it is likely, wish to have some input into procedural matters themselves, but some initial indications of the thinking of the chair would be helpful to them.

Schedule a Meeting Promptly

Once a committee has been appointed, a meeting should be arranged as soon as practicable. A long interval between the appointment of a committee and the initial meeting gives the impression that the assignment is unimportant, that the chair is uninterested, or that the chair is conducting activity on behalf of the committee without the committee's knowledge. Sometimes delays occur because pertinent data collection has not begun. To avoid such delays, as much data collection as possible should be done before the committee is appointed, and after appointment the committee should be kept informed about the status of such activities.

Many readers doubtless have attended initial sessions in which the chair has revealed a long list of projects to which the committee has been committed without its members having had a chance to express an opinion. The chair usually makes such comments as, "There was nothing I could do," or "We are already committed." This situation may be avoided by a prompt meeting. Since most new committees need to be fitted into the already full schedules of their members, special attention by the chair and the staff person is necessary to find a time when everyone can conveniently meet. This process may involve a good bit of work on the phone, checking and rechecking schedules. It may involve scheduling an initial meeting at an unusual time, such as 5:00 P.M. or Saturday morning. It may involve a dinner meeting. Time and energy devoted to this task pay rich dividends in terms of fuller participation and also avoid complaints from members unable to attend a meeting scheduled in an arbitrary manner.

> The new chair of the Sewage Fee Committee was conferring about the first meeting with his staff person, Yancy. "I'll send out a notice as soon as we can get it run off," said Yancy. "No," said the new chairman. "We only have fourteen members. Let's type up a personal letter to each, welcoming them to the committee and alerting them to the fact that you will be calling them with respect to the first meeting. Then call each one." "OK," replied Yancy slowly, "but that sounds like a lot of work for a meeting notice."

Initial Packet

In the process of contacting everyone about the initial meeting, a list of names and home and business phones of the members must be compiled. That list should be distributed, along with the information about the meeting and the sponsoring organization, in an initial packet so that everyone on the committee knows who is in the group and how to get in touch with the others. The initial packet for each member should also contain a copy of the charge to the committee. This charge may be a formal declaration by a parent organization, it may be contained in a law, it may be set forth in the minutes of another committee. Members must know, however, what it is they are being asked to do in the terms used by the authority establishing the committee. The chair will have an opportunity to clarify his or her understanding of the mission and role of the committee, but this clarification should not be the only basis for member understanding of that mission and role. Indeed, that understanding should be a matter of some discussion at the initial meeting. Many is the committee that, for doubtless many reasons, has misunderstood its charge and/or the character of the sponsoring group. If every member has a copy of the charge, then the likelihood of inadvertent ignorance is diminished.[1] In all other respects, the packet for the initial meeting is like the packet for regular meetings.

> On his way into the meeting of the Executive Committee, Ernest found himself irritated. "I asked Ed to have the agenda and the purpose statement out in advance," he mused, "and Ed agreed. Now we do not have it, and that is a real problem." He was afraid that he would not be able to hide his annoyance under a mask of good humor. He and Ed had clashed on this before. As the new year got off the ground, and with so many new members, Ernest had hoped there would be a change.

Schedule of Meetings

As we all know, scheduling meetings is a constant source of problems. It is useful to take some time at the initial meeting to develop a schedule or at least arrive at some general idea of meeting times. It may be that the actual schedule cannot be established until the second or third meeting—but the committee should be developing some idea of how often and when it wants to meet and about how long the meetings should be. A proposal about these matters in the initial packet, clearly labeled "Preliminary," will encourage the members to think about their other commitments in relation to this committee.

> By phoning the members, Dick Yancy, the staff person to the Sewage Fee Committee, had assembled a list of times when it seemed possible for people to make meetings. There was no time when everyone could come, but some times were better than others. "I don't know why it has to be," he thought, "that committees I staff are always having troubles with the time of meetings. I wonder if there is some way we can schedule meetings in a longer time frame—then maybe people could adjust their schedules a little to us, rather than our always trying to accommodate schedules that cannot be adjusted."

The Chairpersons' Rules of the Game

Good chairpersons, like all good leaders, like to let those with whom they are working know how they would like the "show" to "run." Sometimes

---

1. We say inadvertent because there are times when a committee refuses to be limited by the charge. The group may wish to become involved in some matter not included in the charge or may even become committed to an action from which they are by charge excluded. If a committee cannot accept its charge as stated, it should seek to negotiate a change or even resign if the differences are substantial enough.

the chair simply tells the committee that meetings will begin on time, etc., etc. Other times, the message will come in more subtle ways. For example, scheduling meetings soon after the committee is formed and supplying a crisp initial packet containing all the required information go a long way toward informing the committee members that this particular chair is going to run an efficient committee. Committee members take their cues from the chair, much as students in class take their cues from the initial session of the class. One can generally tell after the first meeting how the chair or the teacher is going to proceed. Members' conclusions about this matter are important in determining whether or not they will devote sufficient effort to the work of the committee.

> In his opening remarks, the board president told the board, "This is my first year as president. You know that, as the firm has grown in the past, we have proceeded rather informally. I fear that such practices must now yield to more formalized ways of getting work done, because we are very, very much behind in our work. Therefore, I would like to suggest that we think of beginning and ending meetings promptly and using perhaps even one-person subcommittees to look into matters and bring us reports. And if you want items on the agenda, please just give me a ring. It is hard, unless the matter is an emergency, to discuss it simply off the tops of our heads." The members nodded approval. One could tell that they felt things were getting off to a good start.

A key element in committee process is the balance between formality and informality. Clearly, a committee constituted of a group of friends is not going to go into full-fledged *Robert's Rules* procedures. Neither is a relatively large group that meets infrequently going to become informal. All involved should remember that the ultimate purpose of a committee is to make decisions about a particular set of problems or circumstances. All else is prelude, including discussion, working documents, and the like. Usually, some balance between formality and informality is in order, yet this balance must be fair; one cannot plead informality in the periods in which one's causes would be favored, then insist on formality in other situations.

One of the reasons that *Robert's Rules* can be so unhelpful in many committee situations is that the rules may not be applied so as to facilitate a decision. They may not be well known to committee members, and they may be selectively applied. If those rules, or any other set of parliamentary rules, are to be used, then copies of them should be made available, and someone who is knowledgeable should become the parliamentarian. In the main, however, relatively conventional, commonsense procedures that are understood within the group will suffice. Other aspects loom larger in terms of committee dynamics.

Members and Staff Roles

Although the chairperson takes leadership in establishing procedures, the members can take it upon themselves to express their own feelings and views about how the committee should be run.[2] Any special procedural or logistical concerns should be mentioned at the start. Once the initial period of committee organization is past, it is unfair and difficult to insist on a change in policies or procedures. Hence, the alert member can take advantage of the clean slate of the new committee to ask that committee business be conducted in a certain way. Similarly, staff members can avail themselves of the opportunity to share a little of their work plans (which have been, of course, previously discussed with the chair). The committee members thus have the opportunity to hear how the staff will be working and in what ways and for what range of tasks the staff person will be available to the committee members. They may then state their own preferences about how the staff should serve the committee.

> Ernest looked about the Executive Committee and thought he could get support for a motion. When recognized, he said, "Mr. Chairman, I move that this committee establish the procedure of having the agenda in the hands of the members two weeks ahead of the meeting date. Emergency items can, of course, be taken up at any time." There was general support for this procedure.

Substantive Considerations

Procedural aspects of the committee's operation are an important part of the set of concerns addressed at an initial meeting. Another side of the meeting, of equal or greater eventual importance to committee performance, is a range of substantive matters that the committee needs to address. Thoughtful consideration of these matters is essential if the committee is to function properly. In addition, the alert chairperson seeks at this stage to lay the groundwork for shaping committee activity by analyzing and interpreting the committee's task. This is an important first meeting task.

The Charge

An essential ingredient for successful committee activity is an understanding of the committee's charge or purpose. Therefore, the charge should receive full consideration at the first meeting. As previously indicated, the

2. The matters discussed here are exclusively procedural. Substantive concerns are considered in the next section.

statement of the charge from the appointing body should be shared with all committee members. Such information often needs clarification. If discussion reveals points of confusion, or desires to modify, curtail, or expand the charge, the matter should be referred back to the appointing body for consideration and authorization.

The importance of the clarification of the charge cannot be overemphasized. It helps to focus the committee's approach and define the scope of its task, eliminates or minimizes efforts of committee members to—consciously or unconsciously—direct the committee into areas not encompassed by the assignment, and enables the committee to carry out the purpose as conceived by the appointing body rather than by the committee itself. Understanding and clarification of the committee charge are also great aids to the chair and staff in their guidance of the committee work.

In brief, when one is asked to do a job, the nature of the job should be understood.

> The committee appointed to search for a new executive was having its first meeting. Things were not going too well, because the chairman of the group had forgotten the letter from the board president. That letter was needed. The group was in the throes of an argument. "I do not care what you say," Irving announced. "We cannot find the proper executive unless and until we have some clear idea of the mission and role of the organization and a specific job description." Franklin's face was glazed with annoyance. "We can't do that, Irv, because we are not authorized to set the mission and role of the organization. Besides, the new exec might want to have something to say about that. If he does not, I don't want him. Let's just look for smart people.

Constraints

One substantive matter of great importance that affects the discussion of the charge has to do with the constraints on the committee's work. Constraints come in many forms. Two common ones are money and staff—and most committees have neither. But there may be political constraints or matters of interpersonal delicacy or interorganizational domain implicated here. Certain matters may need to be avoided, or certain ones considered. Time is another constraint. The members may have only a certain amount of time to contribute, or there may be a time limit on the task—perhaps a report must be on the table by a firm deadline. These constraints should be spelled out as fully as possible, not only because this permits members to organize their time, but also because the constraints provide a key mechanism through which the chair and the members can guide the committee process. The use of time—time for a task or time for members' attendance—becomes a way in which the committee can be kept to its task and helped to avoid wandering.

As the committee discussed whether it should start by finding the person or by defining a set of organizational goals, the chairman commented, "Let me bring something to the attention of the group. We have two months to do whatever it is we have to do. So let's keep this time factor in mind as we proceed."

Establishing Limited Objectives

The committee charge only indicates the direction in which we are going or the destination we are trying to reach. It does not tell us what road we should take. This decision requires the development of rather specific objectives and plans or steps for the accomplishment of those objectives. Once the charge is understood and accepted, a study plan and strategy should be developed that has the acceptance and support of the committee. In formulating its plans, the committee must be realistic about the constraints under which it must operate, whether these are money, staff, political considerations, time frame, or interpersonal or interorganizational matters. Usually much discipline must be exercised in order to limit the objectives in the light of the existing constraints. It is extremely frustrating and discouraging to find, too late, that a committee has charted an unrealistic course, with the result that it misses deadlines and the work drags far beyond the point where it can have maximum impact or effectiveness.

Interorganizational Considerations

Committees rarely function alone, in isolation from other working groups. Often there are other committees, sometimes with partially overlapping jurisdictions, sometimes with partially overlapping domains. Naturally, the Committee on Finance does not want to spend a great deal of time working on something that the Committee on Budget Priorities is also looking into. But again, perhaps it does: if people on the Committee on Finance feel that their perspective is one not shared by the Committee on Budget Priorities, and they or others in the interorganizational system wish to have that perspective represented, then the Committee on Finance will look into the matter too. Sometimes it is not a question of perspective on the same issue, but different aspects of the same issue that two committees are considering. In that event, while the focus is different, each committee is likely to make assumptions about what the other part of the issue is or will need to be. So, for example, if the Curriculum Committee and the Personnel Committee of a school are working simultaneously but not together, each must make some assumptions about the work of the other—the curriculum planners are assuming a certain type of staff, and the personnel managers are assuming a certain type of curriculum. The assumptions each group makes about the other for purposes of its own work may be regarded as premature, or otherwise problematic, by the other group. Clearly, thoughtful attention is needed here by the chair, the staff person, and the members. Interlocking memberships are often used to facilitate communication. First-meeting assessments are crucial.

> The Sewage Fee Committee was having an initial meeting. After introductions and formalities had been completed, the committee began discussing several aspects of its functions. "Part of the job," said Dick Yancy, "is to relate sewage fees to the city budget. Sewage fees are an important part of city income, and if the budget is going to be in trouble, we may be asked to reassess our fee basis." "Well," asked Elenore, "when will we know that?" "There's a problem," replied Dick, "that has been bothersome for years. By law, we need to set our rates by December 1. On the other hand, the next year's budget is not approved until the May council meeting. Usually we have a joint member with the budget committee to get a feel for what is going on."

Working with Other Committees

For a variety of reasons, some of which we have just mentioned, one particular committee will want or need to work with another committee. When this possibility develops, discussion within the committee is proper, followed by a consideration of the ways in which cooperative work may be achieved. A *joint task force* in which a problem is studied by members of both groups is one possibility. At other times, an agreement to *work in tandem* is advisable. Under this style of operation, there are no explicitly joint efforts, but the two groups keep in very close touch. Tandem working styles develop where there are not clear indications that a joint task force's recommendations would be acceptable to both groups. For the initial meetings, tandem operation is usually a good suggestion, because it commits people to joint work without committing them, perhaps prematurely, to joint committee membership in the sense a task force would. A third pattern is for groups to proceed separately and then come together *in conference* at the point where their recommendations differ. This plan is the one used by the U.S. Congress, and the Conference Committee is the form it has devised to work out such differences.

> The dispute in the Executive Search Committee between those formulating goals and those searching for personnel was resolved as follows: The Long-Range Planning Committee would provide some goals, ones they had been considering, and the Executive Search Committee would use these as a basis for looking at candidates. The only problem was that the Long-Range Planning Committee was not producing the goal statement, and the two months' time was running out.

Preceding and Following Other Committees

Sometimes one committee "works with" another committee only in the sense that the second committee follows up by taking the decisions and recommendations of the first and doing more work with them. If this procedure occurs, then the second committee has an interest in the kind of decision or recommendation it is going to receive, and the initial committee is concerned about the kind of decision or recommendation that will prove acceptable at the second phase. If, for example, a finance committee or personnel committee is making recommendations to the full board, then that functional committee is concerned about the type of recommendation the board will find acceptable. The functional committee will seek this information in the form of "signals" from the full board. Similarly, the subcommittee should seek to give signals to the recipient committee in regard to the direction being taken at the moment. While both sets of signals may be formally premature, conversations between the chairpersons can provide each group with some idea of what is happening, and each group can make necessary corrections or plans accordingly.

> The Bargaining Committee knew that its agreement had to be approved by the general membership in a committee of the whole. Its members had to hold firm and yet compromise with the membership in the least significant areas. Yet the exact nature of what the membership would and would not accept was unclear. For this reason, the committee decided to hold periodic informational meetings with the membership. While the explicit contents of proposals would not be revealed at this time, the general outlines of discussions would be shared, and the membership's views could be ascertained.

Working with Units and Organizations

Sometimes committees work closely not with other committees but with staff and organizational units. A finance committee is likely to work closely with the controller's office, the personnel committee with some members of the personnel department, and the like. In these situations, the committee has a central concern to which it must be alert—cooperation. Bureaucratic units have a tendency to act at times as if they have the one and only definition of the situation. Not only do such units usually have a near monopoly on information, but they have more permanent members than committees do. Hence, their people often can simply wait out committees that are doing things they dislike. Careful attention to relationships is important here because of the potential of cooperation in the situation.

> The Sewage Fee Committee had run into difficulty with the Water and Sewer Department of Blissfield. The head of the department was a crusty civil servant

who liked to have things his way. The Sewage Fee Committee, under the leadership of Elenore Shonts, wanted to have a discount for citizens over sixty-five, and the director was opposed. The question now came down to, as Elenore said, "Who is running the show?" And, she would add, "It's the Fee Committee."

While this situation may or may not work out in the direction desired by the committee, close relationships developed through exchanges of membership and minutes can help prevent problems.

Conclusion

The first meeting, or series of meetings, is highly important because of the tone and pace—the "lifestyle"—it sets for the committee, and because of the messages it conveys about the way the committee is likely to operate as it goes about its business. Some initial impressions become self-fulfilling prophecies; an initial assumption that the committee is going to be very effective may lead to the increased participation that creates that very effectiveness.

In order for a committee to get off to a proper start, attention must be paid to a special set of procedural and substantive considerations. The substantive considerations assume special importance because they lay the groundwork for later activity. Specifying the mission and role of the group and thinking about any constraints that might affect committee operation are particularly vital.

Although constant attention throughout the committee life needs to be paid to the problems and potentials of working interorganizationally—with other committees and/or with other units and organizations—in a variety of relationships, the first meeting is an especially important time for such considerations to be introduced. In this initial period, arrangements are sometimes made that with a little more thought would have been seen as inadvisable. Or, on the other hand, potentials for interorganizational links may not be perceived because too little thought is given at the start. Thus, interorganizational scanning and mapping become key initially and require attention throughout.

One further point on the initial meetings that has not previously been discussed in the chapter needs to be mentioned: The importance of personality. We have taken the view in this book that personality is of less importance than is generally thought and that proper understanding of the roles and functions of committees plus adequate preparation are the keys to committee effectiveness. Nevertheless, in the initial meeting of a committee whose participants are new to each other, the personalities of the members assume perhaps their greatest importance. One should be particularly alert to the risk of untimely actions, on the basis of initial impressions of the chair and the members, that the committee may later regret. This point is especially pertinent to the election of officers, if that is an early duty of the new committee.

CHAPTER 12

Pulling It All Together

Introduction

Committee progress and successful achievement are, of course, the responsibility of the entire committee. The conductor, or chairperson, and the staff person share responsibility for the activities, yet the reader should understand that all members bear some responsibility for committee operations.

Charting Direction and Progress

In the initial series of committee meetings, a basic tone and sense of direction is established, taking into account member preference and the formal charge to the committee. As meetings progress, the chair needs to be sensitive to the progress the committee is making and must endeavor to keep it on course. If, as is often the case, initial agreements about objectives and goals become confused and progress is slow, then it is the responsibility of the chair and the staff person to help the committee assess its structure and operations. Time is also a factor. There are usually report dates, meetings, and the like that are important with respect to committee activity. If, for example, a report is due by April, certain things must be accomplished in January and February. Every member must be sensitive to the time constraint, but the chair has the overall responsibility for keeping the committee on course and on schedule.

> "You know," said Bill, "committees are so different." He was talking to his friend Irv, with whom he served on two committees. "The Staff-Training Task

Force is one example. There we move along, and we really have a sense of accomplishment. The Library Committee, though, seems to be plodding, and we always take a lot of time, even though we never accomplish anything." "I know," replied Irv. "And the thing I resent is spending so much time! It always seems that we could be finished so much earlier on the Library Committee. I think we all act crazy, just out of boredom."

Communication

Our normal experiences in daily life clearly reveal the complexities and difficulties of accurate communication. This is particularly true when we are dealing with mixed groups, or individuals with varied backgrounds and experiences. As an example, various professional groups have their own jargon that may convey different meanings to others. Consequently, in chairing a committee or serving as a staff member or committee member, one must continue to strive for clarity and understanding in written and verbal communications.

There are a number of points at which the process of communication can be strengthened. The initial step is the point at which one is asked to serve, when a clear understanding of the committee's purpose and the member's role is necessary. A second phase is the period during which the committee's objectives and goals are refined and member roles are further specified. A third phase of committee communication relates simply to the ongoing process of interaction among members, the chairperson, and the staff. We have already mentioned the need for the chair to meet regularly with the staff person. Such meetings serve to open and keep clear the communication channels between them. The chair, however, needs to be sensitive to the fact that the committee as a whole also needs some access to the staff, and time should be made available for staff reporting and meetings with other committee participants.

Similarly, opportunity for discussion and communication among committee members is important. The chair must be aware of the importance not only of formal attention to problems of communication—clarifying points, providing opportunities for discussion, focusing alternatives—but also of informal opportunities. Here, a social event arranged by the chair or a committee member might be helpful. Some balance that provides an opportunity for the committee members to interact in quasi-committee ways is most important.[1]

---

1. We say "quasi-committee ways" because most of the interaction at these affairs is around committee business—yet it is not formal. Also, the members have the opportunity to see and interact with one another in a more relaxed and more human situation than in a formalized session.

The chairman of the Finance Committee was talking to the executive. "I want you to propose a series of meetings this year, Ron, in such a way as to include some lunches and dinners. Perhaps one dinner and maybe three lunches would be appropriate." "Why is that?" asked Ron. "It has been my experience over the years that some of the meetings have to have time for informality as well as formality," replied the chairman. "We can meet at about 11:30, have lunch, and then between about 12:45 and 2:00 finish a great deal of business. I use the lunches to provide a time when people can chat in a friendly way and perhaps get more of a feel for some of the positions their co-members are taking on issues."

Use of Written and Other Materials

The committee process is almost always helped by the use of written materials. Often, when the committee is considering an item, a written report by a subgroup or a single person serves to clarify the issues. When something is written down, one can focus better on what is stated and on possible omissions. If the committee is considering policy statements, it may need to go through many drafts before the statement is exactly what it wants, and in the process it will achieve a common understanding of the document. A draft document serves to avoid vagueness and misunderstanding. Alternative formulations, concerns, opinions can be dealt with in terms of How would you say it? or What would you like to see changed in this draft, and in what ways? Writing it down and rewriting it not only serves to clarify intent, it also serves to facilitate and focus discussion and participation. Other materials such as filmstrips, films, photos, and maps may be used to help committee members increase their understanding of an issue and to communicate with each other in clearer and more common terms.

"Mr. Chairman," said Roger R., "I would like to compliment you and your staff for the excellent film on our new band program." Roger R. was a member of the Board of Education, and there had been much controversy about allocating money for instruments and uniforms. (The film class had made a movie of the band, and the chairman of the school board had asked that it be shown to the full board.) "Thank you, Roger," the chairman replied. "The superintendent and I felt that if the board could see the band in action and get a 'feel' for the way these young people perform, it would be helpful in thinking about budget. And let's not forget the wonderful job the film class did."

Use of Experts and Consultants

There are times in the work of all committees when they need expertise that the committee does not possess. If the committee has a staff person, that person should be able to perform most tasks but may not be knowledgeable in all areas of concern to the committee. All too often, committees languish at this point, and the illness has two manifestations. One occurs when, even though the group is dealing with a subject about which no one present knows a great deal, the committee continues to discuss it. This kind of unproductive behavior usually results in frustration and conflict on the part of members.

Another kind of problem can arise when a committee recognizes the need for more information and seeks to have one of its members or a staff member hastily "bone up" on the subject. While we recognize the need for individual participation, we must understand that it is not possible for a novice to become an expert on a technical or complex subject in just a short while.

At either of these points, when the committee is confronted with some set of technical problems, it is useful to bring in a consultant. Sometimes such a person will donate time, sometimes compensation must be arranged. But the appropriate use of specialized help, around specific problems, is the most efficient and effective way to deal with some issues.

The Advisory Committee to the district judge was meeting on Wednesday, as usual. The question at hand was on certain provisions of the mental health law regarding mental illness and insanity. "The problem," said Mrs. Leavitt, "is that these two terms have different meanings in the legal context." "I agree," said Fred Brown. "Besides, a lot of work is now being done here that we don't know enough about." "I suggest then," said Mrs. Bailey, "that we call the law school of the university and invite a lawyer who knows about these things to come and discuss this problem with us." "OK," commented Fred, "but we also need someone with a psychiatric or psychological background." "Perhaps," added Mrs. Leavitt, "we should spend a day with experts from several fields, sort of a training day. I think it is unlikely that we can find any one person who knows all the ins and outs here. Since we are supposed to advise the judge, we had better get some broad-based exposure, including some legislators and the local prosecutor." Everyone agreed that a full day spent with some expert consultants would assist the committee to more fully understand the subject matter and save a considerable amount of time.

Facilitating or Limiting Participation

The key to participation in the committee process is to guarantee ample opportunity for the study and discussion of agenda items and yet not make the process so lengthy that members have the sense that "we have been over this, and over this, and over this, again and again and again." The job of the chair, and of members as well, is to facilitate participation in some instances and to limit it in others. We have mentioned the utility of using written materials and consultants as a means of facilitating participation. However, these approaches as well as others can be abused. Committees reach a point of saturation. Such a point is attained when a committee is satisfied that all essential aspects of an issue have been touched upon, and it would take a great deal more work to produce any further improvement in the quality or quantity of information on which to base a decision. Up to this point, the chair has been seeking to encourage and develop participation, but now the chair needs to move the committee to a decision. At this point, some limits must be established. There is always a member who will call for more drafts, more materials, and more discussion. There are always members who feel that a decision is "premature and hasty." A proper balance must be struck. There comes a time when proposals, directions, and actions must be "voted up or voted down."

> As the Building Committee was moving through a series of draft plans, Chet thought to himself that the process had bogged down. At that moment, his thoughts were broken by the sharp, pungent voice of Hermione Laswell. "Harry," Hermione said to the chair, "these drawings are good, but I can't decide on making any recommendation. I need to see a landscaped model, something that is much more fleshed out than any of these." At that point, Chet felt angry. He said in an exasperated tone, "Hermione, we have this additional set of plans today because you made the same comment last month. It is the comment you always make. We have put off making a recommendation for six months while we all looked at more detailed plans. And it should be noted, building costs have gone up 4 percent during this time alone." "Well," replied Hermione, "we cannot be premature." "True," said Chet, "but there is such a thing as being postmature as well. And that's where we are now, in my opinion. I move we accept plan C!" There was a second, and the plan passed.

Postmeeting Activity

Among the great problems and difficulties committees encounter is lack of follow-through. Decisions are frequently made that require that some action be taken, but, somehow, nothing happens. Generally, two types of mistakes are made in this connection. The first is that no specific person is assigned to do the follow-through; hence, no one feels responsible for taking the action that was specified by the group. Second, in those situations where someone was assigned responsibility, supervision may be lacking; often, some prodding is required in order to get results. In both instances, the chairperson and the staff person have important responsibilities in assigning tasks or checking on progress, and often one of these two shares the task of follow-up with the assigned member. In the final analysis, it is the responsibility of the chairperson to be certain that the work is completed. These activities are part of the committee process.

> Sally and Beatrice were talking after a meeting of the Red Cross Volunteer Coordinating Committee. "One thing I have to say about Sam Beaver," commented Sally, "is that he sure does a thorough job of being chairman." "You are right," added Beatrice. "He never lets us forget anything we promised to do or anything that needs to come up on the agenda. He must study old minutes to be sure he has not missed anything." "Well," Sally added, "I think it's good. A group like ours that meets less than once a month and has representatives from different groups could really fall apart if someone like Sam didn't do that kind of homework."

Report Conference

One problem many committees face, and a problem we shall consider in more detail in the final chapter, is accountability. How are committees made accountable for their performance? Are there ways of assisting them to improve their performance? Can they be rewarded for doing a good job? Or stimulated and guided if the job is dragging or getting off target?

One helpful device is reporting back to the appointing body. If the committee assignment is complicated and requires considerable time, periodic or progress reports are a useful device. This tactic has the added advantage of placing before those who will finally act on the report its center and direction and thus giving the committee some feel for the kind of reception the final report might receive. In the case of standing committees, more formal reports submitted at least annually are helpful.

> At the March meeting of the Personnel Committee, the chair, Mike Flicker, asked the group about a report. "I think we should be granted a section of the final report that the board makes," said Mike. "The annual report will only have a paragraph or two about us. But the agency report, from which the annual report is made up, will have statements from each of the committees of the board reporting on activities, efforts, and key issues that have affected us over the year. I am going to ask Mrs. Simpson if she would help me in pulling together a draft. In two meetings, we can then go over it together." Mrs. Simpson agreed.

Conclusion

As a form of social interaction, a committee process has peaks and valleys. The peaks, the actual meetings, are heavily influenced by what has gone on before each meeting and what may be expected to go on afterward. All participants in the committee process—the chair, the members, the staff—must do their part to make the whole committee process function effectively. This chapter has suggested some techniques and mechanisms that may be helpful in getting all the participants in the committee process pulling together, not necessarily toward the same substantive goal but toward the goal of reaching a high-quality decision.

COMMITTEE TYPES

AND FUNCTIONS

In Part I, and subsequently, we have considered the roles of the chairperson, the member, and the staff person and their importance to committee functioning. The main elements of these roles will remain constant regardless of the type of committee, the functions the committee may be performing at any given moment, and the social context within which the committee operates. Yet, these other elements—type of committee, committee functions, and social context—do make important differences in shaping the role performance of key persons on the committee. Some would say it is six of one or half a dozen of the other, that the roles and the other elements are of equal importance. While essentially agreeing with that, it is our opinion that this issue is better viewed as a question of theme and variations. The central core of role requisites provides the theme, and the various functions of types and contexts provide the variations.

As committees are performing different functions, or as they are constituted as different types of committees, there are some special problems, many of which are quite common and easily identifiable, to consider. We believe it would be constructive to alert potential committee participants to some of these difficulties in advance of their actual occurrence.

Policy-Related Committees

There are doubtless many ways one could conceptualize and organize the "committee field." Basically, we believe that committees, whatever their genesis, are concerned with policy. For our purposes in this volume, we define policy to comprise legislative recommendations, institutional codes, organizational guidelines, et cetera, that have broad application. We do not mean to imply that all committees make policy. Indeed, only one of the seven types of committees we will discuss in Part IV actually decides, in a formal and legal way, whether or not to establish a policy. To be concerned with policy can mean sharing information about policies with others, and hearing about their policies; it can mean making policy recommendations to officials and policy-deciding groups; it can mean seeking, coordinating, and implementing policy agreements in situations where the committee has no formal/legal authority to actually set policy, as well as, in some instances, deciding policy and overseeing its administration. We have identified seven functions or types of committees: (1) policy-sharing committees, (2) policy advisory committees, (3) policy-coordinating committees, (4) policy-implementing committees, (5) policy-deciding committees, (6) policy-overseeing committees, and (7) policy-administering committees (task forces).

Policy Development and Policy Action

Generally speaking, committees have one or two emphases within the general framework of policy. They are either developing policy, as in the sharing, advising, and deciding committees, or they are seeking action on policy already developed (by them or other committees) as in coordination, implementation, oversight, and administration committees.

Interorganizational and Intraorganizational

The first four committee types are most common in the space between organizations—the interorganizational system. Members may be from many organizations seeking to acquaint themselves with each other, or they may represent many settings that collectively advise some "host" organization. Action also occurs interorganizationally. Organizations need to come together for concerted action on many bases, from writing a common proposal for a grant to developing shared responsibilities in time of disaster. Coordinating committees are frequently used for such purposes. Implementing committees are often created when there is no official body with exclusive responsibility to carry through on a set of recommendations, or where there is no agreement that any one of the participating organizations should assume the responsibility.

The other three types of committees either represent the organization—for example, a board of directors—or are otherwise within the framework of a specific company or firm or agency. Policy-deciding committees are often boards, but not always. Sometimes a subcommittee of a board, or some other type of committee is authorized to proceed in some set of matters. Overseeing and administering committees are more specific versions of policy-deciding committees. After the board has approved the budget, for example, it is usually up to the finance committee to oversee the spending and make certain that guidelines are observed. Sometimes a building committee will be given authority to administer several contracts of a construction project. In any event, it is important to keep in mind that both policy development and action occur in the interorganizational setting as well as the intraorganizational one.

Formal Authority

Committees may have different types of authorization to proceed with their mission, and it is important to mention here what these might be. One type is legal authority, in which the committee is legally obligated to carry out some course of action. A board of directors is one type of committee that often has such legal authority. Statutes may confer authority. For example, a statute might create an "advisory committee" on urban renewal. The law might be vague about the specific responsibilities of such a group, or it might specify in more detail a set of roles and duties. In any event, such a group, unlike some others, has formal authority to proceed. Other committees, often those in the interorganizational area but not always, do not have legal authority to act. An implementing committee, appointed by a community planning body to effect the merger of three settlement houses, cannot order that merger to occur. For those committees without legal authority, the question of the extent of their authority may be an enduring issue.

Function and Type

We have referred to these seven committee modes as both "functions" and "types." For purposes of discussion, committees are classified here on the basis of their primary responsibilities. It should be noted, however, that two factors make classification difficult. One is that many committees have a sufficiently mixed mandate that they perform multiple functions. A coordinating committee, by way of example, may become for certain items a policy-deciding committee, leading to confusion within or outside the committee in regard to its role. The second factor is the attitude committees often take toward policy issues: they seek to "take the next step." Policy-developing committees may seek to decide and implement their recommendations. Individuals and groups have a tendency to seek to complete a task, once begun. It is hard to give advice and then bow out of the picture.

In order to facilitate the reading of the following chapters, we have organized all of them in the same format. Each has the following parts: "Introduction," "Types and Functions," "Special Issues and Problems," "Key Decision Issues," "Key Role Requisites," and "Conclusion." All but two of these headings are self-explanatory. In "Special Issues and Problems," we will identify the focal difficulties that committees of the type discussed, or committees of any type performing this function, will experience. In "Key Decision Issues," we will try to solidify the main elements that need to be decided on in that function/type situation.

CHAPTER 13

The Policy-Sharing Committee

Introduction

As the complexity of the modern community increases, the need for shared information becomes imperative. This need arises whether the complexity occurs within an organization, within some ethnic or racial community, or within some specified territory. It arises somewhat differently, but with equal pressure, in two types of groups—corporate and categoric.[1]

Categoric groups are organizations or units within the same category—realtors' associations, bakers' associations, social workers' associations, and the like. Individuals in these groups need to know about others' activities, problems, new approaches, experiments. Sometimes it is also necessary to come to agreement about domain, or "turf," so that competition does not adversely affect the members. A corporate group, on the other hand, is a gathering of people who are mutually interdependent, such as steel makers and retailers, suppliers and users of a given sort, producers and transporters, and the like. These groups need to know what sales look like so they know what to produce, what production looks like so they know what to expect to have to sell, what the transportation situation is, et cetera. Committees whose members are appointed to share information and act individually on the basis of that information are policy-sharing committees.

---

1. See Amos Hawley, *Human Ecology* (New York: Ronald Press, 1950).

Types and Functions

As a type, the policy-sharing committee is quite common, although its name is often something else—frequently "association" or "council." The policy-sharing committee is generated by some form of mutuality—mutual dependence on some group of clients, resources, or territory; mutual performance of some function—such as philanthropy, child care, medical, or real estate service; or interdependence on each other. Usually, the directors of the organizations involved will form an ad hoc group to do some initial sharing of information. Over time, this group may actually develop into an organization that comes to dominate its founders. Any committee with the word "exchange" in its title is likely to have some form of policy-sharing function. Committees set up to exchange information on markets, procedures, city functioning, and volunteers are examples.

The policy-sharing committee can operate best if it sets for itself the minimal initial goal of exchanging information. A key assumption is that any action that results might be called "autonomous coordination" in the sense that participating organizations, upon hearing what other organizations are doing, may make adjustments to be in line with the prevailing practice. Sometimes, if it becomes clear that two agencies need to confer, that can occur outside the committee scope as the natural result of the desire to achieve a mutually satisfactory accommodation of interests.

Special Issues and Problems

Policy-sharing committees have a number of problems. If it is acknowledged at the outset that they exist simply to share information, problems can be minimized because differences of expectations are avoided. Yet, in the sharing of information, the participants are often unsure about how much to release and how much to hold back. Organizations need their secrets, as it were. Furthermore, they may fear they will receive little or nothing in return for the information they reveal. Hence, even the exchange of information about policies and practices is usually limited until the participants acquire confidence in one another.

The participants themselves become a problem for this type of committee. Usually, organizational executives give such committee activity second or third priority. Frequently executives come themselves initially and then delegate the responsibility to representatives. The shift is a crucial one. The responsibility for participation has been shifted from the people who can make decisions, in this case about what information to share and what action to take in regard to that information, to those who must check with the "front office." Secondly, and as devastating, is the practice of sending a succession of different representatives to meetings. Ignorant of what has gone on before, new people require orientation. Sometimes such a committee spends much of its time in orientation.

The sharing of information, however useful, often is not sufficient to hold attendance after the first few meetings. Policy-sharing committees often develop problems of morale because the task just does not seem central enough. As morale slips and attendance wanes, the key reason for coming—to hear what others are doing—becomes obviously imperiled.

These problems occur as a result of the limited mandate. Therefore, policy-sharing committees are often asked, or may decide for themselves, to do some actual coordination. What often happens is that the group meets and decides on relevant issue areas, and then the members go back and try to "sell the agreement." Unless there are very compelling reasons related to organizational interest why constituent organizations should comply, they often do not. They may ask for time to study, for more information, and the like. This process is a frustrating one for the members, who then fall into two modal orientations. On the one hand, there are those who remain loyal to their respective organizations, putting their interest in the committee into eclipse. And there are those who become loyal to the "community interest" and thus run into trouble with the organization they represent. In any event, the original purpose of the policy-sharing committee is aborted and its effectiveness is nullified.

Key Decision Issues

For a policy-sharing committee to be effective, it must insist that it will take no action committing its participants to a certain position or implying a commitment. Its decisions or actions should be restricted to its major goal—the sharing of information. This decision is a very hard one for a committee to make and an awkward one as well. Yet the moment a policy-sharing committee starts making decisions, it will develop frustrations, because its mandate and its membership do not permit their implementation. Further, the committee is not usually structured, staffed, or prepared to go through the lengthy process of analysis and the development of recommendations on which sound decisions might be based. The only decision the committee should make is an initial one to avoid becoming involved in anything other than policy sharing. This happy state can be defined and achieved with the leadership of the chair and the staff. Although there will always be some members of such committees who cry for "action," they should be dissuaded and reminded that the sharing of information is the purpose of the committee.

The second issue on which the committee should seek agreement is the stabilization of membership. This goal may take a few meetings to achieve but, by that point, a full complement of regular members should have developed.

Key Role Requisites

The Chair

Several roles involve important special problems here. In a policy-sharing committee, the chair needs to lead the committee to an early agreement to avoid "action." This responsibility, however, cannot be effectively carried out by the chair alone. The chairperson should initially set up a schedule around which members can begin their reports and, if possible, develop a common format in which the reports can be made. In a policy-sharing committee, the members play a more central role than is true in some other committees; among other responsibilities, they must obtain and report specific information on a more regular basis. For this reason, the chairperson should seek firm agreement about participation in the initial stages of committee organization. The chair should also encourage reporting on strategic matters related to policy—emphasizing the importance and value of sharing such information—in order that the meetings will be significant enough to attract and hold participation.

The Member

The member of a policy-sharing committee is often more a representative of his or her agency than would be true in other types of committees. For this reason, the member must be clear, insofar as possible, as to what types of policies the agency is willing to share and how these are to be presented to the committee. After the meeting, the member should report back and check with superiors in the agency in regard to the nature of further presentations and participation.

As mentioned above, the member has a more specific role in this type of committee, since the purpose of the committee is to hear the information the members bring. Hence, the member should try to attend in person rather than send substitutes and should always be prepared to report in turn. When representing the executive, the member should be able to accurately reflect agency policy as well as the position of the agency on matters before the committee.

The Staff Person

In a policy-sharing committee, there are some special tasks the staff person can do that are helpful to the committee. First, since the members may not represent the universe of relevant policies, the staff person can seek other examples of actions and activities from elsewhere in the community and the nation. So, for example, if the committee has been convened to consider a health plan policy for a group of organizations, the staff person can usefully secure examples of other plans from other places—perhaps some large organizations and some small ones, some from insurance companies, and so on.

Second, the staff person needs to develop a form of record-keeping in which the different policies can be coded as to their essential components and presented so that the committee will be able to make comparisons. While the individual reports of the members are very important, they often do not permit good comparisons because the members may not choose to emphasize similar points and may use different formats and approaches. It is very important for the staff person to work with committee members to develop and present comparative material.

Finally, the staff person needs to check with the individual members to see if they can provide copies of the original policies for the committee files. The committee files can then serve as a point of reference for future study and research on specific topics.

Conclusion

Policy-sharing committees begin as, but rarely remain, solely information-sharing bodies. Convened for that purpose, they often shift their focus and become interested in making policy recommendations and actually serving as a vehicle for coordinating programs. If the mission of information-sharing can be specified and carried out, then a useful task will have been accomplished.

CHAPTER 14

The Policy Advisory Committee

Introduction

Policy advisory committees are established to provide advice to some person or organization. They generally assess a policy issue about which significant differences in points of view have evolved. Such a committee may be made up of experts, or it may react to materials prepared by experts in the subject matter being considered. (We here follow Banfield's definition of an *issue* as a topic over which there is contention and for which resolution is either difficult or uncertain.[1]) Sometimes the work performed by these committees and commissions becomes a key policy document, which sets the stage for work to come for many years. One such example is the National Advisory Commission Report on Civil Disorders.[2] Whether the impact is great or less than great, the hope of the advisory committee is to propose to its sponsor a course of action that will be considered and appropriate.

Types and Functions

Advisory committees and commissions, or groups performing advisory functions, often act in two rather distinct ways. The first occurs when a committee has been appointed to focus on a specific problem or issue and prepares policy recommendations for solving it. A second operating mode occurs

1. E. Banfield, "Politics, Planning, and the Public Interest," in Fred M. Cox et al., eds., *Strategies of Community Organization*, rev. ed. (Itasca, Ill.: F. E. Peacock. 1974).
2. *National Advisory Commission Report on Civil Disorders* (Washington, D.C.: U.S. Government Printing Office, 1968).

when the committee is appointed to give advice to an operating executive or group on an ongoing basis. In the former case, the advice is usually transmitted in a formal, and often substantial, report; in the latter case, recommendations are often transmitted serially and may be oral or informal written reports. In both cases, the task of the advisory committee is to recommend policy actions or directions, both immediate and long range. The ultimate success of the committee, determined in terms of the extent to which its advice is accepted, tends to depend on the relationship between the committee and the appointing body as well as on the quality of the advice as such. While acceptance of the advice is usually the measure of "success," there are occasions when high-quality advice is overruled because of "political" considerations.

There are some independent policy-advising organizations that fund themselves and appoint committees to report to the nation. The Committee for Economic Development is one such group, and this large organization convenes national figures and develops committees to study and report to the organization and the nation on many social issues such as regional government, housing, welfare, and education. The Brookings Institution, the Urban Institute, and the Rand Corporation are other examples.

Many organizations and groups that have broad responsibilities appoint advisory committees to make recommendations on particular policy issues. Sometimes schools and colleges have "visiting committees." Large organizations and boards often have technical advisory committees to make recommendations on technical matters that might be beyond the scope of the organization's normal resources. So, for example, an organization that has a research department might set up a technical advisory committee of researchers who could help the staff deal with problems as they relate to research and provide direct technical assistance when needed.

There is one other type of committee that we will mention here but not discuss in detail. That committee is the "study" committee. A "study" committee is set up when some elements of a community or an organization have determined that a problem exists, and they empanel a committee to study it and make recommendations. Naturally, one would think that this type of committee would be a policy-advising committee. However, our experience indicates that it really falls somewhere between the policy recommendations committee and the policy-implementing committee. This is because there is a strong push for implementation from the very start. The committee is often selected with implementation in mind, and the charge is developed to permit or encourage implementation. At other times, an appointing group may imply to the committee that its recommendations will be accepted. (This device is occasionally relied on to capture the services of community leaders who do not care to serve if they believe their suggestions will not be followed.) While this does not make the committee a policy-deciding committee, it comes close. Some of the political elements involved in this type of committee have been detailed elsewhere.[3]

Special Issues and Problems

Policy advisory committees have a number of special concerns and difficulties that need to be considered. The problems of the advisory commission or committee dealing with specific issues are somewhat different from those experienced by the general advisory commission or the committee with a technical mission. Therefore, let us examine them separately.

Specific Advisory Committees

One of the first problems often faced by the more specific advisory committee is a feeling on the part of some members that the appointing body does not really want their recommendations—that the committee will be preparing just another report to gather dust or will be merely a "rubber stamp." It is for this reason that, early on, such members sometimes express hostility directly at those who appointed them. Committee members may discuss among themselves their assessments of the purposes the sponsor had in mind. If a breach of faith develops, the committee can cease to function effectively within a short time.

If the committee remains functional, a second difficulty faces it immediately: how far can and should it go in its deliberations? Most matters on which groups are asked to advise include a range of problems from moderately complex to very complex. Committees can, very justifiably, go into lesser or greater detail on any one item, depending upon the press of other items, committee judgment, and other factors. Related to this situation is another judgment about how to approach the substantive problems the issues may include. There may be different policy positions available—punishment versus treatment in the processing of offenders, for example—that need to be considered and for which technical solutions or definitive knowledge are unavailable. The committee needs to decide whether it should take the posture of recommending what it believes can be implemented or whether it should recommend what would be desirable, even though it is reasonably confident that more-utopian recommendations stand little chance of implementation.

The committee has to contend with the issue of conflict over its recommendations. The first areas of conflict may develop inside the committee, and differing positions need to be worked out. In the most serious case, the

3. Robert D. Vinter, with John E. Tropman, "The Causes and Consequences of Community Studies," in Cox et al., *Strategies of Community Organization*.

dissident group will issue a separate report and thus resolve the issue of internal conflict. Then the committee members must consider what will be the effects in the external community of its recommendations and try to keep a sense of that reaction in mind as they are developing a report. Internal conflict and external impact interlock. Generally, committees that believe they will be getting some "heat" about their recommendations from the outside like to have a unanimous report. Two or more reports may result in the disesteem of the committee's recommendations. Yet a question remains as to the extent to which one will compromise to secure agreement, and the extent to which members are confident about their substantive position. Where individual members believe strongly in opposing positions, compromise is difficult.

There is another aspect related to the majority/minority report and conflict/consensus questions. Is the committee going to present a single set of recommendations, thus endorsing them, or will the committee present several alternatives for the appointing body to select from? If the latter course is taken, the committee must decide whether or not it wishes to endorse certain ones, prioritize them, or identify member preferences.

As recommendations are developed and the above questions answered, the committee has two more problems to confront. The first of these is the manner in which it wishes to transmit its report. There are several possibilities, ranging from a "hushed-up" internal release to a spectacular or potentially explosive public release of a report with media involved, and the like. This decision is a strategic one. It is possible, as an example, for an advisory committee that believes its recommendations are likely to be buried to plan a public release, thus compelling the recipients of the report to give a public reaction. Finally, the committee has to decide whether it wants to address the matter of the implementation of its recommendations and, if it does, what mechanisms and structures are involved in following, checking, and the like to oversee and monitor implementation.

General Advisory Committees

It is useful to note some of the special problems of committees charged with general policy advisory responsibility but not asked to make a report on one or more specific matters. Such committees are usually organized to assist a governing board or an executive. Three procedural difficulties often emerge with such committees: (1) matters to be considered by the committee; (2) the relationship between the committee and the board or executive it is assisting; and (3) the manner or form in which the advice is to be presented.

The agenda of a general advisory committee should be formulated by the chair in consultation with the executive or group being advised. If there is a clearly defined mandate, the committee should be careful to not permit it to be subverted by the press of the daily business of the sponsoring group. The committee should secure clarification as to whether or not it can give advice on its own initiative, when the board or executive has not asked for any comment on a particular topic. Most often, such groups initiate advice as well as respond to requests for it.

Also, there may be confusion about what constitutes advice, since committee decisions may be reported in various ways. If the meeting is orderly, and the agenda properly formed so that each item is presented to the committee in a way that makes a decision possible, all decisions are then recorded in the minutes. The minutes serve as a record of the committee's actions and may be transmitted as a report to the advisee. Or a committee may decide that certain actions need to be highlighted and prepare a special report to its advisee.

Frequently there is a question concerning whether or not the executive or board should meet with the advisory group. Meeting with advisees present provides a fuller picture of the issues to be considered and offers an opportunity for informal interaction. On the other hand, committees must be careful not to be used as "rubber stamps" for decisions already formulated. General advisory committees are prudent to establish a mixed mode of meetings—sometimes with, and sometimes without, the advisee. Then, as the situation dictates, the committee can meet by itself or invite others to be present, without having that action misunderstood.

Technical Advisory Committees

Many of the above concerns affect technical advisory committees as well. However, there are a few additional matters that are of special concern to them. The first relates to the point that "experts," whether on the committee or in the literature, may disagree as to the best way to approach a problem from a technical standpoint. In such a situation, multiple recommendations, noting the strengths and weaknesses of each, are almost a necessity. Secondly, technical experts are human and possess the same frailties as others. Like the rest of us, they have policy preferences. What makes the situation difficult is the possibility that they might, knowingly or unknowingly, advocate their own position in the guise of expert judgment. The reverse of that problem, for the committee, is to avoid automatically discounting an opinion advanced by an expert because it is known to be in accord with his or her general policy preferences. And finally, technical experts often have a difficult time understanding that technical considerations may not be the only considerations involved in a policy decision.

Key Decision Issues

The committee must remember that its main charge is to develop a set of recommendations. That is the goal toward which all work points. Making decisions about the matters we have referred to as concerns is very important and should facilitate the work of the committee. However, because of the complexity of an advisory committee's task and some of the issues confronting it, such a committee often strays from its course and produces no recommendations or very flimsy ones. Therefore, the basic decision of such a committee must be to stay on course and complete its assignment irrespective of the intrigue of seemingly related yet diversionary matters.

A second matter of importance is time. Advisees often want advice right away. Such speed is sometimes contra-indicated by the issues and their complexity. It is frequently necessary to make compromises, to look at a piece of an issue, and to comment first on the most crucial points.

Key Role Requisites

The Chair

Each role has some special characteristics. We have just mentioned the strong possibility that the committee can stray from its course because of the complexity of issues it encounters. It is the job of the chair to manage this complicated situation and make certain that the committee develops a set of recommendations.

In carrying out this function, the chairperson needs to be an intellectual, as well as a procedural, leader. The chair's guidance and judgment are absolutely necessary on difficult questions. Without leadership in developing creative solutions to the problems facing the committee, it will almost surely flounder.

As the committee goes about its work, the chair may realize that some of the issues, especially substantive ones, are really highly specialized in nature. For this reason, he or she may want to suggest that the advisory committee seek other expert opinions on particular items. Such additional advice may come from a subcommittee of especially competent members, or a small group of outside people, or a combination of the two.

This approach is by way of carrying out another of the chair's functions that is always present but of especial importance here because of the sensitivity and importance of the mission. The chair needs to balance discussion and decision. The complex and sometimes technical matters reviewed by such committees make this role more than usually difficult. By referring some of the issues that do have technical aspects to a small group, the larger committee does not become bogged down.

The Member

Members of policy advisory committees have extraordinary responsibility for their work because of the potential "flack" when recommendations come out. This is an unusual dimension to committee service and compounds the normal complexities attributed to such an assignment.

In the internal workings of the committee, the member must balance his or her own interests and desires against those of the total committee and the impact of the committee. These are always questions of judgment. How far should a member go in pressing a point? Should a minority report be considered? And so on. These issues affect members directly and are among the more difficult aspects of committee membership.

The Staff Person

The staff person is the one who must bear the brunt of many of the complexities we have been discussing. The role has two central aspects in the policy advisory committee and possibly more, depending upon how the committee itself resolves some of the issues it must confront.

The staff person is the one who must generate the data on which the committee makes its decisions about policy recommendations. This task may involve a lot of research; it may involve writing and talking to many others to develop appropriate information. The information should always contain the following elements:

1. sources
2. reliability of the information
3. validity of the information
4. thoroughness and completeness with which one was able to review relevant sources
5. any political implications of the information

Each of these elements is necessary if the committee is to accurately digest the material presented to it. Staff people are frequently irritated by these data-gathering roles because committee members are continually asking for more and different information, sometimes requiring the staff person to cover the same ground again. The staff person needs to work out with the chair the "rules of the game" so that the committee does not victimize staff.

A second key role is to help the committee decide on the policy issues confronting it in making policy recommendations. This help is usually best given if the staff person can present, in a memo, the major alternatives available to the committee at any moment in time, and the costs and benefits of each. These memos need not be too copious or lengthy unless there is some technical information that the committee needs to have. Through this process, the staff person can sharpen the view of the committee members toward the problems and issues they are facing, and help them to be aware of the implications of their decisions.

As the committee progresses, the staff person may wish to aid it by making substantive suggestions in regard to difficult points; and may be asked, as well, to aid in developing solutions to some of the problems. Sometimes it takes one who is not a member of the committee to act as a proposer of ideas. There may be points when even the chair cannot be helpful, and the staff person must be ready to assist. The staff should take care here, as elsewhere, to avoid overinvolvement in the recommendations he or she develops. The committee, in the end, makes the final decision.

Conclusion

The advisory committee is one of the most difficult kinds of committees to serve on because of the inherent problems facing it in terms of policy issues, and because of the procedural difficulties and complexities facing it at work. These committees are among the most common, and, in our experience, work on them is more subject to disillusionment and more frustrating than on almost any other type of committee.

CHAPTER 15

The Policy-Coordinating Committee

Introduction

Policy-coordinating committees are created for more than sharing information or advising. They are developed to take action on policy recommendations—recommendations framed either by themselves or by someone else.

Action takes two general forms. The first form—coordination—usually refers to an improvement in the division of labor with respect to some goal or objective, usually within the interorganizational system. Often, of course, it will involve information sharing, but the principal assignment is to develop and effectuate linkages in the operational programs and assignments of the units represented. The second type of action committee, to be discussed in Chapter 16, is to implement policy. Implementation contemplates more basic structural changes than are implied by coordination, and often involves the elimination or creation of whole organizations. In the terms of some old and still useful distinctions about system change, coordination means change *in* the system, while implementation involves change *of* the system. To put it still another way, coordination focuses upon adjustments of the interorganization linkages and connections, while implementation usually emphasizes the units themselves.

Types and Functions

Coordinating committees are among the most common of committee types, and many other committees will be called upon to perform coordinative functions as part of their overall role. Indeed, the press and citizens-at-large are continually calling for more and better coordination. Generally, however, coordinating committees will not develop—or if they do develop, they will flounder—unless at least one of three conditions is met: (1) the members are forced to get together by law; (2) there is some financial inducement available to the units for coordinating their efforts; or (3) the member organizations and units see some gain for themselves, other than money, in initiating or joining such an effort. Precisely because coordination implies some adjustments in the division of labor and hence more work, or different work, or less control than any participating unit might have previously had, the costs (losses) need to be compared with the benefits (gains). If the members cannot see gains for themselves in such a cost/benefit calculation, then they are not likely to contribute and may, indeed, oppose coordination efforts.

Coordination may also fail to occur because of another feature of the coordination process: the committee is usually not empowered to act itself, but rather must get others to act. The actualization of the coordinative policy is handled by the member units. Thus, their continued cooperation and participation are vital.

The types of coordinating committees are legion, and their importance in a complex, diversified society is increasing. In any setting where complex functions are carried out by discrete units and where there is not central authority that can achieve coordination by orders, such committees are likely to appear.

Several loci are common. Urban communities across the country are replete with committees coordinating everything from transportation policy to garbage collection. Public welfare and social service functions often have coordinating committees. States create coordinating committees to achieve a more harmonic and efficient distribution of state resources. The federal establishment is simply full of coordinating committees relating this department to that department, and the like. And even though such committees are somewhat less likely within formal organizations than between them, they are common within very large formal units, such as the federal government or General Motors, or in formal units, such as universities, that have highly autonomous subunits.

Special Issues and Problems

Perhaps the most central problem facing the coordinating committee is to retain the interest of members, especially as the costs, even if they are short-term ones, begin to accrue. When people talk about coordination, the language is usually pleasant and neutral. No one mentions the costs and problems involved for the "coordinatees," but these rapidly become a special problem. To produce a more effective division of labor, the participating units must either add to their workload or give up something they have been doing—actions that may not be well received. Additionally, the phrase "more effective division of labor" is not neutral but suggests some goal. Some of the participants may not share that goal, so coordination, even leaving aside the change in workload, may hamper the ability of an organization to achieve its own goals. Should, for example, a family welfare agency allocate staff time to a coordinating committee for children's services? Perhaps, but one will have some convincing to do.

A second issue faced by the coordinating committee is the design of a specific plan for coordination. While in a general sense the concept of such a plan may be simple, in specific terms it becomes quite complex. Organizations have differing personnel patterns and differing budgetary styles. A specific organization may not be able to cooperate in some particular way because it cannot free up the personnel or the money, or because it would be left with surplus personnel, some of its functions having been assigned to other organizations, et cetera.

The coordinating committee must follow through, once the plan (or set of plans) has been developed and approved. Sometimes, follow-through means that the members themselves do something—perhaps each writing a section of a grant proposal or contributing information from their agencies to a central location for processing and referral. At other times, the members must obtain support from their agency staff, and it is that staff, not the committee members, who must perform certain tasks. In either case, oversight and monitoring are necessary.

The issue of cost is often raised with respect to coordinating committees. Sharing and advisory committees have relatively limited demands for money, and costs of the advisory committee's services are usually covered by the advisee. In policy coordinating, however, a staff person is usually essential, and his or her salary becomes an important item, as does space for any supplies and equipment the committee needs. The action focus usually requires more detailed attention to issues and a closer following of activities over time and hence is likely to involve greater needs for funds. Who pays, and the possibility that the organization that picks up the tab may have some hope of being more influential for so doing, become important issues for the coordinating committee.

Finally, we should point out that a very special problem with respect to coordinating committees is the echelon at which costs and benefits are calculated. Often coordination is offered as a vehicle through which some overall system-wide efficiency or effectiveness can be achieved. Agencies are generally hesitant about working on such a basis, even though they might agree that greater overall sense would be made if they did. They will frequently complain that they, as agencies, should not subsidize such a program, but that funds to finance the coordinative effort should be obtained from some other source. The clash between system goals and agency goals is one of the most common conflicts in coordinating committees.

Key Decision Issues

There are perhaps two key decision issues in policy-coordinating committees. First, the committee must decide upon a *basis* or goal for developing the coordination plan. Without such a basis, the different echelons of interest and the different attitudes about participation, as well as the individualistically oriented goal structures of the individual members, will erode committee action. Not infrequently, the initial decision here will be to act in policy-sharing ways as a beginning step. This decision is proper and useful, providing that the committee keeps its eye on the central action focus of its mandate.

Once the relevant information has been developed and the appropriate basis developed, the committee must decide upon an actual *plan* of coordination. This decision is equally hard because, in the actual plan, the interests of the several members are advanced or retarded, and those whose interests are retarded are likely to oppose that plan. If proper process and discussion of the basis have occurred, the committee should be ready to develop its plan. Even those who are going to experience short-term losses should by now be aware of the longer-term benefits.

Key Role Requisites

The action focus of the policy-coordinating committee creates some demands on each of the participants.

The Chair

The chairperson in a coordinating committee should have the personal respect of the units within the coordinating system. Typically, such a person would be both prestigious and influential, traits helpful as the plan develops and moves into operation. He or she should naturally possess the general skills that any chair should have, and, in addition, be skilled at negotiating, because it is through a process of negotiation that the plan will be developed and put into action. Since the chair is often from one of the affected organizations, special care must be taken not to give the impression that the attempt at coordination is only a "cover" for increasing the influence and prestige of that organization. If that organization has taken some leadership here, it is not unlikely that substantial gains will accrue to that agency, and most members will recognize this leadership. However, if they come to feel that they are being "used," they will simply stop their participation. For this reason, it is better if the chair does not come from one of the organizations involved but is independent, yet has acceptance from all the groups represented.

The Members

The key responsibility of the members is to act as an effective liaison between the committee and their places of employment. They should keep their employer informed about (1) what is happening and (2) what the agency will be expected to do. To the committee itself, the members should relay information concerning (1) what, if any, limitations their agencies have put on participation in the effort, and (2) agency reactions to developing ideas and suggestions.

When a plan has been approved, the member will need to be prepared to be the key person for actualizing it in his or her own agency. Often during the process, especially if the coordinating committee is producing some joint written document, such as a grant request, the member will need to engage in "homework"—getting facts, writing drafts, and the like.

The Staff Person

The staff person, along with the chair, occupies a crucial position in the coordinating committee. Since the focus of the committee is action, the staff person is usually the one who follows and monitors the development of the plan and tries to see to it that the plan, once developed and ratified, is followed. The staff person works with the individual members to develop information on their procedures. The staff person is sensitive to the political realities implied in coordination from the perspective of the several agencies or organizations involved. The staff person, along with the chair at appropriate times, contacts those organizations not on the committee whose participation is necessary. And the staff person becomes the contact person and information center as the plan goes into effect.

Coordination requires a reason to get together influential backers, and much work. The reason is the mandate of the committee, the influence comes through the chair and the members, and much of the work is done by the staff person. For this reason, staff must be very careful to take a neutral posture. The danger here is similar to that facing the chair—that members will think the staff person, often loaned from a local organization, will overtly or covertly, consciously or unconsciously, favor the interests of that unit.

As with the chair, there is merit in having a staff person come from outside the organizations represented on the coordinating committee. Independence helps to provide the neutrality needed. If this is not possible, then the staff person must assume the additional responsibility of neutrality and, with respect to coordinative functions, act as an agent of the committee, not of the employing organization.

Conclusion

The coordinating committee is a common form of committee charged with effecting some change in the extant system with respect to the division of labor. Although coordination is popular language, it is less successful in practice, because the units involved frequently believe the costs exceed the benefits. Benefits, of course, are usually seen in the units' terms rather than in overall terms.

CHAPTER 16

The Policy-Implementing Committee

Introduction

Implementation of decisions, agreements, and recommendations is an objective of all committee activity. Implementation, however, requires different skills and foci than coming to a recommendation does. Not the least of the requirements of implementation is a careful following of the situation. Unless some individual or group oversees implementation, it is not likely to happen. Implementation is difficult enough when one is working within the organizational system. The greatest difficulty develops in the interorganizational system, where there is no clear authority.

There are many reasons why a committee is needed to implement recommendations within the interorganizational system. Usually there is no transorganizational authority that can force organizations and other units to follow through. It is for this reason that so many coordinating committees collapse. And even those interorganizational authorities that do exist are not too powerful. Most of us would agree that the urban system, taking just the governmental area alone, is so complex that it almost defies description, let alone management.

In addition to the absence of formal interorganizational authority is the fact that most recommendations, if they are nontrivial ones, will advance the interests of some elements in the system and retard the interests of others. While those whose interests would be advantaged are not loath to implement the recommendations, those whose interests are disadvantaged are obviously less willing. And finally, there is the issue of resources. Implementing recommendations often takes money, and additional resources must be garnered before implementation can begin. Overall, the implementing com-

140

mittee is more concerned with strategies, politics, and leverage than with resolving issues or resolving value conflicts; it is more concerned with action than deliberation. And specifically, that action usually involves some rather substantial change *of* the system—establishing a new or modifying an old policy, creating or eliminating organizations. Implementation is, of course, implicit in all committees. However, when the difficulties become severe, a special committee whose members have the skills and influence to promote changes in the system needs to be appointed.

The changes may involve at least four types of approach: (1) *education,* in which a change occurs because those affected accept a new view; (2) *negotiation,* in which change occurs through bargaining; (3) *community organization,* in which political force is mobilized; and (4) *advocacy,* in which partisan groups back a particular approach. Sometimes the strategy must cover all four approaches because, before one can reach the point of negotiation, there is need for the other efforts.

One of the authors had the experience of attempting to persuade the county commissioners to establish a mental health program recommended by a study committee. We had pleasant negotiations with them, but nothing happened. A rather astute observer of the situation, who had a good political sense, commented that we had gone at it all wrong. Our first effort should have been a series of articles about the seriousness of mental health problems and the extent of need; next there should have been a community conference to show community concern with the problem; and only then should we have approached the commissioners, who would be responding to something viewed as a community problem around which there was wide community concern. These kinds of strategic and tactical considerations are the "bread and butter" of the implementing committee.

Types and Functions

An implementing committee is one charged with that specific responsibility. Its action might range from a broad educational program to secure understanding, interest, and support of recommendations to much more specifically focused efforts such as conferences and negotiations with groups whose support is essential and with the individuals who will make final decisions.

Generally, implementing committees come in two styles and two forms. The style depends upon the scope of the committee assignment. Some committees are given the responsibility to both study a situation and follow through on their recommendations—so that implementation is a part of their assignment. Such committees are sometimes called study committees—although not all study committees have responsibility for implementation. (The study committee was discussed under Policy Advisory Committees.)

The second style is the committee appointed after the study has been completed or the decision or recommendation has been made, and its assignment is specifically to implement that recommendation.

There are two committee forms that are compatible with either of these two types. The two forms—partisan and cooperative—attack the task of implementation from two different postures. Members of the partisan committee all agree in substance with the recommendations, or, if it is a study committee, all have agreed on the nature of the recommendations. They then proceed to push against whatever opposition develops to seek implementation. Implementation here is viewed as a contest, and it often develops into "our" interests versus "their" interests. The basic underlying strategy of the partisan committee is political force.

The cooperative committee seeks to achieve results through accommodation rather than conflict. Again, it can be appointed at either point—study or implementation. The difference here is that the members represent, or embody, the different perspectives and positions that relate to the issue at hand. The appointers hope that, in essence, the committee will include those who are affected by the decision. If they can agree, then the decision is, in a way, automatically made. If a cooperative implementing committee does not have all the relevant decision makers on it, at least the appointers hope it will be a microcosm of the larger interorganizational system. Hence, the issues that arise can be dealt with in the committee. Even more favorable would be a situation in which resolution of issues within the committee means that these issues are also resolved in the larger interorganizational system.

Special Issues and Problems

The most pressing issue confronting an implementing committee is that of mandate. In the absence of clear interorganizational authority, the authority of the committee is likely to be suspect. Indeed, this suspicion occurs within large organizations as well, where lines of authority might be unclear or functions cloudy.

Implementing committees are often appointed by community-wide or organization-wide bodies to develop the political support needed for implementation. This becomes the second issue that an implementing committee must face—a political problem. Once the committee agrees that it has the responsibility to implement, the question becomes, How does one do this without authority? One answer, of course, comes from the study committee. "The facts speak for themselves." But behind the facts there must be one of two elements—agreement or pressure.

Implementation without authority can occur if those involved give their assent. In that situation, a sort of democratic legitimacy is developed. If those involved agree, who remains to question the decision? Alternatively, implementation without authority can occur through the use of political pressure. The implementing committee attempts to guide the political situation in such a way as to pressure those from whom agreement is sought. Generally, the implementation committee, whatever its initial posture, tries to use some combination of these elements—the facts, agreement, and political pressure—to achieve implementation.

Depending on the style and combination the committee uses, there may be some specific problems. The partisan implementing committee may find itself isolated and working uphill against strong opposition. Because it comprises only partisans, the arguments that seem so appealing to other committee members may fall on deaf ears outside the committee. So, with the difficulties of working "under fire," the committee may become more introspective and cut off from reality.

The cooperative implementation committee has a different type of problem—faction. The different views represented on the committee may not, as hoped, be amenable to compromise. In an advisory committee, this situation sometimes results in a majority and a minority report. In an implementation committee, the situation is even more serious, because the opponents are the very targets of change. If the cooperative committee forms factions in a study phase, then it may be impossible to even get the study off the ground. Some members know that the long-run effect of any study will adversely affect them, and they oppose it.

In passing, we might also note that those who appoint cooperative committees should be wary of filling membership slots with intractable opponents of the committee's mission. Under the guise of agreement, they accept membership to sabotage the committee effort. They know that, because of the cooperative posture, opposition at the committee level may well be fatal to achieving the recommendation's effects. For this reason, it is always well to structure a cooperative committee in such a way that it can be dissolved if a stalemate occurs. Many committees exist like a "man without a country," floating around the system, unable to proceed and unable to return.

The two implementive styles—where the recommendations are already developed and where a study committee has been appointed—develop different problems. Try as one might, it is difficult to get a committee to take existing recommendations and implement them without seeking to have some effect on the recommendations themselves. Sometimes this situation develops because the difficulties of implementation lead the committee backward, as it were, to a posture that blames the difficulties on the "poor quality" of the recommendations. Thus it feels justified in reworking the recommendations in lieu of working on the implementation itself. At other times, the substance of the recommendations or absence of certain items may create difficulties for some members. For whatever reasons, the potential for revolt is always there.

A related, but different, problem occurs in the study committee. Here, perhaps more than in any other kind of committee, a question of motive on the part of the committee appointer is an issue. The appointer will, usually, completely deny that anything other than "study" and the "development of recommendations" was intended. Yet sometimes the committee members will note a very powerful chairperson or an unusually competent staff and sense there is more going on than meets the eye. Sometimes the appointer will be candid with the chair, sometimes the appointer will lie to the chair, and sometimes the appointer just has hope that the study will emerge into action.

Whatever the "real" situation is, one can be certain that the committee is unlikely to know it, probably because there are several "real" situations, depending upon the persons with whom one is speaking. What are unquestionably real are the political fact of the committee's existence and the fact that the committee must deal with the problem. Committees often wait for guidance from elsewhere rather than act on their own volition—something fatal in this type of case. In any event, the committee is likely to worry about what is actually expected of it.

One special issue that relates to the implementing committee is the extent of "community power" (or organizational power, or religious power, or whatever) the committee as a whole enjoys. It is desirable for this reason that the implementing committee be made up of "doers," people who get things done. Exactly who might fit this category is often open to question, especially since the agenda for implementation is often quite varied. But the search for community power is nowhere more clear than here.

Key Decision Issues

One of the key decisions for implementing committees is made before or as the committee is appointed: what form and style, what implementive strategy, is to be followed. This decision will be reflected in the choice of chairperson and the committee composition. A second key decision relates to the nature of the implementive strategy after the committee has been formed. Within the parameters put upon it by composition, the committee must make many decisions about moves and countermoves in the implementive process. These become critical as time moves along.

As with all strategy, the committee will need to be responsive to events as they develop. Little in the political world ever proceeds neatly according to a preconceived plan. Once it is clear how events are going to develop, the committee must decide how much effort it wishes to invest in implementation. Sometimes the task is not too difficult; sometimes the committee runs into a storm of problems and resistance. As resistance mounts or, preferably, as the committee's intelligence system alerts it to the appropriate expectations, the committee may need to reconsider the level of effort it believes is proper to put forth. Alternatively, it may wish or need to call for additional resources and assistance in the performance of implementing tasks.

Key Role Requisites

There are several special aspects to roles played in implementing committees.

The Chair

Political and strategic considerations dominate the roles of those on implementive committees. While the role of the chair in advisory committees is to be an intellectual and task leader, the role of the chair in implementive committees is to be a political as well as a task leader. The tasks, of course, refer to those we have outlined in previous chapters. The political portion of leadership is partly what the chairman brings to the role in terms of political knowledge and connections and partly how he or she responds to the situation as it develops—a test of political judgment. The chair needs to have a range of political skills: to be able to move ahead while deflecting, neutralizing, and even converting the opposition; to be able to mediate within the committee group itself. Again, depending on the nature of the committee, somewhat different skills are needed. Mediation is more likely in a cooperative committee structure, while neutralizing the opposition is perhaps more necessary in a partisan committee structure.

Since implementation is often a question of resources, the chair needs to pay special attention to the degree to which additional resources would be helpful in neutralizing opposition. Chairmen need to be especially careful about noting possibilities for either developing new resources or reorganizing old resources for greater benefit. In many cases, the latter course is difficult, because there really is no way to reorganize old resources in any substantial way without cutting program. Since cutting program means developing opposition, it should not be done unnecessarily. The good chairperson of an implementing committee knows that fresh resources are the quickest route to successful implementation, and will seek early ways of providing them as a lever into the situation.

In implementation especially, but in other functions as well, two prime political elements are the special responsibility of the chair: timing and follow-through. The timing of strategic moves is critical. No one can specify in advance the best time for this or that—all we can do here is alert the chair, and the committee, to that issue. Often errors in timing are fatal to implementation of plans.

After the initial overtures have been made, follow-through, in terms of whatever is necessary—additional drafts of agreements, arranging transfers of persons or funds, or whatever—is essential. If one fails here, one loses the momentum of implementation. Committees often become tired and fail to follow through at the crucial point. It is the chair's responsibility to see that the momentum is not lost.

The Member

In the implementation committee, the role of the member is substantively similar to that of the chair. The member has the same responsibility for great discretion in these committees. With timing so important, and political elements so uncertain, a slip could "blow" the entire strategy. The member of a cooperative committee has the responsibility to approach work in that spirit but not to move so far ahead as to fail to perceive reality as the "principals" see it. The member, after all, is the one most likely to be asked to "sell" the agreement to those self-same principals, and, if too far off target, will eventually look very foolish. Conversely, the member of the partisan committee must take some responsibility for bringing in views that the committee would otherwise not hear. Partisan committees often are most successful at identifying the "foolishness" and "false premises" of their opponents, and they often continue this practice until their failure to succeed becomes obvious, even to them. Members of partisan committees must occasionally play the devil's advocate to "reality test" the other members of the committee, and even themselves. Especially in partisan committees, but in others as well, the debates may become centered around issues of personal opposition. As such a tone begins to overtake the committee, implementation moves from a strategic task to a cause. A Pyrrhic victory may sow the seeds for later dissolution of the implementation. Members have the responsibility to modify their own behavior in this situation.

The Staff Person

The staff person's role is predominantly in the strategic area, drawing more on political than technical skills. Much of the information on which decisions about strategy will be made comes from the staff person, who should strive to be painfully accurate in reporting here, because political strategy evolves in the field of action rather than in successive drafts. A mistake in a draft report can be rewritten; a mistake in political strategy is difficult to correct.

As usual, the staff person can lay several options before the committee and attach the best estimates of probabilities as well. But the choice is up to the committee, and this fact is often difficult for the staff to accept, especially when the role of a master political strategist is so personally appealing, and when one has, in other committee situations, played a more substantive role.

Staff must be concerned with fairness, thoroughness, and balance. The "opponents" must feel their position and input have received attention. The staff member must not go through the motions merely to create the impression that his or her approach is a balanced one—it must truly be balanced. Both the impression and the reality that the committee process is being manipulated must be avoided.

Yet, as staff members are gathering information from inside the committee, they are also laying political groundwork and giving information to people outside, whether they are aware of it or not. The very questions they ask, the very people they see, provide clues to the committee's intentions, and these clues are eagerly noted by interested committee watchers. Sometimes, for these reasons, staff must see people they do not actually need to see and obtain information they do not actually need, in order to present a balanced impression to outsiders who may be seeking information about the committee's intentions. Two rules of thumb govern here. First, be discreet. Again and again this point becomes important. Second, since information will inevitably be revealed, one should act in a balanced fashion, as we just mentioned, in a way that will not foreclose any options for the committee and may gain options for the committee.

Because of the sensitive nature of the political work here, the staff should be very careful to keep in close touch with the chair. Sometimes contacts should be made by the chair itself, or by a committee member, or by a senior or junior staff person.

Conclusion

The implementation committee is a politically sensitive one because it involves, ultimately, the allocation or reallocation of resources—money, prestige, valued interactions, perquisites, and so on.[1] And the task of the committee is often made more difficult by its dubious legitimacy within the interorganizational system and by the resistance it encounters even in the simplest tasks.

For these reasons, questions of a political nature, beginning with the

1. For a discussion of the "nuts and bolts" of implementation activity on a policy level, see John E. Tropman and Milan Dluhy, "Policy Implementation," in John E. Tropman et al., eds. *Strategic Perspectives on Social Policy* (New York: Pergamon, 1976).

membership of the committee itself, run throughout the committee's work. What seems to be most crucial here is to achieve and maintain a momentum of implementation that can involve partisans and opponents alike and encourage them in the belief that implementation is possible, probable, and better than the status quo.

CHAPTER 17

The Policy-Deciding Committee

Introduction

The policy-deciding committee is the first in our ranking of committees in terms of formal/legal power over the implementation of decisions. Policy-sharing, policy-advising, policy-coordinating, and policy-implementing committees all have power over their *own* affairs—when to meet, what kind of report to issue, what kind of strategy to pursue—but they do not have the authority to implement their decisions. Indeed, as we have mentioned, much of the activity of all four kinds of committees has to do with the problems generated around that very point—i.e., the fact that they think about a thing, exchange information, and work toward implementation, but they cannot "command" it.

Naturally, the other side of the pasture always looks greener. Policy-deciding committees, as we will mention, frequently find that they do not have the information other types of committees have; that "command" sounds fine, but actually things do not work quite that way; and that staff assistance, since we now move into an executive/board type of relationship, begins to generate its own problems and concerns. Despite these caveats, there is still an essential difference between this and other committees: policy-deciding committees do have formal authority, and they also have formal responsibility for the operations of the organization.

Types and Functions

The most common type of policy-deciding organization is the board of directors. The agency or organization may be large or small, new or old. The main point is that the board of directors is the formal, legal body in control of the corporation. Its members are responsible for the activities of that corporation.

From this example, one could assume that policy-deciding committees generally operate internally to the organization and that their concerns are intraorganizational. This assumption is only partially correct. There are policy-deciding groups that operate in the interorganizational environment, and it is well to note them here. Many municipalities and local regions have set up various authorities that decide on salient elements assigned to them. For example, a hospital planning council may have authority, under a health-planning act, to give or deny permission for hospital construction. Under a similar act, a mental health regional authority may have the power to give or deny permission to certain grant applicants or to certain programs within the mental health field. A United Way board might decide whether or not a member agency can conduct a capital fund campaign. Often, under some of the new federal patterns, local governmental units must ratify local programs for which there are federal funds, through the mechanism of approving the budget. Often this is pro forma, but it need not be, as the controversies between municipalities and the local city programs amply attest. Whenever a committee acts to carry out a formal/legal decisional mandate, whether it is internal to the committee and the organization or in the interorganizational environment, it is a policy-deciding committee.

Special Issues and Problems

The policy-deciding committee has a number of unique problems, although many of the problems facing other types of committees are also present in greater or lesser degree. But a twin set of problems, one seen from the board's viewpoint and one from the executive's viewpoint, provides a unique and continual hazard for the policy-deciding committee. These problems are the policy-versus-administration dilemma and the information-versus-action question. They can be worked out if the relationship between the executive and the board is good. If it is not good, these problems will loom doubly large. This relationship was discussed in detail in Chapter 5.

Policy versus administration is a difficulty that has involved many boards and their working staffs. It is really the question of how far the board should go in entering into the ongoing, daily activities of the agency. Formally, of course, the board can go as far as it likes. However, it is presumably paying an executive to handle the administrative problems. Generally, the board feels it is time-consuming and inappropriate to become involved at the administrative level, and it handles the policy issues. Yet, often when an issue arises there is not clear identification as to whether it is a policy issue or an administrative issue. With the exception of personnel matters (e.g., hiring and firing), we suggest a rule of scope: if an issue is of concern to one person, it is of narrow scope and an administrative matter; if it is of concern to many, it is broad in scope and a policy matter. By a problem of concern to one person, it should be emphasized, we mean one that is unique, not general. An issue is usually presented by one person. If that issue concerns this person alone and has relatively few elements that extend this scope, then we would call it an administrative issue. If, on the other hand, the issue appears to have broad implications, then it becomes a policy issue. There are, of course, policy aspects to administrative issues, and they can be considered without bringing the whole issue to the board.

The executive needs to make decisions on an information-versus-action continuum. That is, he or she must decide which items to take before the board and which of these to present for information only and which for action. Both the board and the executive want the board to be informed, and both recognize the need to have the board take action where appropriate. Neither board members nor executive likes the board to act on every little point, nor do they like boards that do nothing.

There are also other issues of importance. One relates to the experience of the board and the executive. Experienced boards and executives can often come to an agreement on their roles quickly; less-experienced ones usually take much longer, and membership on such boards is more frustrating.

And more specifically, there is the crucial issue of how issues are selected for board decision. Reaching a balance between information and action does not speak to the mechanism by which certain items are, or are not, brought to the attention of the board. Typically, the executive and the chairperson confer, but often members will want additional information on specific items to satisfy themselves.

Finally, an issue always latent in policy-deciding committees is the resource issue. Because the committee is ultimately responsible, and because resources are inevitably limited, there is always the question of which programs, persons, or activities should receive fiscal preference. This is where the buck stops. Boards may not be able to resolve differences of view, but they must make decisions. This process is often a painful one but unavoidable. Not only are resources the issue in specific resource problems, but they often underlie, as a sort of hidden agenda, other issues. Many of the board/committee discussions concern the resource implications of a matter, or how to get additional resources.

Key Decision Issues

Policy-deciding boards make many decisions, and all of them are, in some sense, key decisions. However, it is possible to identify four kinds that are particularly crucial because they implicate all other decisions. The first of these is the appointment of the chair—which, although important in all committee activity, is especially important in the policy-deciding committee because of the impact of the leadership on the entire organization.

Second in importance is identification and agreement in regard to the central mission of the organization. Often difficult to achieve, agreement here, at least in the broadest terms, becomes the set of assumptions on which the remaining two decisions are made.

The final two are internal organizational decisions. Of crucial importance is the appointment of the executive, or principal staff person, since much of what subsequently happens will depend upon the executive working in conjunction with the board. This decision is very important, yet boards often fail to protect themselves appropriately in the appointment process. Despite care in screening, people with excellent qualifications often do not work out in a specific situation. However, they are in the situation before it becomes clear to others and possibly to themselves that it is not working out. At this point, the lack of precaution creates a problem. Boards undergo elaborate procedures to obtain the executive's resignation, feeling that the situation is not serious enough to warrant firing him. The executive, perhaps only dimly aware of what is happening, cannot face the possible loss of a job; so the situation deteriorates. Several precautions, if taken in the initial hiring, would have made the situation much easier. The first is the limited-term contract. Little used but incredibly useful, this form of contract specifies that the executive is hired for a limited period of time, usually three to five years. After that time, the contract is void. It can be renewed, but it should be understood that this is not necessary or even likely. The board may feel at that time that someone else would be good, and that decision is quite unprejudicial to the skills of the executive. Another position can be sought with the full support of the board and with their good recommendations. One is not then faced with the possibility of a quasi-competent executive who cannot leave and cannot stay.

The second precaution is a specification of a yearly conference, in which the executive's performance will be discussed with the chairperson. It is surprising how many executives, especially if they are senior executives, work without having their performance reviewed in any substantive way. Yearly review is a technique that can keep the relationship from deteriorating, or at least can acquaint the executive with the feelings of the board, good and ill. Conversely, it gives the executive the opportunity to share some of his or her reactions and impressions with the chair. We believe that both the limited-term appointment and the yearly review work to the advantage of the board and the executive. Nonetheless, it is rare that a staff person will request them, and so it is usually up to the board to insist on them.

The final item of key importance to the board is the approval of the budget. The budget is the lifeblood of the organization, the physical manifestation of the mission and role of the organization. Each year, budget approval is an important item. Because of the details and technicalities involved, the finance committee usually oversees much of the work here, and so we will discuss this matter in more detail in the next chapter.

Key Role Requisites

There are a number of special aspects to the roles played in the policy-deciding committee.

The Chair

The formal authority creates some unique situations for chair, committee members, and staff. The chairperson is the formal head of the corporation or organization and, as such, the single person most responsible. The chair's tasks relate especially to the issues we have just mentioned: to aid the board in developing, or renewing, a generalized concept of the mission and role of the organization; to work out with the executive a modus operandi for bringing items to the board for action or for information; to restrain the board from delving too far into items of administration when they express a desire to do so; to convey the wishes of the board to the executive; and to act to protect the executive from the board.

The chairperson is crucial in appointing the executive and would be the person with whom the executive meets for the yearly formal review, and who also is the person who confers on a continuing basis with the executive about a host of matters throughout the time between meetings. These are responsibilities the chair cannot avoid.

The Member

The board members share with the chair the formal responsibility for the corporation or commission or agency. The member assumes a trusteeship responsibility and must therefore make special efforts to devote the time, energy, and leadership necessary to carry out this trusteeship. For example, he or she must be willing to attend meetings regularly, serve on special subcommittees, and help with tasks where his or her knowledge, connections, or expertise will be helpful. The member must also resist the temptation to feel that the executive director can handle everything. Each member should be a working member, not a "letterhead" member.

The Staff

The staff person to a policy-deciding group is usually the executive of the corporation. Although assisted by other staff, he or she is the key person to whom board members will look for information, answers, and consultation.

The staff person has several responsibilities, many of which are detailed in Chapter 5. However, we can mention some additional points here. The staff person needs to be aware of the action/information dichotomy and to work with the chair to develop a pattern appropriate to the particular board. Often, and usually to the irritation of the staff, the board's desires in these matters will change as the board changes. The executive must be willing to work out new arrangements as they are called for, not assuming that, once formulated, an arrangement is perpetual. Additionally, the executive must be responsible for the delicate balance between agency continuity and agency change. Often boards, especially those with many new members, like to begin as if there were a completely fresh slate. The executive needs to interpret to the board the nature of existing commitments and the requirements for changing them and, with the board, arrange a training program for new board members. Care must be taken not to appear arrogant or to imply superiority to the board. From the board's viewpoint, an experienced executive is an asset unless or until he or she becomes unresponsive to board wishes.

Perhaps the most difficult situation for the executive is to implement a board directive with which he or she disagrees. Disagreement can be expressed in the meeting, but, once the decision is made, the board must expect that the decision will be carried out. If the executive cannot do it, both parties should begin considering a replacement.

Conclusion

Policy-deciding committees are among the most common and also among the most difficult on which to serve. They differ from other committees in that they possess legal authority and legal responsibility for the actions of the corporation. Committees closer to administration—policy-overseeing groups and policy-administering groups—usually act under the authority of the policy-deciding committee. The former types of groups should meet regularly with the latter to secure approval and ratification.

CHAPTER 18

Policy-Overseeing Committees

Introduction

Sometimes, policy-overseeing committees are needed. As we mentioned in the preceding chapter, policy-deciding committees are often dismayed about the difficulty they have in getting their decisions carried into practice. For this reason, policy-deciding committees often require some additional structures to oversee the implementation of their decisions. There may be resistance to policy decisions, or it may be that the policy is general and the details require additional consultation. Often the board or policy-deciding committee relies more on the "spirit" of the resolution than on the actual language, and executives may unintentionally fail to implement certain items because they are unclear.

Additionally, any policy document will cover only a portion of the area intended. Guidelines are frequently needed to specify the details of implementation or to deal with the special cases that always seem to crop up immediately after a policy is decided upon.

Finally, many policy-deciding committees feel keenly the formal legal responsibilities they possess under the law. Therefore, they may delegate some of their members to work closely with the executive on an ongoing basis, in order to have more or less continual assurance that events are proceeding appropriately.

Some matters, particularly those involving personnel and salaries, may not lend themselves to detailed discussion by the full board, especially if the board is large. Often the considerations around these details are better handled in a smaller group, with only the final recommendation going to the board. Additionally, there are tasks that a full board cannot handle—for example, the screening of applicants for the post of new executive, or the detailed review of the budget. For these reasons as well as others, many boards seek a closer relationship with the operating staff and wish to have some of their members involved in a prescreening of items, so that only the policy matters come to the board.

Types and Functions

Committees that provide close functional supervision of operating personnel under the circumstances just described are called policy oversight committees. Typically, these are executive committees, personnel committees, and finance committees. Congress, at the highest level of government, occasionally has a Committee on Congressional Oversight, aimed at assuring that the will of Congress is not being sabotaged in the operating bureaucracies.

The policy oversight committees typically function in close working relationship with the executive and his or her staff. At this working level, there can be the frankest exchange about problems and potentials. Members of the executive committee both guide and help the executive director, who acquaints them with details of problems for which the full board does not have the time. They guide in seeing that the policies of the board are carried out. They can order him or her to take certain actions. However, there may be a series of legitimate dilemmas as to what would best serve the letter and spirit of a board directive, or there may be several alternatives, each of which has some costs and some benefits. Consultation in a quasi-collegial manner may benefit the executive in being able to draw on the experience and "savvy" of the members of the specialized committee.

The committee also helps the executive in another way. He or she can often avoid conflict with the major board if key items are cleared with the executive committee. Should questions arise, it is not a case of the board versus the executive; rather, it is the executive and some members of the board talking with other members of the board.

Most experienced boards, and most boards of any size (more than fifteen or so members) work through the subcommittee system. In this way, they receive reports not only from the executive's viewpoint but from their own members on key matters of personnel and finance as well as general functioning. Any distortion for which the executive is responsible, purposely or inadvertently, should be eliminated through prior committee review.

The subcommittees we have mentioned are crucial ones. There is one more area that is perhaps even more crucial yet is only sporadically represented by an oversight committee—the area of program. Most organizations are set up to *do* something. Finance and personnel, of course, are always factors. But many organizations, including symphony societies, social agencies, and philanthropic foundations, have tasks for which these are but means. Such decisions as what to play, whom to serve, which projects to finance are among the most important they must make. Yet the program area often has no direct representation in the decision-making process. To some extent, as we shall mention in the next section, conflicts relating to this area occur via budget and personnel decisions rather than directly.

Special Issues and Problems

There are several problems that the oversight committee must handle. First among these is the likelihood that the committee members will be seen by the rest of the board as a "power group" that does things and tells the board later. Often there is substance to this impression; yet, at least in part, this is the way things are supposed to be. But it is an issue that can cause opposition to reports, on the basis of general board cantankerousness alone. It does point to a second problem. Charged with oversight, and often needing to make rather quick decisions, the oversight committee is always faced with the question of how far to go before checking with the whole board. The executive may base a case on the pressure of time, thinking it will be easier to get agreement about a project from the executive committee than from the whole board. Executive committees need to be wary of this kind of pressure.

On the other hand, there is an almost reverse pitfall that may occur over time. As the executive committee works closely with the executive staff, it may develop an appreciation for and sympathy with executive corps problems and perspectives, thereby losing the central board thrust. Homans has noted that "interaction breeds affection," and this process has been noted with federal regulatory agencies, which wind up being lobbyists for those they are supposed to regulate. For this reason, a change in the membership of these key subcommittees is often useful. The problem, however, is that there are usually not enough well-qualified people on the board for such interchange to be fully effective.

Finally, the oversight committee needs to be able to tolerate more candor and conflict than is likely in ordinary committees. Conflict may occur when the executive balks, or "foot-drags," in the carrying-out of board intent. Sometimes there is no pleasant way of saying, "Get moving or else!" Such groups are usually small, and the close working relationship, coupled with this small size, leads to a more direct expression of opinion than is usual in other committees. More directness, even bluntness, is necessary too, because without it work would not be done. If ever there is a place where all the difficult difficulties, the cantankerous conundrums, the perennial problems, and the agonizing appraisals occur first, it is in the overseeing committee. We are not suggesting that there is rudeness, only that the central issues must be dealt with, and, when one reaches that point, one is likely to find plain speaking.

One area deserving special attention is the question of whether the apparent issue under discussion is the actual issue under discussion. As we noted, some organizations have important programmatic missions, but these missions are not directly represented in committee form. When this is the case, then some of the discussion about finances is not really about finances at all, but about program; the same can be true with personnel. Members should be clear, therefore, when the issue is program and deal with it directly.

Key Decisions and Issues

The important decisions that need to be made by the overseeing committee are usually either more specific than decisions made by the board or prior to full board decisions—or, in an emergency, they are made in lieu of full committee action. One can never speculate on what emergency action may be required. However, the other decisions are more routine and can at least be outlined.

Within the framework of the mission and role of the agency as indicated by the board, it is a policy-overseeing committee, usually the finance committee, that gives approval to a tentative draft of the budget in time for full board review. After the budget has been passed, members of the finance committee will usually approve specific salary levels for specific individuals, consistent with the executive's evaluation and the overall budgetary limitations. Throughout the year, as transfers from one account to another are needed, the finance committee gives approval when necessary. If budgetary problems come up, the finance committee is closely involved in the strategy for improvement.

Major appointments to the executive corps are channeled through a personnel committee. Such a committee may or may not actually make the appointments, but it is usual that the appointment is discussed with that committee, even if it is in the hands of the executive. That committee will have a role in setting up personnel policies and recommending them to the board, and it will develop guidelines when a new executive is to be appointed. At that juncture, the board may ask the extant personnel committee to handle the search, or it may convene a special committee for that purpose. In either case, the appointment of a new director involves a group that does preliminary searching and screening and may have the de facto power, its recommendations being automatically accepted by the board. Alternatively, it may make a list of possibilities available to the board, and the board chooses.

The executive committee has a less-formalized set of responsibilities. The committee is usually involved in reviewing progress reports from the executive concerning his or her implementation of actions called for by the board, and discussing with the executive problems and issues on which guidance or clearance is sought. It is often the executive committee, on the recommendation of the finance committee, that gives final approval to the executive's yearly salary. And it is the chairperson of the executive committee—who in most cases is also the chair of the full policy-deciding committee—who holds the annual review with the executive. Should problems with the executive arise, they will initially need to be considered by the personnel and executive committees.

Beyond action on specific issues, the policy-overseeing committee makes another process-type decision. Since this group is usually the first to hear of many issues and the first to take action on them, the decisions it makes on how to handle these issues and its style of approach are likely to be influential with the full board. The committee may, for example, suggest that an ad hoc subcommittee be established to look into an issue, and move to develop specific information via this route. It is often a good one.

Key Role Requisites

The overseeing committees place special stress on the major roles.

The Chair

Being a chairperson of one of the key policy-overseeing committees is one of the most important tasks in the committee repertoire. It means that the full committee has entrusted that person with a great deal of authority and responsibility. Reciprocally, the full committee is usually ready to go along with the recommendations of that person or, at the very least, give very serious consideration to the position he or she is taking. Often, the chair here has a special factual competence in finance or personnel management. Fulfilling this responsibility requires at least two things—openness and work.

By openness, we mean to convey the notion that these chairpersons have a special responsibility to listen to the items and views presented by others. This special responsibility exists here because of the rather large area of discretion enjoyed by chairpersons and members of these committees. Particularly as time passes, a chair is eager to get on with the job and may fail to remember that one of the responsibilities of the chair is to maintain an "action/participation balance," not only within the committee, but between the committee and the board. Often, the chair needs to hold his or her own policy preferences in check until the "evidence" is in. The listening is as important as the "evidence" in many cases.

By work, we mean to suggest that the range of responsibilities of such chairs goes beyond reading and checking the substantive material presented by the executive staff. The chairperson needs to become acquainted with some staff, visit the operations of the organization and, in short, become widely familiar with the operations of the organization. This does not mean that the members of the oversight committees, and especially their chairpersons, are to intrude into the work of the organization. But it must be remembered that boards are sometimes quite removed from the actual operations, rarely see them, rarely talk to staff, rarely talk to customers or clients or suppliers. Without overdoing it, the chair should become familiar with these elements. This will enable him or her to be specific about changes that are necessary and to defend the operations of the organization when that is necessary.

Finally, the chairs of the key oversight committees will usually accompany the executive on important external-affairs missions—going before the United Fund budget committee, seeking a grant, making certain types of important public appearances. Others know that there is always the possibility that the executive might misrepresent the position the board will take on a grant, or whatever, in order to secure his or her own ends. The presence of members of both the executive corps and the key committees is reassuring, if nothing else.

The Member

Here, as in some of the previously described committees, the role of the member is similar to that of the chair, with somewhat fewer prerogatives. Serving on these committees is rewarding for the simple reason that they are some of the key structural elements in the social system where real decisions are made. They are places where one can have an impact on the course of events, something many desire and few attain. The same requirements of openness and work apply here for the member as for the chair. Because of the importance of membership, attendance (that old saw) is even more essential than at meetings of the full board. Often, if one member does not attend, action must be deferred.

Members, like the chair, should take the opportunity to develop a good working knowledge of the organization. Knowledge of the operations cannot be left to the chair alone. Issues on which this knowledge will be relevant continually come up, and the member needs to be prepared.

The Staff Person

For several reasons, working with a policy-overseeing committee is perhaps one of the most difficult assignments for a staff person or executive. First, the very notion of oversight implies "checking" on the executive, at which the executive might well develop low-order pique. Secondly, the executive committee may issue instructions for handling a matter that differs from the preference and style of the executive, who is certain to find that annoying or even threatening. Thirdly, the various oversight committees with which the staff person works may have different postures and different requirements, and they also may differ from the board. This situation may lead to confusion.

The difficulties, however, are balanced, if not outweighed, by some advantages. Oversight committees provide groups with whom the executive can check items and secure early, if preliminary, clearance. They usually represent a fund of experience and wisdom on which the executive can draw. And they can help in some of the executive's tasks. They may make speeches, and they may handle important external affairs missions.

Because of the advantages and disadvantages involved here, the executive, or any staff, must be careful about maintaining the proper balance in relationships with overseeing committee members. In many ways, the relationships are collegial. In other ways, they are subordinate. The staff person needs to develop a close working relationship while, at the same time, maintaining proper distance and respect.

Conclusion

Policy-overseeing committees are commonly created as subcommittees of policy-deciding committees to pursue specific additional tasks. Usually these tasks involve developing a more intimate knowledge of the agency or organizational operation and being helpful to the executive in the carrying-out of board wishes.

The policy-overseeing committee is an important committee type, because many preliminary decisions are made there, even if they are later ratified or modified by the board. Further, policy-overseeing committees can set the style of organizational response even if they are not able to make the final decision.

CHAPTER 19

The Policy-Administering Committee (Task Force)

Introduction

Our progression of committees has been coming closer and closer to actually doing administrative work. We believe that the policy-overseeing committee is the point where policy concerns end. At that point, the professional paid staff usually becomes involved to "administer" the policies. Occasionally, however, a committee is developed that has the responsibility for actually carrying out policy. Its focus as a committee is on action rather than thought, program rather than policy. For specific tasks and/or for brief periods of time, the committee as a committee implements directives and acts like an executive. Such action groups are commonly task forces. While not as common as some other committee forms, the task force is usually used in very specific, difficult situations where concerted action is needed within some important constraints of time.

Types and Functions

When are task forces found, and what are their forms? Usually they occur in the following instances: (1) in a crisis; (2) in a complex implementive situation where resistance is expected or speed is essential; (3) under certain specifications of law. The crisis action group comes together when it is absolutely necessary for many groups to work together, as in providing disaster assistance, and coordination is essential. Under such conditions, representatives from various organizations may form an ad hoc task force for the duration of the crisis, and these representatives may have authority from their respective agencies to make decisions in the field. What might have been

162

simply a policy-coordinating committee becomes an action group. Similarly, but in a different type of crisis, when an executive becomes ill and there is no one immediately available as replacement, the executive committee may become an action group. They may run the organization until other arrangements can be made. Sometimes the executive committee, or the whole board, serves in this capacity when a new organization has been formed and there has not yet been the opportunity to appoint staff.

Often in a situation where implementation is occurring, the executive will personally pull together an action group of relevant persons to "honcho" the implementation of some new policy or the introduction of a new technology. Such an action group might be called a type of oversight committee. We have located it here because the main purpose of the committee is action, not oversight, but it is not an implementation committee because it has formal power to accomplish goals. Such special-action groups usually occur when the situation is very complex, where resistance is expected, or when the system involved is very large, speed is essential, and one cannot wait for the normal channels of implementation to work. So, for example, if a bank is installing a new computer system, the bank head might call together the heads of all the departments and the representatives of the computer company as a special-action group to work together on installing and planning utilization of the new equipment. Or the executive of an organization might call on a group of employees to work together for several days at the task of implementing new policies established by the board of directors.

Finally, there may be certain situations in which the law provides for the formation of a task force. For example, if a disaster is declared in an area, a committee or task force may automatically be created, with certain powers lasting for the duration of the disaster.

Whenever a committee moves to do the actual work involved—preparing memos, advising staff of changes, clearing with different units on their needs, making policy and then taking that policy right to the street level and using it—it may be called a task force. The needs of the group still involve policy, in that it is interested in developing the appropriate rules and regulations. But at the moment, for some short or specified period of time, it is doing the administrative tasks as well. Usually, after time has passed, the group is dissolved or stripped of its special authority, or it returns to its usual functions. In general, a task force is a time-limited, specific-purpose committee, with formal authority to take action focused upon specific tasks of an administrative nature.

Special Issues and Problems

The task force encounters a unique set of problems. In a sense, it is a "group executive," which has the assignment of action. In this sense (and unlike the executive committee), the member is more a "doer" than a deliberator. The member actually has some of the roles of a staff person; the line is not very distinct.

Initially, of course, this "group executive" needs to establish a set of decision rules, and very quickly. In certain instances, an executive assumes the chair by self-appointment, thus becoming the committee boss and making the decisions. In other instances, a rule—plurality, majority, consensus, or whatever—is established in order to speed decisions.

The problem of establishing a decision rule sometimes overlaps with the problem of finding a committee leader. The leader must keep the committee making decisions and taking action; he or she may or may not be the one who also is the decision maker. But in the crisis situation that typically generates a task force, there is special pressure to have someone who is key in the committee as its leader. In an intraorganizational situation, the chair is often an executive at some level; in the interorganizational situation, it is likely to be someone already designated by law or custom—the chief of police, mayor, head of United Way. In short, the leader of the task force is often one who has an analogous role in conventional life.

Task forces have the authority to act, and there is usually external pressure for them to do so. However, the groups do not necessarily forgo the special interests of the members on that account. In both intraorganizational and interorganizational situations, department heads and agency representatives generally seek to further their own advantage, if they can. Indeed, this is the reason why an executive sometimes brings in a special action group composed of people not involved—such as the partisan implementive committee—who are loyal to the executive and specifically insensitive to the moans and groans of the other operating staff. There seems to be no simple way of resolving the disputes that arise, even here, out of competition and desire for upward mobility. Usually the situation dictates a natural leader, and this person or agency attempts to pull others together insofar as that is possible. Generally, the appointment of a chairperson helps to resolve difficulties.

A third problem is work space and equipment. Some other committees need only a meeting room on occasion or limited office space for staff. An action group often needs a headquarters office, perhaps offices for some of the committee members, phones, files, secretaries, messengers, access to funds and cash, et cetera. Usually one of the members takes on the role of staff person and sees to these arrangements. Sometimes the necessities are provided as the task force is appointed. Whatever the situation, the action group usually needs much more by way of facilities and equipment than other committees.

A fourth problem is time for members' activities. Usually some arrangement must be worked out so they can serve full time on the effort. This arrangement must be worked out within the organization or with other supervisors and executives. Failure to mobilize for adequate committee time can spell death for the task force, since its missions cannot be accomplished without personnel.

A fifth problem is one of decompression. Authority to take action in this way is a product of special circumstances and tolerated by the system in that sense. When the circumstances are over, so is the task force. Yet on occasion members have difficulty in returning to their more ordinary, and less authoritative, roles.

It should be noted that the concept of a task force, as used here, has a very specific meaning. In general, however, "task force" is applied to every committee that someone feels some urgency about. Many advisory committees are labeled "task forces," as if assigning the words could give the mission an enhanced sense of importance. Perhaps it does. Our view, however, is that the overuse of the concept will lead only to eventual disuse.

Key Decision Issues

An issue that immediately confronts the task force is the extent to which it wishes to check back with the appointing body or another group about its actions. Often task force operation, with its emphasis upon action, circumvents "normal" or "typical" channels of committee process. Some checking and clearing is useful; the question relates to the amount of this activity possible.

A second problem is that of priorities. The conditions that bring a task force into existence are almost always difficult. Often there are many items that need attention. The questions of which items, and how much attention, are crucial. The priorities problem, of course, affects all committees, but rarely with the urgency and immediate relevance involved in the task force.

A third issue relates to how to physically organize the task force's efforts. Space, equipment, et cetera need to be found, quarters established, and the like. These tangential tasks must be taken care of quickly so that the actual work can begin.

Key Role Requisites

There are some unique requisites to roles in task forces.

The Chair

The chairperson faces a difficult situation here, winding up in one of two postures—becoming either the "boss," formally or informally, and acting to resolve disputes and give orders to the troops, or a "coordinator," seeking to mediate between various factions that have secured membership in the group. Action groups function better under the "boss" model but usually are organized under the "coordinator" model. Perhaps successful chairpersons in groups of this type do some of each at the appropriate times.

Both approaches violate what we feel is the usually appropriate role of the chair. However, in these special circumstances, there is a pressing need for disputes to be resolved and decisions made. After listening to the various opinions, it is not improper, if the authority is present, for the chair to resolve a dispute by his or her own action. In no other committee would the chair be likely to take such an action, except in ruling on a procedural point.

The mediator role is usual because it is difficult for the chair to really secure the authority to become a "boss." Either it is not possible to grant such authority—as in the interorganizational situation—or the objections are too great.

Whatever the case, the chair is going to take actions that are unpopular, and a considerable amount of criticism and "heat" is likely to be generated. The chair should be prepared.

The Member

There are two phases to the role of the member in a task force. The first phase occurs during the development of the mission and the decisions on priorities. The second, which might better be called a function, relates to the activity the member undertakes after these decisions have been made.

Initially, the member must be candid about his or her own interests in the situation. If the committee is partisan in structure, the individual member may have no particular interests to advance. In an interorganizational situation, the member needs to acquaint the committee with the perspectives of his or her organization, the lengths to which that organization is willing to go in this situation, and the extent of the representative's authority. It is within this framework that the committee develops its mission. If, for example, one member says that his or her organization will provide so much money for the enterprise, and that offer is actually unconfirmed, then planning on the basis of those funds would be unwise. Once each member has made an initial report, the missions and priorities are developed. The member has an obligation to participate here, but once the decision has been made (by whatever decision mechanism), then the member should shift gears into the role of a partisan functionary.

Carrying out decisions involves much detail work. Task forces have a number of functions that members need to assume. Someone needs to establish a link to the media, someone needs to be in charge of funds, someone in charge of space and facilities, someone in charge of special requests to the group, someone in charge of preparing revised drafts of policy documents, and so on. The specific functions will vary depending upon the overall situation and the set of missions the committee has chosen.

Each member needs to take on several of these functions and carry them out. Usually, arrangements will have to be made to terminate or scale down regular activities while one serves on the task force. Normally, these arrangements are not difficult because of the short duration of the group's existence. Should it seem that the responsibilities are more extensive than anticipated, the members will most likely need to renegotiate with their superiors and agencies. But because of the operating rules of the task force, some adjustment of regular responsibilities will have to be made for the member.

The Staff

In a task force situation, the distinctions we have emphasized between staff and committee tend to blur and disappear; the membership is, singly and severally, the staff. If there are paid staff, each committee member may be allocated some portion of a staff person's time, simply to extend the implementation and action tasks the member is carrying out. Thus the staff role in relation to the committee member is more an extension of the member than in the other committee situations, where there is a distinction between the policy tasks of the committee and the administrative tasks of the staff person.

Conclusion

Under special circumstances, there develops a necessity for a committee—we have called it a task force or policy-administering committee—to undertake the administration of policy for short periods of time. Almost any of the committees described may become task forces, but the most likely candidates are the policy-coordinating committee, in times of disaster, and the executive committee, when the executive is unable to function or has not yet been appointed. The implementing committee may, under extraordinary circumstances, be given formal authority, and it then might become such a task force.

THE SOCIAL AND ORGANIZATIONAL CONTEXTS OF COMMITTEE OPERATION

Committees exist within a social world. Elements outside the working life of any committee affect it both generally and specifically. These external elements we call contexts. Contexts are organizational—that is, having to do with the specific operational format or structure of the committee—or social. In either case, there is little a committee can do by way of changing or affecting the contextual element.

Organizational contexts are not "good" or "bad" in themselves. At any given moment, one element or another might create problems for a committee. Three elements in particular constitute important external dimensions affecting committee functioning: the auspice under which a committee functions, the mode of committee appointment, and the scope of committee functioning. These rather theoretical dimensions have some very practical instances.

In explaining the auspices of committee functioning, we generally look at the major system that appointed the committee. Most inclusive of these auspices, of course, are the well-accepted distinctions *public* and *private*. Public committees are appointed by public (usually governmental) authorities or elected within that context. Private (or "lay," or "voluntary") committees are appointed or elected by agencies, organizations, or other private groups. There are other dimensions to the element of auspice—one could think of a religious dimension, a racial one, et cetera. Yet it seems to us that the most salient dimensions stem from the question of public or private auspice—most salient, because analysis from this base permits identification of systematic rather than idiosyncratic ways in which functioning is affected.

There are really only two modes of committee construction—election and appointment. The committee itself rarely controls this element, yet it is crucial in understanding committee behavior and in acquitting oneself properly in a committee role, because it dominates the politics and support structure of committees and also establishes constituencies.

The last contextual element is the scope of committee operations. Scope implies two dimensions, horizontal and vertical, which we believe collapse essentially into one. The horizontal refers to the breadth of the committee's responsibility at some specific vertical level. The vertical dimension refers to the level of social organization at which the committee is operating—individual, group, community, organization, state, society. Generally, as committees have broader geographic scope, they have narrower responsibilities, although there are many exceptions.

Each of these organizational characteristics involves elements of a social context for the committee. One issue is especially important—the issue of committee constituency: What group or groups "out there" in the world are interested in, affected by, supportive of, responsible for, the work of the committee? Committees have many constituencies, many publics. Only infrequently do these groups agree with each other or among themselves. It is rare to find a course of action that advances matters, harms no one, and advantages everyone. The committee's social context is made up of such constituencies, some of them formally specified in the appointment, some of them informal but influential. The committee, as it is going about its work, must deal with these constituencies. It must keep them appropriately informed, and constituents always think that more information is appropriate than committees do. Committees must call on constituents for help and support but not let them come so close to committee functioning that they in effect become part of the committee. The committee must maintain the appropriate social or working distance from each of its constituent publics. It is difficult to determine what this proper working distance is, and to establish it vis-à-vis one public may make one too close to or far from another.

In a variety of ways, the committee must limit and focus both the number of publics that might be interested in its work and the breadth of the interest of those publics. The committee must seek to discover the publics most salient to its work and with serious intent and/or effect. Making these assessments and acting upon them is part of the task of all committees.

Moreover, constituency is only one of the elements that the social context creates for the committee. Issues of resources, political and otherwise; regional and local styles and characters in the solving of problems; the linkage of the mission of the particular committee to prestigious or nonprestigious groups within the social context of each of these; and many other issues come into play when context is considered. The fact, for example, that a committee is elected is an element of that committee's context, as a member enters it; yet the reason why a committee is elected, as opposed to being appointed, is an additional element of context. In other words, organizational context is the way in which structured elements of the social context are expressed and given meaning within the specific instance of a particular committee. For this reason, the social context, the organizational context, and their linkages must be considered seriously by committee participants.

The committee, then, operates within two contexts—its own structure, which we have called the organizational context, and sets of structured social relationships within the larger system around the committee, which we have called the social context.[1]

---

1. The whole matter of committee structure and context, and of the links between this context and the larger social context, is a very interesting theoretical area. For example, we have generally called by the name *social context* a differentiated social system that comprises at least three elements: political, economic, and cultural. The constituencies of a committee are essentially elements of the political subpart of the general social context. One could talk about the economic and cultural linkages as well and their bearing upon the committee. And the linkages between committee context and social context provide an additional area of exploration. These are noted but not explored here.

CHAPTER 20

Committee Auspice: Public and Voluntary Committees

Introduction

One important way in which the committee knows to whom it is responsible is through its auspice—the persons and systems that charged it with its mission. We can divide auspice into two broad types—public and private. A public auspice exists for the committee that has been formally constituted and charged by a governmental body. Such committees may be elected or appointed and may operate at any level of government. Indeed, in certain cases, the government itself is such a committee. Alternatively, a committee may be appointed by any nonpublic body. Such a committee has private, voluntary auspices.

In the middle is a group of committees appointed by quasi-public bodies, such as COMSAT, or state universities and public utilities. The exact nature of the auspice of such committees is an issue that is raised continually. Also, there are certain other committees appointed by essentially private institutions—for example, business firms and United Funds—that have a quasi-public status because of the nature of their roles.

Simply because a committee has a public, private, or mixed auspice does not mean that its area of activity, or domain, concerns that context. Some private committees make governmental matters their domain and seek to influence these matters. Some public committees (those of federal regulatory agencies would be one example) make the private sector their business. Most often, however, there is auspice-domain symmetry.

Public Committees

The public committee usually has greater responsibility than other commit-tees to make its business open to the citizenry. Several elements may be in-volved here. First, the chairperson and members should be accessible, within reason, for meetings with the public. Many questions of both fact and pol-icy can be handled by the staff, but the principals nonetheless need to be available.

Secondly, meeting time and agenda must usually become a matter of public record. Committees vary on whether all their meetings are open to the public or some business is conducted privately. Some have executive ses-sions before the major meeting or at some other time. Sometimes reporters are allowed to attend these private sessions for background information with the understanding that they will not publish directly anything about the pro-ceedings. Today, many states have "sunshine" laws forcing certain meetings of public boards and committees to be open. What is essential in our view is that there be regularly scheduled public sessions, that the agendas for these sessions be available, and that the facilities be adequate for the public to attend. Further, special arrangements must be made with press and other media, because they are prime channels through which the public becomes informed about emerging issues. If there are to be private sessions, then the public needs to be informed about them, or they will be seen as they are— clandestine. Citizen suspicion in this area has led to the aforementioned "sunshine" laws.

Important other ways that the public is informed about committee ac-tivities and invited to participate are available too. The chairperson and members need to circulate around the community to make reports and seek opinions. Innumerable occasions will present themselves, lunch being one familiar example, for such mutual exchange.

There is little question that public committees usually work more slowly, because they are continually processing a wide range of public infor-mation. They must accept this as both a critical opportunity and a constraint in their role. On the other hand, they must seek to set up appropriate limits and occasions for public participation, or no issue will ever reach closure.

Public committees must realize too that, like it or not, they become important, not only as a functioning unit in the system, but as a model and example of proper procedure. Hence, they have a double responsibility for openness and candor. If the chairperson cannot see to it that these requisites are met, it is up to the members to do so. The chair and members working together with staff make the vital difference.

A counterpoint, though, is in order. Every committee needs some pri-vacy to work on delicate details or handle difficult problems and to attend to committee process. One cannot work continually in the glare of footlights.

Those footlights have a strange effect on some members—they begin playing to the galleries or refrain from expressing themselves, and real work becomes impossible. Both chair and members, and staff as well, should be aware of the need to schedule some time for in-depth discussions. Sometimes, as we mentioned, these are billed as executive sessions, and every committee should have the right to call them for some portions of business, although such meetings may be challenged. Other times, weekend retreats are scheduled, perhaps as much for socio-emotional reasons as for task accomplishment.

All committees need to keep records. They should be kept in excellent form and be accessible to the public. Summaries might be published every so often in local papers.

Public committees are likely to have formal legal mandates to fulfill. It is the job of the chair to see that the committee and its members are fully informed of all requirements and restrictions and abide by them. If the restrictive elements become too burdensome, they can be renegotiated with the appointing authority. In carrying out these mandates, the public committee has the obligation to hear from all types of constituencies. Being "public" indeed means that a predecision was made that this mission should be carried out.

Finally, the public committee needs to schedule some regular reporting mechanism. Strangely, the private committees, especially boards, are more likely to do this through the form of an annual meeting/report than are many of the public bodies. (This point is discussed more fully in the section on committee accountability in Chapter 25.)

Private Committees

The private, or voluntary, committee has some problems that differ from those of its public counterpart. Many of these differences are rooted in the central issue of accountability. Public committees are often more accountable because they have relatively constant feedback on their work, from a variety of publics. Their problem is usually not so much accountability as it is the necessity of limiting their inputs and structuring these inputs so that work can be done.

The private committee is under no obligation to have open meetings or to have any sustained interrelation with the public-at-large. Yet, it is advisable for these committees to consider some systematic way for such a relationship to occur. In the proportion that public committees face the danger of input overload that halts work, private committees suffer from input underload that is perhaps ill-informed.

Private committees do have some groups with which they interact regularly—their closest constituents or contacts. Sometimes these are stockholders/members, sometimes contributors, sometimes foundations and funders, sometimes consumers—in general, people important in the funding of the committee or the constituency to which the committee is responsible. Too often, the views and attitudes of the funders come to dominate private committees, not necessarily because they are the most impressive people, or have the most impressive views, or even bring the most pressure. Often it is because the committees see almost no one else or are oversensitive to the funder resources. Thus, while the public committee must shape and mold its constituency into a usable form, the private committee must expand and cultivate additional constituencies and publics. Private committees have more potential for innovation, and greater prospects for conservatism, than is true of public bodies. The relative freedom that private committees have from constant public scrutiny and legal limitations permits somewhat greater flexibility and, if desired, a potential for moving faster than may be true in public committees. However, the relative isolation of many private committees creates a situation in which this potential is not realized.

Chairpersons and staff especially, but members also, may be helpful here. The staff has the responsibility for bringing new ideas and approaches to the private committee. Sometimes this may be accomplished by inviting guests, or arranging for the board to visit some appropriate other program or organization, or through information obtained from the literature or experiments in other communities. Sometimes it is through working with the chair and mentioning need to achieve broader perspectives. The chair can help through acting in similar ways, encouraging the committee to seek broader perspectives, and scheduling, during his or her term as chair, annual meetings, annual reports, meetings with other groups, and the like.

Mixed Committees

As we noted previously, some committees live in an uncertain world. They are neither clearly public nor clearly private. Depending upon the issues with which they are dealing, they may have elements of both. They may have both a mixed structure and a mixed emphasis as time goes on. In many ways, these committees provide the greatest amount of flexibility for the chairperson and members because, to a certain degree, they themselves decide upon the mode in which they wish to relate to their publics. The difficulty of the situation is that neither the public nor the private attitude is completely proper. So, while this gives the committee flexibility, it also creates a situation of complexity with no clear course to follow.

One of the issues facing this type of group, then, is the likelihood that some considerable time will be spent, especially among new members, both in trying to decide the appropriate posture the committee should take generally and in looking at specific instances as they come up. For example, how often should a United Fund budget hearing be held? Although it is a private corporation, it is also a nonprofit philanthropic organization that has an unspoken contract with its donors to provide good services with the money. With this understanding, just how responsive does the United Fund need to be, and are there issues on which greater, or lesser, public response is necessary? And to push the issue a bit further, one needs to ask about the proper balance between the satisfaction of the donors and the satisfaction of the clients. Private agencies that do not charge clients the full cost of services are in a special plight here, because if the needs of clients are not served, they may withdraw in disgust, but such loss of "business" would have less effect on the agency than would occur in a nonsubsidized agency.

Another example might be a committee formed by a public utility to explore the social role of the utility in a time of pollution and energy crisis. Exactly how accountable to the general public should such a committee be? Even private business is now struggling with this question somewhat. Ralph Nader's consumer-oriented organization, John Gardner's Common Cause, and other similar organizations are making these questions much more salient than they were only a short time ago, particularly to private business.

To complicate matters even further, many private organizations are now receiving public funds for substantial portions of their operation. With public funds come public auditors, as well as the need to follow certain legal restrictions. What has not yet become clear is the extent to which the operations of these organizations also take on some of the requisites of a public auspice. How much information does an organization receiving 70 percent of its business from federal contracts need to reveal to the public about its affairs? Again, these are questions now taking up the time of mixed-structure committees across the land.

What members, chairpersons, and staff must realize about issues of this sort is that they take up committee time, are an absolutely necessary component of committee business, yet focus more on the functioning of the committee than on the work of the committee. They represent aspects of "committee maintenance" in the sense that they tend to focus on the social-psychological elements of committee activity and on acts of organizational self-preservation, which contribute only indirectly to task achievement.

Conclusion

The auspice under which a committee operates may be public, private, or mixed. The "mix" can vary in basis—it can be private with public funds, public with private funds, private funds with a nonprofit stance, et cetera. Public committees have a greater responsibility than private ones for reporting to the public constituency and a greater need for privacy, as well as a need to focus and channel their variously interested constituencies into usable form. Private committees, on the other hand, need to seek more public interaction and must take care that their privatization of business does not cut them completely off. Because they have less-well-specified responsibilities to report to the public, dealing with the issue of how this is to be done will occupy some time.

The mixed committee, with elements of both public and private structure, will find itself in the most difficult position in this regard and will need to spend more committee time dealing with issues of the proper public posture and the appropriate ways to deal with specific cases. We have noted that, in the mixed committee especially but in the others too, there will be time spent on organizational maintenance, which is not task oriented per se; it only prevents task thwarting. What is important to keep in mind here is that many who serve on these different types of committees tend to be unaware of how the structure extrinsic to the membership creates issues and presents opportunities and frustrations. Such matters are so often ascribed to "personalities" when a look at structure might be much more helpful.

CHAPTER 21

Elected versus Appointed Committees

Introduction

The manner in which a committee is composed makes a critical difference in the way it relates to its environment and in the ways the internal processes of the meeting are handled and proceed. Basically, committee members are either elected or appointed. Each of these methods has different implications for the committee process because of the different constituencies that are involved. The appointment of the chairperson is a special case, and we will need to deal with the manner of his or her appointment separately.

The critical issue in the appointment/election question is committee accountability. As we have pointed out, all committees have several publics interested in their activities. The auspices under which a committee functions have an interest; elements of the domain have an interest; various special-interest groups feel particularly affected by committee work, or potentially affected, or somewhat left out; and so on. Questions concerning to which groups the committee owes accountability and the ways it is accountable become critical concerns that committees need to continually weigh. On the other hand, various publics and interest groups work to make committees accountable, and committees in turn are either forced, or seek, to find the proper places to which they should be accountable. It is to a discussion of these matters that we now turn.

The Elected Committee

The committee that is most directly accountable is one that is elected, provided that committee is ongoing and the member needs to stand for another term. As in all election situations, the member must then report to that group that has formally elected him or her and seek support for another term. Within some limits, this process does create a policy review situation, where the record and performance of the incumbent are costed out against the potential contributions of some newer person. If there is disagreement about policies, and if the electorate does not care for the position of the particular person, another contender can be elected.

There are numerous problems and difficulties here, however. First, the elected committee is often one of limited term. In that event, the constituency needs to find other ways to make the member feel responsible and accountable. Second, there can be individual/group problems, in the sense that an individual who supported policies endorsed by the electorate can be defeated because of actions of the committee as a whole. Third, issues become intertwined, and we all know how members can be defeated for reelection on the basis of extraneous criteria.

Committee process and activity is affected by the election mechanism. Accommodation is often more difficult to achieve in these committees, because members feel they have a mandate, or they know that their constituents would not tolerate certain actions. They may continue to press for the actions they know their constituents want, even if it means that other committee business is delayed. Yet, in some important sense, these matters *are* committee business.

Members may on occasion take public positions for the benefit of their constituents or the press—positions they do not really hold or in areas where they would indeed be willing to make some accommodation. The difficulty here is that the meeting process becomes full of statements that are both theatrical and serious. Not only does this process occupy much committee time, but it is frequently difficult to judge which is which, since the credibility of a position for the record is completely destroyed if the member also announces that he or she is simply taking the position for the record.

Members of elected committees need to realize the political necessities that affect themselves and other members. A certain respect is due the representative who is presenting and fighting for the wishes of his or her constituents, and who will need to continually seek their advantage. On the other hand, members know that constituencies are rarely unanimous, and there is considerable room for leverage around most points. Committees are wary of a member who is completely certain of his or her constituents' positions— wary that this member's own position is being pushed under the cover of constituents' wishes.

Members need to strike a balance between posturing and performance, and they need to consider the long-run, as well as the short-run, interests of their constituents. They need to recognize that more of the committee process will be consumed by matters relating to constituent appeal.

This process may seem inefficient, especially in the short run. It must be remembered that the provision of accountability, like everything else, takes time.

The member has the responsibility to cultivate his or her constituents, to spend time meeting with them and ascertaining the depth of commitment and "feel" that they have for the issues under consideration. It is not proper to meet with only a few, and this restricted procedure is likely to result in subsequent defeat. Frequently, individual members will schedule times in the week at convenient locations where constituents can come and meet with them. Whatever the mechanism—meetings, letters, conferences, or other means—it is important to know the dimensions of the constituents' views and to seek to reflect them accurately; one's own position may, of course, be different, but it should be knowledgeably so.

The Appointed Committee

Members who secure their positions through appointment rather than election have a somewhat different pattern of accountability. The elected members have a specified electorate, for good or ill. Everyone in that electorate may not vote, of course, and there may be some groups that are more interested than others. In the main, however, such members are working with known components.

This situation is much less true of the appointed member. He or she has some responsibility to the person who made the appointment, but that responsibility is very unclear. Indeed, some take the view, as we are inclined to, that, once appointed, the member has no further responsibility to the appointer other than to listen, and is not obligated to "follow instructions" in the usual sense.

There are some cases where the member is appointed as a specific representative of the appointer, who has the authority to appoint and remove the member. In this case, the member usually pays more attention to the appointing authority. Further, there are usually provisions for reappointment, if removal is impossible. The member who hopes to have the term renewed must consider whether heeding the wishes of the appointer will aid, or detract from, that potential. Usually these arrangements are modified by the sense the member has of other constituencies involved.

The appointed member is usually selected because of connections with some constituencies it is important to have represented on the committee. Sometimes these matters are considered openly in the initial discussions about the appointment. At other times, the assumptions are more subtle. In any case, the member is placed individually in the position of determining which elements of the public form his or her constituency and developing relationships with them. Sometimes these elements will seek out the committee member. At other times, the elements that seek contact are not those with which the committee member desires to work. Nonetheless, it is important to have some sense of the general situation of several relevant constituencies as the member goes about the committee work. The job is much less clear, and hence more difficult in some ways, than for the elected member.

It may seem that the member's performance is not evaluated in this situation, and certainly the evaluation is not as direct as is the case with the elected committee. Nonetheless, opinions and views about the member's performance filter back to the appointer, to the chair, and to other members. It is on the basis of this rather crude evaluation that the member finds new opportunities opening up or seems to find the role being restricted.

Overall, the appointed committee has less connection to a constituency, and the committee is likely to be a mixed bag of persons with different skills and talents, ranging from those with technical qualifications to those who merely "have the time" to serve. For these reasons, the appointed committee often spends considerable time "finding" the constituency—which always turns out to be that initially unknown group of citizens, employees, colleagues, et cetera, who are interested in and/or affected by the work of the committee.

Committee Commonalities

There are certain commonalities in the problems of accountability with which both elected and appointed committees must struggle. Both kinds of committees need to spend some time thinking about their constituencies and how they want to relate to them. In this sense, the elected committee, whether public or private, is something like the "public" committee of the previous chapter, and the appointed committee something like the "private" one. The elected committee needs to shape its constituency, and the appointed committee needs to develop one.

In both cases, the final control of committee operation rests, not on defeat at the voting booth, nor on lack of reappointment, but rather on the loss of reputation suffered by members and chairpersons of malperforming committees because of the failure to get some results from the committee's efforts. We believe that this single element—fear of losing reputation—is what controls much committee behavior, for good or ill. Defeat at reelection is a post hoc method of control, punishing someone for something that has already happened. Failure to secure reappointment is similarly post hoc. In both cases, then, the matter of status, standing, or reputation becomes a focal element. Where it can work for ill is that, in both types of committees, it places a conservative cast on committee action, which may or may not be present in the constituent group.

Conclusion

The way in which a committee is composed—by election or appointment—exerts strong influence on its activity, and it may even affect the ultimate substance of the decision. Each kind of committee has its own characteristic processes.

The elected committee must be responsive to the people who elected it. Often this responsiveness means changes in agendas and adjustments in attitudes, and almost always it means that much more time is taken in processing the business of the committee. Indeed, part of the business of the committee is responsiveness itself.

While the energies of the elected committee are consumed with the problems of relating to the constituency, the appointed committee must spend time finding its constituency and then deciding how it wants to relate to that constituency.

Much here depends, as usual, upon the chairperson, whose situation is confounded by the different types of allegiances that may result from the way he or she came into that position. (See Chapter 1.) Only in the situation where the committee elects its own chairperson is there a minimum amount of potential friction between the chair and the members' agendas.

CHAPTER 22

Committee Scope

Introduction

Committees have not only a mode of construction and an auspice under which they operate but also a scope—an area of domain. One example of scope is the local, state, or national domain many committees have. We are all familiar with the differences that such various points of reference imply. And, in the world of "committeeology," this hierarchy of scope is also something of a hierarchy of prestige—better to be on the state committee than the local one, et cetera. There is little question that committees of broad geographic scope—national committees—are usually the most prestigious.

The geographical domain of a committee creates a "set" within which the committee thinks of itself. National committees take the nation as their point of reference and try to think of the national implications of their decisions, however hard that might be. State and local committees behave similarly, but with geographically appropriate points of departure.

The formal domain of geography, however, is not the only meaning of *scope*. It also refers to the breadth of the task. Two state committees, one charged with eradicating poverty and the other charged with eliminating litter along the roads, have a similar geographic domain but quite different functional domains. The domain of the antilitter committee is very narrow in scope, while that of the antipoverty committee is very broad. Generally, as either type of scope increases, the complexity and difficulty of the committee's task also increases.

Although we will deal with the two types of scope in detail, we might note the appearance of a convergence, which also was briefly mentioned in the introduction to this section. Geographical and functional scope appear to be inversely correlated, viz., a committee operating at the national level is more likely to have a very focused mandate or to focus its own mandate, while the local committee is likely to have a broader mandate or to broaden its own mandate.

We might further hypothesize, following Roland Warren's discussion of communities as a model, that committees perform either vertical or horizontal integration.[1] National committees are concerned with vertical integration, working with relevant counterparts at state and local levels. Local committees are involved more in coordinating their efforts with other committees at the local level. These two foci are metafunctional, in the sense that they are functions performed by the committees in reference to the system in which they operate, but have little to do with the formal assignment of the committee. True, committees may be, and are, given broader or more narrow formal assignments, and these formal mandates will, we believe, be consistent with the hypothesis just mentioned. But committees themselves do some specification of their mission and role, and this work is accomplished within the framework of other inputs from other systems. The systems more likely to contact national committees are local versions within the same substantive area, which thus create an agenda for issues that over time acts as a force to shape the mission and role of the national committee. Within the local area, on the other hand, contact is more likely to come from local committees in different substantive areas, and the resulting agenda also acts to shape the committee goals. In the former case, they become narrower, and, in the latter case, wider. While certainly it is not only the external input that shapes committee mission and role, it is a significant factor to be recognized.

With this background in mind, let us consider committees in relation to two aspects: geographic scope and functional scope.

Geographic Scope

For our purposes, let us assume that there are four levels of geographic scope: local community, regional, state, and national. Each committee level has some special problems and some special elements for staff, chairpersons, and members to keep in mind.

The Local Committee

Committees with the local community as their domain will obviously be focusing on problems and issues that affect that community. Important here, though, is the attempt on the part of the local committee to interact

1. Roland Warren, *The Community in America* (Chicago: Rand McNally, 1962).

with other local groups or organizations within the interorganizational system to keep each other apprised of activities. Sometimes local committees (or those at any level) form policy-sharing groups for such purposes. Local committees have the responsibility to adapt their programs and decisions to local needs. Although membership from the locality serves to strengthen the information base involved here, additional fact gathering is often needed. We have been impressed with how little many committee people know about their own communities, and this is especially true where committee membership is composed of "cosmopolitans" rather than "locals." A central issue, then, is being sure that the committee is aware of local preferences, desires, and issues. A major problem is the maintenance of contacts with other relevant committees and organizations.

Chairpersons of local committees should have or develop contacts within the community that is their domain; this is also a responsibility of members and staff. This point may seem an obvious one, but as people begin to serve on many different committees, we have observed that they seem to continue to draw their information from the same constituent base for all these efforts rather than to vary the constituents to suit the domain of the committee.

The Regional Committee

Of the four domains we are discussing here, the regional or metropolitan committee is the newest. Historically, the domains of committees have tended to follow legal boundaries—the city, the county, the state, the nation. Even private committees have been incorporated within one state, and their by-laws have usually specified some geographical limitation.

Within the past decade or two, the concept of region has become a more important one for functions of all sorts. As suburbanization continues, the region and metropolitan area will at least equal, and may surpass, the city and state as the key unit in which much localized action is taken. Regional committees are now forming for local governments themselves (i.e., regional councils of government; regional planning organizations for health planning, land use planning, United Fund campaigning, human service planning, et cetera). Citizens are increasingly asked to serve on such regional bodies.

Regional bodies are new, and there is little in the way of precedent to guide them. They represent, in both theory and fact, a direction of development that threatens the historical fiefdoms of local politicians and bureaucrats in virtually every field. Because the region is a concept rather than a legal entity, regional committees are beset by the most serious problems of interorganizational complexity and stress. Very often such committees receive their funds and their allegiances on a contributed basis; any time they do anything that their "members" (those who contribute money or manpower) do not like, they must deal with threats of less support. A strength some have, however, is the requirement of the federal government that funds for certain purposes are available only if there is regional planning.

Central issues relate to establishing legitimacy and stability and overcoming the idea on the part of communities and members alike that the committee is "for show." Further, regional committees must establish a record of effectiveness, an extremely difficult problem since effectiveness is likely to cause some hard feelings in the larger interorganizational network and result in threats of loss of support. Again, the review-and-comment authority given some regional bodies by the federal government gives them a stature that is most helpful.

For members and staff, the sense of accomplishment and stability is important. If they do not have this sense, and reality behind it, there will be a dwindling of interest on the part of the members and an inability to secure good staff. For the chairperson, this type of committee is one of the very difficult assignments because the potentials and problems are both at very high points. Staff, chairpersons, and members need to be quite patient with this type of committee and learn to accept the relatively slow pace at which work is accomplished. Further, much time is spent outside of meetings of the committee developing and maintaining relationships in the many municipalities and units involved.

The State-Wide Committee

While committees operating at the state level have a clearer domain, and thus fewer problems, than the regional committee, there are two pervasive problems that afflict the state committee. The state stands somewhere between the locality and the national society. Since the federal government began revenue-sharing programs, initiative seems to have moved away from the state level to the urban and regional area on the one hand and the nation on the other. As a result, state-level committees may still feel that they have neither the action potential of the community and region nor the power and influence of a national committee, and wind up in a position like that of the middle child. But this is changing as the federal government places upon the states responsibility for developing comprehensive plans and fund allocation in many areas.

Additionally, state committees, more than any other, receive mixed external inputs. They are high enough in the hierarchy to receive much upward flow of information. They are low enough to receive many lateral contacts from other committees at the state level. And, they receive comments and regulations from the national level. Such committees may have aspirations and orientations too, and, depending upon the membership, they can go to either the more community-oriented level or the more nationally oriented level. Usually, it is the latter. Many readers will have participated in longish sessions of these committees where some members argued for more national contacts and perspectives, some wanted a more urban focus, while others support a rural perspective. It is up to the committee itself here, more than at the other levels, to shape its mission from these conflicting pressures. And it has to perform this function under the stresses we have just described. Here again, the role of the chairperson is critical. Conceptual leadership as well as procedural skill become important as he or she works to help the committee define a focus and mission and role.

Members and staff, especially staff, have a great responsibility in a statewide committee, because it is very difficult to set up meetings. Travel is a problem, and most members need to plan on taking an entire day for each meeting. That means that reimbursement should be arranged for travel costs. If only those who can afford to spend money and time are able to come, the membership will not include people with all the perspectives that are needed.

Staff should recognize that the limited amount of time committee people can be together means that (1) staff must travel more to meet with members; (2) staff must do more preparation and be extra careful about getting material to members, including more, and more detailed, material than would ordinarily be the case; and (3) staff must make more use of both mail and telephone to facilitate communication.

The National Committee

National committees have certain unique features not present in other kinds of committees. Frequently they are part of a system that has state, regional, and/or local committees or structures through which people move or from which they are elected to the national committee. Membership on the national committee in these cases is recognition for active involvement at these other levels. But even when not part of such an organized system, national committees reflect broad concern with a problem, and hence there might well be leadership, interest, and activity at other geographic levels. So national committees have a rather ready and logical channel through which to select membership, and, because of the prestige of national committees, people are willing and sometimes anxious to serve.

This tendency creates some difficulties in terms of membership balance and perspective. Youth and minority points of view might be omitted because they are not part of the system from which membership is selected. Also, because of the nature of national committees, there is need to select people of stature and experience, and this eliminates many potential members—especially youth. However, this situation has been changing, and efforts are made to include them in the membership of some national committees.

Committee selection that draws from within its own system also has a tendency to limit perspectives because it is rather ingrown. National committees should be sensitive to this possibility and use devices to ensure a range of inputs, not only from minority people within their own structures, but also from outside their own systems.

Communication—important in all good committee operation—is especially important for national committees. Because of the geographical coverage, it is not possible to have the informal type of communication that takes place in a local or even regional committee. Therefore, special efforts must be made to keep in touch with members and get their input for agenda and other committee planning. Perhaps more frequent use of telephone, memos, information bulletins, working subcommittees, et cetera, is necessary. It also means that preparation for meetings must be most thorough, with material going out well in advance.

The national committee has one advantage over local and regional committees—namely, it often meets for more extended periods of time, i.e., all day or a few days. This makes more-intensive deliberations possible. But it also means that, since meetings are less frequent, much more must be accomplished at them. Special attention needs to be given to meeting accomodations, so that members can arrive smoothly at an interesting location and have comfortable surroundings.

Functional Scope

As we indicated initially, scope is not only geographic in nature, it is functional as well. By functional scope, we mean to point to the breadth versus the narrowness of the responsibilities assigned to the committee.

Broad-Focus Committees

Some committees have an exceedingly broad focus—"coordination of services," "planning to combat poverty," "eliminating juvenile delinquency," "developing a 'model' neighborhood." While these committees exist mainly at the local level, there are examples of such broad-mission committees at every level. They have a series of problems that are very inimical to effective functioning, and serving on these committees is often disappointing. The principal problems such committees have are obvious: they may never be able to settle on a system of priorities long enough to do any work intensively, and they may also be unable to develop sufficient agreement to remain at a broad and superficial level over a wide range of issues. Such a committee, perhaps more than any other, is in need of priority determination. Yet, because of the broad focus, it is difficult to (1) find legitimation in any set of priorities, (2) deal with the urgent pleas for this and that coming from other groups. For this reason, broad-focus committees might really be called "bogged-focus" committees.

In these committees, much of the responsibility lies with the members and depends upon their self-restraint and judgment. An excellent chairperson, with a cooperative committee, can prioritize the workload and develop an effective structure. But the best of chairpersons, with a committee of members not disposed to focus their tasks, might be unable to move the committee forward. After some initial discussion, members should be willing to vote on a set of priorities, and the majority of the committee should support the chair in making them stick. Otherwise, the entire session will be devoted to developing priorities, and, in the end, neither will priorities have been agreed upon nor any other work done.

The staff person in a broad-focus committee has an especially important role in shaping and directing the mission of the committee and in locating its efforts within some reasonable bounds. While the staff person can never force a mission or an interpretation onto the group, broad-focus committees are often grateful for the kind of intensive staff work that brings a small range of possible alternative emphases and thrusts within their purview.

Narrow-Focus Committees

The narrow-focus committee has a relatively easier time than its broader brother. Usually, a narrow-focus committee has a delimited mission and role expressed or implied in its mandate. However, this statement itself is usually insufficient because, paradoxically, as the focus narrows, the committee enters the realm of technical expertise, and possibilities begin again to widen. Yet, based on the language and intent of the mandate, and with perhaps some additional clarification from talking with the appointing authority, a respectable series of technically based options can be developed and selected. Choosing from a narrow range of technical options is usually easier than attempting to "zero in" on poverty, for example, if for no other reason than that the level of emotional involvement generally decreases as the technical nature of the material increases.

Chairpersons, members, and staff of narrow-focus committees usually are able to work more easily together, because they are likely to have common grounding in the rather narrower subject matter. The responsibilities on committee members and staff are heavy here, since there is a great amount of detailed material to master and decide upon. Yet often this task seems less burdensome than other committee activity, because there is a greater feeling of the possibility of accomplishment.

Conclusion

We have identified two types of committee scope—geographic and functional. Each contributes some unique problems for members and staff. Perhaps the regional and state committees and the broad-focus committee pose the greatest trials for the members and staff, because it is in those committees especially that external, contextual pressures can become almost the total agenda of the meeting, driving out mission, role, and useful work.

SIGNIFICANT ISSUES

IN COMMITTEE LIFE

Much of the material we have been discussing has been relatively standard—that is, it can be applied across time and space to a wide range of committees. One can, for example, take some of the bibliographic material from the 1930s and 1940s and find many similarities. Each decade, however, develops a set of concerns and problems uniquely important— concerns and problems that infuse and affect all the important institutions. While such issues may have been present at other periods, and probably were, there is a special importance about them during certain periods.

During the past twenty years in the United States, there have been several focal concerns that occupied some of our institutional energies and efforts. One of these comprised "maximum feasible participation of the poor" and its various sequelae. In essence, it was brought to the attention of the country that important segments of the society were left out of decisions that affected them. In a nation for which the phrase "No taxation without representation" was a rallying cry, this exclusion needed remedy.

From the viewpoint of the committee process, this exclusion raised two issues. The first issue was a legal one—Whom does the member, or the committee, represent? The whole issue of representation and (versus) representativeness has been of concern to committee theorists for many years. Withal, the activities of the sixties and seventies have made that issue more salient, and anyone who has heavy committee responsibilities will have to give it serious consideration, both personally and for the committee on which he or she serves.

A second way in which this exclusion affected committee activity was less formalized, and it related to the way in which special groups were members of, and participated in, the everyday committee life of the country. Such special groups, of course, included the poor and disadvantaged, but pressures from African Americans, Latinos, gays and lesbians, Native Americans, students, "unmeltable" ethnics, women, and other groups made committees sensitive to the need to have a broad group in terms of both membership and participation. This initial sensitivity involved other considerations. Participation could not be optimized if the time of the meeting were such that no one could attend, if the place were inaccessible for many, if everyone went out for lunch but some members could not afford it. These technical problems are but part of a larger attempt to involve, in a variety of ways, people not previously involved. And indeed, the pressures created by that thrust, and the lack of familiarity some subsets of these special groups have had with "conventional" committee practice, were among the stimuli for this volume.

A second major development, arising perhaps later in the decade of the 1960s, through the 1970s, and into the 1980s, is the press for accountability. There is great interest in who, or what, is accountable for the spending of money, the allocating of resources, and, in general, the making of decisions. The citizenry at large, the federal establishment, businesses, agencies, and universities are all now pressing, and being pressed, to "account for" stewardships. The thrust for accountability goes hand in hand with a press for evaluation. How well, or poorly, was a job done? Did technique X work? Did it work better than Y? Did it work better than nothing at all? And, if we can answer any of those questions, how do we know? On what basis are the data collected? On what basis is the evaluation made? What are the appropriate statistical and other procedures to use in thinking about such a problem?

While the interest in accountability and evaluation has touched almost every aspect of the American institutional structure, its impact on committee life is just beginning. Committees, as we indicated earlier, are for the most part hard to evaluate and perhaps even harder to hold accountable. With the single exception of those with policy-deciding responsibility, committees have been singularly unaffected by this important trend. In fact, some people would argue that the committee is a device set up to obfuscate accountability and to hide responsibility.[1] According to these people, when the goal is to do nothing and do it in a complicated fashion, the response is, "Appoint a committee." And it may indeed be that committees are, in their functional sense, a social device for muting responsibility. (See Chapter 25.) Nonetheless, committees cannot escape the general trends, nor should they. Some attention will be given to the whole problem of grading and evaluating committee work. We do not expect this task to be any easier in the committee context than it is anywhere else. But several types of evaluation must be undertaken, and accountability patterns must develop.

Finally, we must inject a note of caution. In a society as complex as America's, with its cleavages and differences, one would expect associational groupings with "representatives" from different interests to come together to seek solutions. This expectation should be especially strong if that same society has a penchant—as does American society—for the practical over the ideological, for the pragmatic over the philosophical, for action as opposed to contemplation. Yet we know very little about committees as a social form and hence, from the larger, more analytically evaluative perspective, little about the conditions under which they succeed or fail. We do have a sense, however, that, while committees are a vehicle for creating commonalities of action in a field of basic differences, they do not resolve the difference itself. Hence, we should become disabused of a certain romanticism with respect to committees. Some tasks can be accomplished by committee; some cannot. We don't know a great deal about which are which; nor, for that matter, about the various conditions under which tasks may or may not be successfully addressed. We do not have the information to consider whether a particular success or failure was idiosyncratic, or whether the "deck was stacked" in favor of one particular result or another from the beginning. It is to this end that additional knowledge should be sought.

1. There are many such articles. Edson points to this fact when she says, "Since committee work is not a professional skill, not much professional emphasis is given to it. . . . Few books, however, present basic survival skills for those who spend much of their working life in committee meetings." Jean Brown Edson, "How to Survive on a Committee," *Social Work* 22, no. 3 (May 1977): 224.

CHAPTER 23

Representation and Representativeness

Introduction

One of the issues that always arises in relation to committee process is the concept of representation. To some extent, this issue has been discussed at other points in the volume. Elected committee members have perhaps the clearest idea whom they represent, at least in terms of a specific constituency. Even there, however, the question of representation, leaving aside the matter of how an individual wishes to handle it, becomes separate from the question of representativeness.

Representation

The question of representation refers to the individualized aspect of the issue. It has two parts: The first part is, Whom do I represent? and it links the member to some present, future, or past constituency. The second question, How do I represent? is one of the classic dilemmas.

Whom Do I Represent?

Committee members, from the most insignificant organization to the House of Representatives, all face the question, Whom do I represent? While those members who are elected have by law a group they represent, that is ofttimes not much help, because the opinions and views on many issues within that constituency are legion. Committee members from specific sectors—whether these sectors are geographical or "interest" ("The committee shall be composed of two professors elected from each rank of assistant, associate, and full. . . .") or whatever—always face a problem of finding out what it is their constituency wants, and of course different portions of the constituency want different things.

Present, Future, and Past Constituencies. Some members of committees feel that they need to speak for the interests of not only the present constituency but also the past constituency and the future constituency. Some members may take the view that "There has always been a tradition of such and such, and I cannot in good conscience change it now." Other members may speak of future generations, or other groups who have yet to arrive on the scene. The concept of representation is thus thought of in terms of the interests of these groups. What such groups want, or might have wanted, is of course open to some interpretation.

The Delegate. A delegated representation occurs when a member has been asked to represent his or her agency or organization as a participant on some committee. Policy-sharing, policy-coordination, policy-advisory, and policy-implementing committees most commonly have such members. Here the constituency is the organization itself, and the member is assumed to be speaking as a delegate of the organization. In a small organization this creates few problems, because it is easy to work out an organizational position. Representing the larger organization is more difficult, because the many divisions and departments have varying views, and it becomes harder to achieve agreement on what posture the organization should present.

Judgment. Perhaps the most common form of representation is for the delegate to use his or her "best judgment." Generally, the member reserves the right to make the final decision and cast the final vote. That this right is to be exercised independently is one of the reasons why members must take care to be unencumbered by special interests. However, a concomitant of this personalism is the responsibility to talk to many interested groups and hear their points of view on the matters at hand. This practice is quite well developed in the formalized hearings that public committees hold. And for public committees, the process is clearer. For private committees, there are fewer opportunities for members to check the actions of the committee as a whole with relevant others. It may be unclear exactly whom such relevant others would be. Or, there may be many persons pressing their views upon the member, and the problem is one not of seeking opinions but of making choices. In any event, all members must remember that they have some sort of constituency, and they should take some pains to explore developing issues among that constituency.

Representativeness

Representation connotes formal legal processes that permit constituencies with interests in particular matters to have a voice in the discussion of those matters. Problems arise, however, in determining what groups are the relevant ones in a particular case, and then ascertaining how they are to actually have a voice. These are problems of representativeness.

Securing Representation

Perhaps the best way to think about the problems of representativeness is to assume that most committee chairpersons, with the exception of the chair of the partisan committee, would like to have within the membership persons from different religions, races, and sexes, as well as other relevant segments. A policy implementation committee, for example, might have members from business and labor, if such a committee were convened within the interorganizational area. A committee within an organization might have members from different divisions of the organization. Committee builders, as we shall mention momentarily, give great attention to this problem of representativeness. Committee composition is an important element in good functioning and in the acceptance of the decisions of the committee. What are the groups that should be "represented," or at least have a "presence"?

In general, groups that are important in the social system at large should be represented within the makeup of the committee.[1] This similarity of the committee to the society provides an important link between the committee and the larger social structure. Such representation can be achieved, generally, within any context. Since these groupings are societal ones, relevant persons can be found in the community as well as in the organization. There are several more specific dimensions one needs to consider.

Current Social Elements and Issues. In considering representativeness, one must consider the current issues within the range of the committee. If there are two or three prevailing views on some matter, then the committee membership should include people conversant with those views. If there is a conflict between the accounting office and the purchasing department, members from both departments should be represented. The key point here is that the important differences of view need to be involved.

---

1. We are referring here to the social aspects of representation, not, for example, to technical or other elements of expertise, except as these examples take on a political, or values-choice, cast.

Those Affected by the Decision. People affected by the decision, or those for whom the committee action has fateful consequences—a group often ignored—should have the opportunity to be involved. Sometimes those affected are clients, patients, and user groups. At other times, they are those who will be involved in carrying out the decision. If, for example, the local United Fund is developing a new planning system that will require member agencies to carry out new data collection procedures, then it is important to have those agencies involved in the development. This principle is especially important for coordinating or implementing committees. Ultimately, the cooperation of those affected must be relied upon, and it is far better to bring them in early. The chair and the members must give some thought to who might be affected by the work of their particular committee, in advance of that committee's functioning. Not only the most visible but also the covert effects must be considered. Some of these people can then be invited to join the group itself.

One can take two views about such a process. The less charitable view is one of cooptation, in which a secret agenda is already planned and members invited to join will be "fooled" into accepting recommendations that may go against their interests. The more charitable view is that an issue has arisen, that there may be many solutions to the problems inherent in that issue, and that those involved must have some ideas about both the problem and the solution. In such an interpretation, involvement is for the purpose of seeking information and perspective, not manipulating agreement.

Important Sectors. Apart from those affected by the decision, it is useful to think of representation from important sectors of the relevant system. In community interorganizational committees—such as hospital boards, community council committees, and the like—members representing business, finance, and industry are usual, along with representation from the clergy, labor, and perhaps the political, educational, and foundation communities. Often the local press is involved, although it frequently likes to remain uninvolved because it can then preserve its independence of reporting. Depending upon the issue, some thought might be given to a variety of professional communities, such as the medical community, the natural resource/environment community, and the like, as well as local regions and territories (e.g., rural, urban, et cetera) that have views. Within an organization, there are analogous communities that often require representation. Finance, personnel, marketing, advertising, sales, transportation, office services, and central office administration are but a few of the units typically represented in intraorganizational groups. Essentially, the principle here is that of veto. Such groups are often not able to push something through, but they may be able to veto proposed activities should they wish to do so. Power is often important here, as well as sectoral representation, but seeking influential members, a matter we discuss next, should not be thought to replace adequate sectoral representativeness.

Top and Key Influentials

The issue of committee power, and the power of committee members, is perhaps most important within the first group of committees we outlined—information-sharing committees, advisory committees, coordinating and implementing committees. The power of the members is perhaps seen as (and actually may be) a substitute for the lack of formal legal authority enjoyed by other committee forms.

Ever since committees have been formed, it has been axiomatic that their effectiveness is enhanced by including among the membership powerful people from the relevant system, whether that system is in the organization or in the community. Especially important, conventional wisdom argues, is that the chair be influential; other members can be as influential, but not more influential, than whoever is in the chair. This observation stems from the apparent fact that, if members, or a member, can "deliver" more than the chair, that person will become the de facto chair. To our knowledge, while these observations seem reasonable, they have never been tested.

We do seek influential members. But whether a committee so composed is more effective, and makes better quality decisions, than a committee of less-influential members is not known.

These caveats are important, because immense time is spent looking for "powerful people." While our experience generally agrees with the utility of such a search, we have observed additionally that power sometimes substitutes for committee competence. It is often the case, actually, that powerful people are sought precisely because they are competent committee people; indeed, that may be why they have become powerful. Committee makers do not say or think that; they believe power itself to be the key. In the end, perhaps it is. Yet it bears repeating that no one has yet found a way to measure power, and we often assume that attributes such as money, position, or prestige represent power. While those may be associated with power, they often are not, to the dismay and puzzlement of committee builders. We conclude that power, however conventionally measured, should be one element of committee consideration, but we also feel that it has been overplayed and may act as a "cover" for other important elements.

The Problems of Representativeness

Attempting to build a committee that has both representation and representativeness is an awesome task and one that is given all too little attention. As one seeks the proper amalgam of membership for the task at hand, several problems loom large.

Conflicts Between Representation and Representativeness. At times these two principles approach conflict. Such conflict often occurs when the "representative" appointed or elected to a committee is known not to be representative of the community from which he or she comes—for example, a physician who holds radical views and is elected to a community committee. Such a physician would probably not represent the position of many colleagues, and thus, though being *a* representative, would possess no representativeness in his or her particular role. There is then the delicate situation of securing additional representation. This approach may be offensive to the "official" representative and can lead to problems. Often the perspectives from the particular group need to be sought in other ways, perhaps through hearings and written position papers.

Role Stereotyping. Similar to the problem above is the one that develops when a committee member selected on the basis of some attribute balks at playing the "African American" role, or the "Jewish" role, or whatever. In the rush to secure "representation," too little thought is given to human and personal elements. People resent, and properly so, being "the woman" or "the Chicano" of the committee. Members are members, and they will often reject the categories others develop for them. Hence, the committee maker must be careful in two ways—to attend to the categories people occupy, and to realize that these categories are only partial ones at best.

Conflicting Bases. We have mentioned a number of bases along which representativeness might be developed. It is usually not possible to represent them all, or the committee would become too large. The question is, Which bases are the most important, and which are of lesser importance? Here, as in all matters, prioritization must occur.

Multiple Representation. Sometimes there is an attempt to finesse the problem of conflicting bases through the use of multiple representations, in which one member is seen as filling two or more slots. An African American woman can thus serve as a representative of both women and African Americans. While this ploy sometimes works, it often simply pushes the conflict from the committee maker onto the person. It cannot be said to be solved; it has only been "referred," and the problem is still there.

Conclusion

Representation and representativeness are two important elements of committee structure that are continually problematic for committee operation.

The issue of how representation is to be handled is often unclear, and there are no specific rules to use as a guide. The idea of representativeness, in which the committee structure is somehow a microcosm of the important cleavages and differences in the world at large, is one that committee creators seek to maximize. Yet there are often many crosscutting bases on which representativeness develops, and representativeness in one area may conflict, at times, with representativeness in another. Then, the committee can contain so many points of view that it cannot function.

In the final analysis, "representation" may not be "representative," and, in any event, a committee cannot be representative of all elements in a community. One solution, of course, is to fall back on the legitimacy of the formalized modes of representation. However, additional mechanisms must be found in place of this when it does not exist, and to augment it when it does. The purpose of the committee is one guide; membership can be selected consistent with at least that part of the purpose that is known. Finally, though, there is no substitute for responsiveness on the part of a committee. It is ultimately the extent to which the committee is willing to, and can, interact with the constituent groups that determines the extent to which the wishes of a diverse clientele can be seriously considered.

CHAPTER 24

Optimizing the Participation
of Special Groups

Introduction

Involvement of those affected by the decision is, as we have indicated, embodied in the "revolutionary" American principle of "no taxation without representation." And indeed, the very concept of electoral democracy implies such a relationship in the largest sense. Yet it was our national deficiencies in that area that led, within the context of the Johnson administration's poverty program, to a call under law for "maximum feasible participation" of the poor. America had been negligent in seeking representation from all those affected, notably minorities, women, and service recipients.[1]

Involvement of these groups is no longer a matter of choice. A variety of laws assure their right to be heard, and denial of representation can result in court action. Hence, it behooves us not only to comply with the law but also to proceed further than the law and enhance the meaningful and useful participation of those formerly excluded.

Membership on committees is the mode of participation that comes immediately to mind, and it is the one we will stress here. It is very important, however, to be aware that this is not the only mode of involvement. Conferences, work groups, public hearings, and many other mechanisms are available to enhance participation and should be considered along with the possibilities for membership.

---

1. For a summary of salient characteristics of board members, see Nelly Hartogs and Joseph Weber, Boards of Directors (Dobbs Ferry, N.Y.: Oceana Publications, 1974), and John E. Tropman, "A Comparative Analysis of Welfare Councils" (Ph.D. diss., University of Michigan, 1967).

Participation Symmetry

The successful participation of those who have not participated in the past is a development that involves two types of learning. On the one hand, the new participants need to be aware of the conventions and patterns, often very subtle, that govern the operation of the committee. On the other hand, and just as important, the persons who are *already* members need to welcome the newcomers, act with courtesy and respect toward them, and reflect an understanding and acceptance of the fact that the new participants' conception of and performance at a committee meeting might be quite different from the "conventional pattern." One mistake often made by the board-training planners is to assume that only the new members need training. Sometimes the problem members are the ones already there! Egregious comments about "A woman's place is in the kitchen" will not help a new female member feel welcome. Hence, the need for training, both of new members and of existing members, is pressing. Only in this way will we achieve new levels of proper participation.

Affirmative Action and the Committee

In the current decade, committees of every sort are moving into an "affirmative action" phase, in which they seek to bring in the perspectives of those whose views were not represented in the past. Any specific committee might have a unique list of additions, but in general, committees are moving to include more women and minorities and a greater range of age and social classes.

There are some relatively straightforward cautions to which the new member and the extant member might be alerted. We are stressing here the role of the extant in welcoming new members, because the extant member is in a situation of relative comfort vis-à-vis the new addition to the committee. In general, we caution the experienced committee hands to avoid stereotyping new members—be they African Americans, Hispanics, women, the old, youth, the poor, or other special population.

Finding New Members

One of the reasons such persons are not already on committees is that they are hard to find; one of the reasons they are hard to find is that they are not already on committees. This circularity points to a key problem committees have: the problem of membership "old-boys" networks and the relation of those networks to eventual positions on committees. Committee vacancies are only occasionally, as in elected committees, announced publicly so that many can compete. Rather, potential membership is developed from lists of "people we know."

Not only is it important to establish new procedures for locating new members, but it is important to have enough members so that a member from some previously excluded category will not feel isolated. It is very difficult, for example, to be the only woman, the only Black, the only client on a board or committee.

Training New Members

For most committee roles, no formal training is ever provided anywhere in the system. Indeed, one of the reasons for this volume is to fill part—but only part—of this need. While organizations have staff training and development sessions regularly, members of boards and committees are given little or no orientation. This lacuna is difficult enough for people who have had some generalized socialization with respect to committee functioning. For those whose life experience has never included participation, it is even worse. And in addition, there are the special habits and folkways of particular boards and committees that only the initiates know.

We urge, therefore, that each permanent committee have some kind of training package—booklet, orientation session, discussion, or combination of these items—that it can provide for new members. This can improve the performance of new members to a marked degree. For those special groups whose participation we are seeking to enhance, there may need to be something more—a positive outreach to make them feel welcome and appreciated. Without this effort, the psychological distance such members feel because of prior exclusion often is transformed into simple nonparticipation and then withdrawal.

New members, especially if they have little previous experience in committee life, tend to make certain routine errors that can be mentioned here:

1. seeking to get into great detail on a matter at hand, greater than is necessary
2. personalizing issues by reporting their own experiences
3. being concerned with administrative details instead of policy
4. discussing side issues at great length

One result is that the long-term members become annoyed with the newcomers and, in seeking to move the process along, give rise to suspicions of "railroading." This impression in turn calls forth even more of the behavior they judged objectionable. New members of any board need to be educated, and so do the older members. Many organizations are now developing training programs for both groups, and we would certainly encourage this trend.

Special Concerns and Problems

For many of the groups whose participation we seek to enhance, there are special life circumstances and concerns that are directly related to committee participation. More experienced members of the committee must give special attention to these. Without explicit attention, the committee will simply not be able to attract the desired members, or, at best, participation will be low and eventually nonexistent. The points we are making with respect to these several groups are not startling or new; they have, however, proved problematic in our committee experience.

Suspicion

Many of the groups whose participation we seek to enhance have experienced discrimination of one sort or another. The personal impact of discrimination is never fully understood by those who have not experienced it firsthand. As a result of it, new committee members who were formerly shut off from participation may be more suspicious and doubtful about procedures, about practices that have come to be regarded as "conventional," than others in the group. We all must remember that, even though our own "intentions are good," that does not mean the intentions of others are just as good; those who have had the experience of discrimination are well justified in continued vigilance. And institutional species of discrimination may operate through any of us inadvertently. Furthermore, it is precisely gentlemen's agreements and similar practices that have been, to at least some extent, the mechanisms through which discrimination has been maintained.

Divided Loyalties

Persons from previously excluded groups who join committees are often in situations of role strain. A committee action contemplated in some specific instance may disadvantage, or not fully advantage, members of their group—be that group women, Hispanics, or another special population. Often other committee members see this situation as a test: will the excluded member not vote against or criticize his or her own group? We believe that this expectation is frequently unreasonable. Indeed, sometimes the expectation places the member in the position of having to do exactly the reverse. We suggest that the affected member abstain in such cases and that other members make it possible for him or her to do this if wished. Effectiveness as a link with a group will be destroyed if it is felt by the group that he or she has become one of "them." Hence, on such issues a neutral rather than an affirmative or negative posture seems the most advisable.

Logistics

Certain committee members—especially those of lower income, those with children, the youth, and the aged—may find certain difficulties in attending meetings. The chair should explore any such difficulties with individual members. One woman may need help with transportation or with baby-sitting; a factory worker may find it impossible to attend daytime meetings; another may need extra assistance in giving reports. Once a person has been added to a committee, further attention to special problems is needed. If participation is to be encouraged, then ways to facilitate participation must be considered. This point is a particularly important one, because many chairpersons and members do not routinely think of such matters.

The chairperson should also be alert to financial constraints: does the member have money for a luncheon meeting or money for a cab? For many members who are organizationally related, committee service is seen as a part of the job; their employers pick up the tab for such items, or the member keeps a record and deducts committee-related expenses from his or her income tax. Certain members may not have these benefits, since their committee service is not job-related or they do not itemize deductions, and these same members may not have the ready cash needed, in any event. Committees need to help in a way that is nonstigmatizing and reflective of our respect for each person's dignity.

Location of Meeting

We have emphasized the location of the meeting with respect to parking and facilities. But there is a social aspect of the meeting place to consider as well. For example, if a community coordinating committee has members from different agencies and different geographic sections of the community, it makes sense to rotate meeting locations to their various offices and areas. Or if meetings are ordinarily in one location and certain members must travel quite far, it is courteous to have an occasional meeting in their location. Specific situations will, of course, vary. The general rule is to give the committee "presence" through the use of meeting location and to consider the desires and convenience of all in this regard.

Conclusion

The social purpose of committees cannot be served if some members and groups of the society are consistently excluded from membership. This important social form is largely unscrutinized in American society, so that the formal regulations governing affirmative action may not apply, or may apply only in selective instances, to committee selection. *Our point here is to encourage committees to expand their membership to include those who have not had the opportunity to serve.* To take this action, however, the committee must do more than simply find suitable candidates. Aspects of training are involved, as well as a host of special considerations and arrangements that are necessary if full participation is to be assured. It may appear that we have gone to an unnecessarily specific level of detail in providing examples of our intentions here. Yet this type of attention to detail is illustrative of the elements that must be considered if larger social goals are to be achieved and the quality of committee decisions thereby enhanced.

CHAPTER 25

Committee Decision Quality, Effectiveness, Evaluation, and Accountability

Introduction

To ask, in reference to any committee, How good a job did it do? is to address the difficult areas of committee decision quality and effectiveness. The question is implicit in the preceding sections of this volume, but we would be remiss if we did not give it some direct attention.

Going hand in hand with the matters of quality and effectiveness are the issues of evaluation and accountability. Formal organizations today are increasingly being held to strict measures of performance evaluation, but committees, in their various forms, have, for the moment, largely escaped this social demand. Few committees have even given thought to how their work is to be evaluated.

The problem of committee accountability is, if anything, even more difficult. We can hold individuals responsible by virtue of the fact that they can be removed from their posts, but it is less clear how a group that is not a formal corporation may be held responsible. While space does not permit an extended consideration of these issues, nor would this volume be an appropriate place for such a discussion, this chapter will suggest some beginning elements useful to committee members.

Each of these areas—committee decision quality, committee effectiveness, committee evaluation, and committee accountability—opens up new areas for committee members. While each is discussed and considered by sophisticated committee members, none has yet been given sustained attention and discussion, not to mention research. For these reasons, we are not able to be as specific as in earlier chapters. Nonetheless, the matters should be brought to the attention of committee participants, not only because committees soon will be sharing the same scrutiny as other corporate members of the society with respect to evaluation and accountability, but because attention to these matters is inherently important. Committees must move toward ways of characterizing and setting the quality of decision at which they operate, and then move toward improving that level. Thinking about quality and effectiveness is the initial step; assessing and evaluating them is the second step; and, finally, being accountable for them is the third step.

The Quality of Committee Decisions

In recent years, a considerable amount of research has been done on decision making. Basically, this search has focused on whether or not a decision is made and on the substantive interests favored by a particular decision. It has not focused on the quality of the decision, how "good" or how "bad" it is. Assessment of decision quality is admittedly difficult in any situation; within the committee process it is even harder. Why, then, should it be done?

It seems commonly recognized that decision quality is an important element of our interpersonal assessment of people. It is said of Mr. X that he has good judgment, while of Mr. Y that he has bad judgment. These references usually are based on a crude assessment of the general quality—good or bad—of the decisions made by those people.

When we move to the decision-making group—the committee—the discussion becomes even fuzzier. The concept of judgment does not seem as applicable, and the idea of a good committee seems more to refer to whether the committee does anything, as opposed to nothing, or whether the decisions of the committee were implemented. Hence the reference is to the action component of the decision rather than the quality component. In this regard, we would like to distinguish between committee effectiveness and committee quality. But first, let us define committee quality.

A Definition of Quality

Let us consider a situation in which there are a number of actors, all pressing for a decision. A committee is in charge of making that decision. Let us further assume that the committee could take any one of a number of possible actions, each with very different implications for the happiness of those involved. The committee's generalized options are these: it can make a decision that leaves everyone less happy than before; it can make a decision that advantages some and disadvantages others, but the overall impact is that the system is worse off; it can make a decision that basically changes nothing; it can make a decision in which some are advantaged and some disadvantaged, but overall the system is better off than before; or it can make a decision in which everyone is advantaged. We call these decisions, in the usual academic grading system, F, D, C, B and A. The closer one gets to A, the better the quality of the decision.

In this formulation, a C decision leaves things exactly as they were; an F or D decision means that people are more unhappy than they would have been without the committee decision; a B or an A means that there has been an increase in happiness.

The F Decision. The F decision is a qualitative failure. Everyone is worse off than before. A decision for nuclear war might be one example. A decision to eliminate air quality control standards might be another. There are times, and we are all aware of them, when committee judgment causes everything to be worse than it was before.

The D Decision. The D decision very commonly occurs in "corrupt" situations, where a committee favors the interests of the few over the interests of the many. Some are advantaged in a D decision, but most are disadvantaged. Overall, there is less happiness than there was before, even though not everyone is unhappy.

The C Decision. The C decision is perhaps the most common, although this observation comes only from our own committee participation. In the C decision, the relative balance of advantages and disadvantages remains the same, and so does the relative amount of happiness and unhappiness. It could be, in a C decision, that there is some internal shifting, and so it is not necessarily the same people who are happy and unhappy, but there is no overall increase in amount of happiness in the system.

The B Decision. The B decision increases the amount of advantages enjoyed by the members of the society overall, but for some there are still disadvantages. It is the reverse of the D decision. This decision is in some sense the classic case of benefits outweighing costs. In the B case, the quality of the decision has moved into the plus column, and committee members can justly feel that they have made a positive contribution through participation in this decision.

The A Decision. The A decision is one in which everyone gains. Some, of course, may not gain as much as others; some may not gain as much as they would like to gain or as much as they individually would have gained in a D, C, or B decision. Yet, on balance, all are further ahead. The fact that no one is behind makes A qualitatively different from B in the same sense that F is qualitatively different from D. In A and F decisions, no restraint is placed on what happens to individuals. The decision can only make people better or worse off—better in the case of A, worse in the case of F.

The Happiness Criterion. Increased or decreased "happiness" is not the best criterion for decision quality. It only sets the stage for more explicit, more operational terms. Yet it is not completely theoretical. Committee members frequently use that exact language in talking about committee decisions: "Were you happy with (about) that decision?" "Do you think Mr. X will be unhappy about our action today?" A decision about which no one is unhappy, and many are happier than they would have been without it, is an actual committee reality. It simply has not usually been thought about in the terms we are using here.

Substance and Quality

The qualitative measures we have been discussing have had no substantive referent. This lack poses two problems: (1) how to find substantive solutions that will meet the qualitative criterion, and (2) how to evaluate the possible alternative solutions. It is here that the real "guts" of the committee process are to be found—in uncovering solutions and acting on one of them. Committees are created in the first place to act as solution-generating groups. It is in this sense that we argued previously that the tasks of all committees are policy-related.

Essentially, the first task of any committee is to generate policy options over some set of issues. Staff, members, and chairperson are all important in generating a range of possibilities. Once these possibilities have been identified, a decision must be made about which one to recommend or act upon. Action here assumes that an appropriate set of alternatives has, in fact, been generated. If the first process was a faulty one and did not generate acceptable alternatives, or if it generated some of poor quality, then the action on them will be, perforce, of poor quality as well.[1] To rank a series of options, and thus make a decision about preference, is to choose one set of advantages over another. It is here that the group is often judged, at least in American society, to be superior to the individual, especially where evaluation is difficult. We shall discuss the process of evaluation in a subsequent section. It is simply necessary to note here that a decision of any level of quality is not unique; there may be other decisions that would also be good—different,

1. On occasion, it is possible to take a bad policy option and administer it in such a way as to make it of substantially higher quality than it would otherwise be. Similarly, a high-quality option can be converted into a lower-quality program through inept administration or by administration that seeks to destroy the credibility of the option.

but equally a B or an A. These differences in substance come about through other decisions to fix some aspects and let others vary. For example, in budget decisions it has become common (though not necessarily wise) practice to look only at the incremental portions of a budget rather than review all the components.

Committee Effectiveness

"Good" committees, as we have previously indicated, are often thought to be "effective" committees rather than committees that make good decisions. An effective committee is seen as one that gets what it wants, whatever that is. Hence, if the committee wants to coordinate, then coordination occurs; if it seeks implementation, then implementation occurs. It is important to mention effectiveness here because it is so frequently confused with committee quality.

Committee quality, as we have discussed it, refers to the quality of the decision made by the committee. Committee effectiveness refers to the extent to which the decision made by the committee is put into practice. In this formulation, one can see that a bad decision is still one that can be put into practice, and a good decision includes nothing that says it must be implemented. Generally, people tend to think that only good decisions become implemented, while the bad decisions do not.

A key dilemma arises for a committee when it becomes clear that the better-quality decisions are not always the most effective. While there is a close association between the quality of the decision and its effectiveness, the committee controls only the qualitative aspect and does not control some of the aspects that make for effectiveness. Other actors—administrators, executives, and operations people—become involved here. There are, however, some criteria for an effective policy decision that clearly do not relate to the quality of the decision as such. The criteria developed by Simon, Smithburg, and Thompson in their book *Public Administration* (1950) serve, we think, as admirable guides. Their suggestions fall into two parts: (1) reducing the costs of change, and (2) securing compliance. They identify five costs of change—inertia costs, moral costs, self-interest costs, rationality (complexity) costs, and subordination costs—and suggest ways in which each of these costs can be reduced, if not neutralized, in the development of an effective decision. With respect to securing compliance, once change has been ratified, they suggest ways of (1) securing the support of existing values and (2) detracting from the desirability of old behavior.[2]

2. Herbert Simon, D. Smithburg, and V. Thompson, *Public Administration* (New York: Knopf, 1950), Chapters 21 and 22. This book, more than forty years old, is still stimulating and inspiring, as well as relevant!

Evaluation of Committee Performance

If we are to think of committee decisions in terms of levels of quality, and of committee action in terms of levels of effectiveness, it follows that any overall evaluation of committee activity should take both these dimensions into account. Indeed, such evaluation as occurs within the committee system inevitably does take both into account.

Less likely to be adequately considered, of course, is decision quality, since it is the most difficult to measure. Only when a committee decision falls into the A range or the F range, when it is clear that the decision was a bad one or a good one, does this aspect of committee work come in for evaluation in any formal way. Informally, committees are discussed in terms of their "judgment." More common, at least in terms of discussion, is a rating of committee effectiveness. Perhaps because there is more agreement on what it is, and the criteria are somewhat more specific, effectiveness becomes a topic of much concern. A committee's rating on effectiveness is likely to be reflected in citizens' willingness or unwillingness to join it. Most common is an evaluation of these items indirectly, through committee process. It is through the examination and consideration of the procedures used by the committee in coming to its decision that much evaluation currently goes on.

Evaluation of Process and Procedures

In terms of procedural and process evaluation, some specific items are worth keeping in mind:

Procedures. At a minimum, committees need to follow the rules. Time after time there are instances, occasionally blatant, when committees violate their own stated procedures. It is up to the chairperson especially, but members and staff as well, to insist that accepted procedures be followed. The case in which procedures are abrogated is likely to become the troublesome and problematic one later in terms of the issues, and, in addition, the abrogation itself causes difficulties through lack of fairness and equity.

If the committee does not have specified procedures for its basic work, then these need to be created. This need is especially acute in certain policy-deciding roles that committees play. In personnel decisions, for example, both criteria and a systematic way of applying the criteria to those being considered are necessary.

Records. As important as adherence to the procedures is the task of keeping records. Committees often assume that the minutes are kept for the members' benefit, and they are. But a second key purpose is to provide a record for those not on the committee. In the best of worlds, such persons are those who are thinking of joining the committee and are seeking information about what the committee has done. In more difficult worlds, the minutes provide written substantiation of committee activity and procedure that can answer those who would attack the committee. As a means of protecting the integrity of the committee's decisional process, records can be crucial. If records are not kept up, then attempts on the part of the committee members to reconstruct portions of the activity will almost surely be inaccurate, and hence, their ability to defend themselves and explain the basis of committee actions will always be limited.

Review of Process. One of the ways in which an "evaluative mindset" is developed is through a continual evaluative process within the committee itself. We have all had the experience of discovering that something scheduled to be done at some earlier point has been forgotten, so that it will be completed late or cannot be done at all. Perhaps it was buried in the minutes; perhaps it was not assigned to any specific person. The staff person, the members of the committee, and the chair should continually review the committee minutes for items that need attention but have slipped out of the "action stream." A committee that continually evaluates itself in this way will be on top of its business and likely to avoid criticism in the final analysis.

Committee Accountability

Whatever the evaluative processes developed by the committee, and whatever the quality of its decisions, the committee will not be subject to many social controls unless this evaluative process can be translated into accountability. In our view, within the social system committees form one important system-segment that has very limited accountability. This limitation occurs for several reasons: First, as we have already noted, many committees operate in an essentially privatized arena, removed from any scrutiny. And even if these committees do make some efforts to report to the broader community, there remains the question of the degree to which they are accountable to that public.

Second, committees are often constructed in ways that give them real power but not formal power. The real power comes from having as members those who can make decisions within the particular domain under discussion. After taking action, they dissolve. When people ask, "Who made the decision?" the answer is, "The XYZ Committee." But by now that committee is dissolved, and the analyst, or protester, is left somewhat limply wondering what is going on. This situation is not, of course, the case for all committees.

Sometimes the committee remains and the membership changes. With different members, one wonders how a committee can be held responsible. One could, perhaps, dissolve the committee, but that might bring applause from the members rather than regrets. The committee, therefore, is something like a corporation in that it operates as an individual but often can finesse responsibility. It is true that committees are part of a larger structure, and sometimes one can touch base with that structure. However, this fact does not necessarily provide accountability in any form.

Third, committee action is often complex, and staff members play increasingly important roles. Many members of boards of education, or other boards and committees, have found to their chagrin that the staff is playing a very powerful role and has its own independent support in the political network of the community, so that the board really has very limited effectiveness. In this case, holding the board responsible is formally correct and realistically ridiculous.

Generally, the concept of accountability means that those responsible for the decisions take the credit or the blame; yet, unfortunately, the world of committees is so fragmented that credit and blame are hard to assign, and furthermore, it is unclear what should "happen" when those responsible are pinpointed. As we indicated earlier, one possibility is that someone is removed from a committee, but this action is hardly so terribly serious. Sometimes rewards and penalties can be assessed through the host or home organization of the committee members, but committee work, especially on any single committee, usually represents a modest portion of any person's whole assignment.

Here the situation of the staff person differs from that of the chairperson and members, since the staff person is, ultimately, in a position to lose his or her job if committees function too poorly. But this is accountability on an individual basis rather than a committee or collective basis.

We have already mentioned, in the chapter on the chair, the difficulties of specifying to whom and on what matters the committee is accountable. The purpose of this section is not to restate the problems but to call for more accountability and for more ways in which accountability can be translated into real individual and collective benefits.

While there is much work to be done here, there is one very simple technique that we believe significantly improves the operation of committees and creates greater accountability. That technique is the annual and/or progress report. When a committee each year reviews its charge, its accomplishments with respect to that charge, the problems encountered in carrying it out, and recommendations for the future, the committee members themselves are provided a chance to see what they have done, and the appointing body has a chance to see, too. If there is no formal appointing body, then a report to the community via the press is appropriate.[3] Any procedure that results in public presentation of committee accomplishments is appropriate and helpful. If the committee is only briefly appointed, then a short summary of its mission and its accomplishments would be in order. In our view, all committees should report either annually or at the completion of their work, whichever is sooner.

Along with recommending greater accountability, we should mention one caution—a caution that may make it difficult to actualize the call. Committees serve many functions in the system, and one important function may be to provide a vehicle by which difficult problems can be discussed by citizens freed from specific responsibility. In our society, identified as we are with the individual, there remains the reality that many items are out of individual control. Yet somehow the individual still feels responsible. The committee may be an important and overlooked area of life in which individual responsibility is somewhat lessened, and which permits the expression of opinion and view in a less-personalized context. This point is a speculative one but merits, we think, serious consideration as we move toward better accounting and accountability systems for the American committee.

3. One example here is The Robert M. La Follett Institute of Public Affairs, established as an outgrowth of the University of Wisconsin-Madison Center for Public Policy and Administration. A report to update the community on the Institute's public policy research and outreach programs appeared in the April 3, 1991, edition of *Wisconsin Week*.

RULES TO IMPROVE

COMMITTEE

EFFICIENCY AND

EFFECTIVENESS

As has been clear from the foregoing revised material, our approach to effective committees and effective group decision making is quite different from what has been popular in recent days. Much literature focuses discussion on the interpersonal aspects of group decision making—the informal, emotionally laden "process focused" actions. This literature assumes that if you know the people you are working with and understand their needs and desires, you'll be able to forge a good working relationship with them. There is much truth in this central hypothesis. However, it tends to ignore the fact that meetings are, after all, information-processing systems that produce decisions. *Hence, in order to make good decisions, information is needed, and it needs to be organized in such a way as to make it useful and "readable" by the group. Group failure occurs when individuals do not have sufficient information to make a decision, and thus wander around a topic for hours, agreeing only to table it until next time. But the antidote is not overinforming, either.* Some individuals, either through inexperience or guile, overwhelm decision-making groups with piles of materials, so that the relevant is difficult to distinguish from the irrelevant, the central from the peripheral, sometimes referred to as "a snow job." This informational problem thus occurs at both ends of the information provision continuum. The following material emphasizes a "hands-on" approach to managing effective decision-making groups. Given the preparatory material in the first part of the volume, we now move into some of the specific details—exactly how is material prepared, what are the rules to follow, what are the roles to be played, how do the static and dynamic elements of meeting and committees combine? Chapter 26 deals with thinking about decision-making groups and offers some new principles in contradistinction to older, more popular ones (like *Robert's Rules of Order*) to help us begin to think about groups as decision-making entities and to orient our own perspective toward that function. Chapter 27 deals with rules that "help make things go right." Chapter 28 deals with roles and decision-making groups—the chairperson, the member, the staffer—and how these roles interact each with the other. Chapter 29 deals with decision rules in decision-making groups. All too often information is provided and individuals are ready to act, but are hung up because they really don't know what decision rules to use in order to make decisions. Chapter 30 offers a typology of decision-making groups and seeks to suggest which among the types is more ideal. Chapter 31 explores the steps involved in committee evaluation. Chapter 32 deals with decision crystallization—how to get committees to make decisions at the right time.

CHAPTER 26

Principles and Rules to Improve Committee Efficiency

Introduction

One reason groups do not function well is because of self-fulfilling prophecy. We have certain ideas that decision-making groups will function badly, and thus we don't undertake the preparatory activity and preparatory training that would help us help them function better, and would, at the same time, increase our sense of results and accomplishments from our own participation. Part of the problem here lies in the fact that the way we think about groups and the principles we use to approach them—our mental architecture—is antiquated and unhelpful. The purpose of this chapter is to introduce some new principles, and, at the same time, disabuse ourselves of some that are unproductive and do not work well.

Thinking about groups differently—developing some new strategic perspectives on decision-making groups—is a first step toward improving their performance. These perspectives are phrased in a language of principles: the role principle, the principle of three characters, and so on. In order to facilitate the operational aspect of the principle, we will emphasize the operations focus and not the theoretical point of view. We will save that discussion for another time. These principles, like the rules that follow, come from a synthesis of research as well as participant observation of "meeting masters," masters in the fields of health and welfare, education, and business. These masters would not necessarily articulate their points of view in exactly the list described here. Nonetheless, these principles extract and organize their "knowledge in action."

The Role Principle

It is important that readers understand that groups are not simply the sum of their individual members—they have a history, a charter, and so on. Nor are they simply the products of the strongest individual personalities within a group. Often, decision-making group members lay blame for group malperformance on specific individuals within the group—the chairperson, and, not infrequently others as well—and lament that these others could have done more to help the group function well.

Group members often stress one or more of the following three themes: First, certain problems are essentially individual rather than interactive in nature. The offending individuals have usually just been identified. If one could only rid oneself of their noxious presence, I am told, the committee, group, or board would function supremely well. Over-attribution to specific individuals is thus a key part of the problem.

Second, and related to the first point, the individual's problems are of a characterological nature. "She's just that way," or "She must have been born bad." Here, too, the discussion does not reflect the interactive processional nature of group decision making but rather sees it as simply a petri dish for the display of individual characteristics—presumably present from birth—that are fundamental to the individual in question.

Third, there is the implicit or explicit disavowal of any personal responsibility, either for helping things go right in spite of the problematic individuals or for changing these individuals themselves. Somehow, the omniscient, omnipresent "they" have to "do something." Sometimes, "they" are yet higher authority within the same organizational framework, erroneously permitting this incompetent individual to be a member, a chair, or a staff person. Sometimes "they" is undefined, but its purpose has already been served, since whomever else "they" might be construed to mean, it is certainly not "me." The function of "they" is to remove "me" from a position of responsibility.

The role principle disavows each of these themes (or subthemes) by introducing a countertheme—the idea that Erving Goffman anticipated many years ago in his wonderful book, *The Presentation of Self in Everyday Life* (1959). Goffman reiterates Shakespeare's observation in *As You Like It* (II, 7) that life is a play and all the world's people are actors in it. This truth is centrally important for understanding committee-meeting life. Meetings are indeed plays, or information-processing theaters, in which we assume roles. It is important to understand that the behavior of individuals in meetings is the role they play—the one they have chosen to play, the one that has been chosen for them, or some combination thereof. Furthermore, the role is interactive. The very concept of role implies that there are other roles. Thus, troublesome individuals can often be shaped by changing our presentation of self to them. Their character does not need to be changed—our behavior toward them does.

The role principle, then, suggests that one way of thinking about a meeting is as an information-processing play made up of interacting roles that members assume as they enter the meeting space. Sometimes, because of our prior reputation (let's say as a devil's advocate), roles are "reserved" for us by those who know us. But assignments cannot be made without acceptance, too. Therefore, recognizing that we are playing a role, and that others are playing roles, allows us to have a different perspective both on what is happening in the meeting itself and on the ways available to diagnose and change the situation.

The Orchestra Principle

Frequently, meetings begin with a scenario something like this: The staff of a social agency walks in and sits down. The meeting or agency head walks in and says, "Welcome to the weekly staff meeting. I'm delighted that we once again have the chance to get together. Who has something they would like to bring up?" Often, this question is followed by a long silence. Sometimes an individual within the agency takes advantage of the invitation to bring up some pet peeve. Or, the director begins with a litany of "official" business. Topics introduced in sessions like these do not have the benefit of preparation, practice, or rehearsal. Since no one knows what is going to come up, no one has had a chance to mentally work through a topic's issues, problems, and potential solutions. Not infrequently, the discussion wanders far afield as individuals try to get some sense of the nature of the topic that a fellow group member has suggested—how serious it is, what's involved, and if it is really worth spending time on. If we do spend time on it, is it likely anything will happen? And so on. It's completely the reverse of what is suggested by the orchestra principle.

The orchestra principle suggests that one approach a meeting like an orchestra performance—there is a score, a hall, tickets have been sold, the people needed for the performance are present, the pieces have been chosen and rehearsed, all is in readiness. In short, the orchestra principle suggests that the performance is at the end of a period of development and preparation, not at the beginning. The same seems to be true for meetings. The meeting should be at the end of a process of development. This development brings together the issues, information, and people needed concerning the issues, key interests in parties, and so on. At that point, useful work can be done.

The Three-Characters Principle

A typical agency board or staff meeting begins by hearing from the individuals at the meeting. Sometimes, reports and contributions are made by function—the treasurer might report, followed by the program committee chair, and so on. Or, in a staff meeting, reports might come from the director of clinical services, from the planning director, or others. One might ask, "What could be wrong with this?" Focusing on the individual or the function as the organizing basis for the meeting ignores the fact that the content of what these individuals may have to share in a meeting is of very different sorts. Some may be of an announcement nature, requiring little or no action. Some may be of a decision nature, requiring decisive and prompt action by the group. Still others may be of a discussion nature, where the interest is to think through issues, but explicitly not to make key decisions. Indeed, the absence of decision making, in this particular case, allows for freer, more open discussion and sharing of perspectives.

As just suggested, it turns out that meetings have three types of topics or items—announcements, decisions, and exploratory discussion. The three-characters principle suggests that one identify in advance all of the items coming up in the next meeting and sort them into relevant piles—announcement, discussion, and decision—depending upon the intended action at the meeting. The meeting is then organized by first taking all of the announcement items, regardless of person, all decision items, regardless of person, and all discussion items, regardless of person. In short, the three-characters principle invites the meeting planner to organize the meeting by content or desired outcome of items rather than by people or functions. This smooths the group process, and prevents oscillation between decision, discussion, decision, announcement, discussion, decision, and then back to announcement. Groups get confused with all of this going back and forth and not infrequently wind up voting on an announcement.

The "No New Business" Principle

A traditional heading on most agendas is "new business." This is designed to invite individuals to bring up items of concern for group discussion and consideration. Unfortunately, new business is one of the great enemies of your meeting, if handled in the traditional way. The reason for the inherent danger in this is clear, once you think about it—new business doesn't allow you to prepare the information and people you need in order to discuss an item thoroughly and sensibly. Since no one has had a chance to think about it, questions and reactions go all over the lot. This meandering is frequently mentioned by individuals when they complain about the meeting process.

This meandering, however, is an attempt to feel-out the dimensions of the issue, something that could have been handled before the meeting.

The "no new business" principle suggests that new business as such be removed as a category from your ongoing agenda. Rather, as we will see in the next chapter, there will be a rule—called the rule of halves—by which meeting planners will invite new business items to come to them well in advance of the meeting itself. This will allow for the proper individuals involved in the item to be notified and for information or research to be compiled, so that the agenda item is put together with the information that people need to deal with it significantly and successfully. Or, if time did not permit such preparation, it might be listed just for discussion and possible consideration at the next meeting. New business items, precisely because they are new, are troublesome. Therefore, we must find a way to get the important information inherent in new business items to meeting planners well ahead of the meeting itself.

The "No More Reports" Principle

Many staff meetings, board meetings, and other meetings in the human service community and elsewhere wind up being what one might call "oral newsletters." As the meeting begins, one person shares a report of her or his subcommittee or activity within the agency, and the entire meeting is consumed going from person to person, hearing the reports or "updates" on current activity. Like new business, this report mechanism is extremely destructive for two interrelated reasons:

First, the reports scenario is passive rather than interactive. Individuals are not particularly encouraged to ask questions, and certainly not questions of a probing nature. If one does that to a colleague, one might expose himself or herself to similar questions when his or her turn comes along. Furthermore, the reporter is clearly in control of the situation, and we can generally assume that that individual shares selectively.

This problem is a second key rule with the reports mode. Individuals are showcasing themselves, their departments, their activities, their subcommittees. They want to present themselves in a good light. The very things that the group could benefit most from—the problems and difficulties the particular individual could speak about and to which the group can contribute solutions—are the very things that are covered up. Hence, we systematically create a situation in which we invite, and indeed encourage, individuals to present themselves and their activities favorably and not to share difficulties and problems. These difficulties do not take into account the variable nature of the report, and the several cross-cutting topics—announcement, discussion, and decision topics—that might exist within a single report.

The "no more reports" principle suggests stopping this traditional for-mat. Part of the problem will be handled if one follows the three-characters principle, and thus the individual's reports will be broken up into segments. However, many groups still feel that they need to ask individuals to mention a little bit about what they are doing. What the "no more reports" principle suggests, then, is that for each organizational area or function, announce-ment items be handled in the announcements section, and decision items be handled in the decision segment. Any sharing that goes on should be done within the discussion segment, and each presenter should be invited not to showcase her or his own achievements but rather to bring, within the context of making the report, a problem or issue for the group to discuss. This plan removes the asymmetry from the one-way report, and invites the group wis-dom to be shared on the actual difficulties that a subgroup (or sub-element within the group) is having. After all, groups are good at problem-solving. If the culture permits one to share vulnerabilities—"This particular program isn't going so well, and I really don't have any good ideas about what we might do at this point; perhaps some of you could make some suggestions?"—then organizational problems are exposed rather than suppressed, and can be acted upon at an early point, collectively and with a sense of group ownership and responsibility.

The Pro-Activity Principle

Another bad feature of the "report" mode is that it tends to be focused on the past—what has happened or what has not happened—rather than on the present and future—"Where are we going?" and "What should happen?" Groups need to balance reactivity with proactivity, looking ahead, seeking to anticipate where difficulties might arise and how an organization might deal with these difficulties. There are two interrelated benefits to proactivity.

First, one of the great culprits in group decision making is lack of time. When an issue is brought before a group with the injunction "We have to move fast on this one; we haven't any time," interests in innovation, experi-mentation, novelty, and creativity dwindle rapidly. Many of us have sat in a group in which a great idea has come up, but then someone else said, "Gee, that's a great idea, but we don't really have time to look into it. The decision is due within a couple of days." It is important to plan for time. We all under-stand that "daily routine drives out planning." Therefore, planning for de-veloping and future issues needs to be built in as an ongoing part of the process.

Second, proactivity allows issues to be considered when emotional pressure is low. As affect rises, decision quality tends to decrease. For this reason, we need to plan ways to avoid these kinds of pressures.

High-Quality Decisions

We have already stressed the importance of high-quality decisions, and have already provided a mechanism for evaluating these decisions. However, so important is this aspect that it becomes a principle in its own right. The aim and purpose of the group is to make decisions of high quality. Groups are becoming ever more accountable in our organizations; what they are accountable for are the decisions they make. Hence, part of our way of thinking about groups must involve, from the beginning, a perspective that high-quality decisions is our bottom line.

Conclusion

These principles involve the intellectual architecture we use to think about the meetings in which we participate. They apply to all meetings everywhere. If the meetings that we attend are not like those that are suggested here, then we can take some responsibility for beginning to change them. The process will not be an easy one—change never is. But a great organizational savings can be gained by improving the meeting process, by considering the valuable resources that meetings occupy, the time involved, being pulled away from other productive tasks, and wasteful allocations from within the meeting process itself. Improving group decision making remains our meeting goal. It is to this end that the remaining chapters detail steps that individuals can take to help the meeting process achieve its goal.

The Fraction Rules

Introduction

The purpose of this chapter is to provide some concrete steps and actions that professionals in human service, government and corporate arenas may take to improve their agency meetings, whether within a human service organization or when working with others in some kind of collective community or corporate context. These are activities that meeting managers undertake. We have observed them do it. Presenting the materials in a set of rules is designed to enhance their applicability in practice.

The Fraction Rules consist of the Rule of Halves, the Rule of Sixths, the Rule of Three-Quarters, and the Rule of Two-Thirds. In essence, they are planning rules, involving guidelines for gathering information and people, and organizing and preparing information and in general guiding and managing the process so that committee meetings go well and are productive. Committees need this kind of planning, for reasons that we've already discussed elsewhere in this volume, but issues of preparation tend to receive little attention. Therefore, it's probably most common that no one knows what's coming up at the committee meeting until she or he gets there. Then there's a desperate scramble to try to appear sensible and intelligent under conditions that are not only not ideal but also actually counterproductive.

The Rule of Halves

The rule of halves involves preparation for the upcoming meeting. The planner divides the intermeeting space into two parts. If there is a two-week gap between the last meeting and the next meeting, during the first week of post meeting time the meeting planner sends out little notes or calls those who might be attending the upcoming meeting and asks for agenda items.[1] This process is where new business is solicited. The meeting planner, by reviewing past minutes and other committee records, already knows some issues. More will come in from individuals in the group and others concerned with the functions of the group. At about the halfway point, the meeting planner sits down with a list of candidate items and goes through several processes: sifting, sorting, and organizing.

The sifting process involves looking through each item, determining if it is appropriate, and deciding if it is possible to get the information and people that are needed. Perhaps it's something that should be handled by two people in their respective offices. A bit of negotiation goes on here, both with those who have submitted the ideas and others who might be involved. Jim's item, for example, may need an attorney, but Carla, the attorney, is not able to come until the next meeting; thus, Jim is informed that the item will need to be held until the attorney can be present. This kind of item review helps to cull the number of topics, to focus the issues, and to assure the group that it will indeed have the information and people it needs when it gets together. If the meeting planner is not the chair, then he or she clears with the chair the items for the final agenda.

The second step that the meeting planner undertakes is sorting. Items are sorted into three groups: announcement, decision, and discussion. This is extremely important, because under the three-characters principle the meeting itself will now be structured in this batch-process way. Furthermore, it becomes important to determine, in advance, what the goal is that the agenda-item suggester and potential others have for a particular item. This will allow the agenda writer to specify to the agenda readers exactly what is hoped for. Categorizing the items in this way helps people to think about them and to frame their own approach within that set of outlined expectations.

The third step is organizing the items. Several factors are involved in item organization. One of these has to do with the logical sequence of items. If B, in order to be decided, needs a decision on A, then it's best to take A before B. Otherwise, one will decide on B, come to A, make a decision on A, and then will be required to go back and change B because of the implications that A has for B. There are other types of connections that the meeting manager may wish to be aware of. For example, if two items involve the

---

1. This procedure may seem unrealistic. But the meeting planner can "educate" the committee through asking, in the advance notice for the meeting, that items must be sent in by *x* date before the meeting.

same individual, they might need to be separated by another item in order to avoid the appearance that this individual is dominating the agenda.

Another aspect of organization is determining the political difficulty and intellectual complexity of the items in question. As we'll see when we get to the rule of the agenda bell, decision items are ranked and handled according to their controversialism with easy, less-controversial items first, more-controversial items in the middle of the meeting, and discussion items at the end. The meeting manager also needs to be sure that there aren't too many items. Some may need to be set aside due to time limitations. Indeed, time planning, as will be seen by the rule of agenda and rule of agenda bell, is absolutely crucial. One needs to allow enough time for items to be discussed. This requires that one make some time estimates of more-difficult or less-difficult items, and at least begin the process of approximating a time distribution. It's very discouraging for groups to sit down to an agenda that has 30 or 35 items on it, knowing from the very beginning that there is no chance of successful completion. Thus, we should schedule only the number of items that we have a reasonably good chance of completing. If more time is needed, then the meeting time can be extended, or another meeting may need to be called. (See the Rule of the Agenda Bell for more detail on the actual ordering of items.)

The Rule of Sixths

As the meeting manager sits and reviews the number of items for the upcoming meeting, they can be divided by six in approximately the following way: First, about one-sixth of the items should be from the past—leftover items that have not been decided or that have been tabled for one reason or another. About four-sixths of the items should be from the here-and-now, current issues that require announcement, decision, or discussion. Finally, about one-sixth of the items should concern the future. These are the "blue sky"-type items that allow us to follow the principle of proactivity.

The Rule of Sixths has a number of interrelated, crucial aspects worth mentioning here. First, future or blue sky-type items create fun. Why? People have fun when they can exercise their creativity, when they can contribute within acceptable time frames, and where their ideas actually stand a chance of having an impact. Given the press of daily business, however, there's almost never any time for considering the future, regardless of when it is, until the future arrives. Then, of course, everyone says, "Gee, if we'd only discussed *this* a little before . . ."

A second related item of benefit to the Rule of Sixths is the ability to create emotional ventilation. Many items that come up in decision-making groups are ones around which people have a lot of feeling. In fact, the management of feeling within the context of effective decision making is one of the very crucial elements that meeting managers need to take into consideration. All too frequently we tell people to "shut up." Typically, meeting managers and chairpersons feel under pressure because the time frames required for particular decisions are short.

Unfortunately, controversy and high pressure seem to go together. What often happens in decision-making groups and committees is that the controversial items, because they are controversial, are not dealt with until the last possible moment. This approach creates a situation in which time pressure and the controversial nature of the item compound group tension exponentially. Hence, under the Rule of Sixths, controversial items are discussed first, when decisions are not to be made. This procedure allows for some of the emotion and feeling to be ventilated under conditions that do not require immediate action. Thus, time pressure, at least, is relieved. As most of us know from life experience, the rush of feeling that is often expressed around a difficult decision tends to subside a bit after it is expressed. This relaxation of feeling allows for a wider range of alternatives to be explored.

The Rule of Sixths contains a subrule for controversial items specifically, called The Two-Meeting Rule. The Two-Meeting Rule requires that controversial items be scheduled at least once for discussion only and then a second time for decision. Sometimes there are two, three, or even more time periods when discussion is held and decision is held back. The reasons for this rule are clear by now—it allows for the expression of creativity within an acceptable time frame, it permits emotions to be ventilated, and it encourages new ideas and useful approaches.

Creativity and emotional release are two virtues of the Rule of Sixths, but there is one remaining virtue that needs to be stressed. The Rule of Sixths allows for the exploration of ideas and approaches to problems that may reduce their difficulty and increase the acceptability of a solution. When committees get together to solve problems and come to action steps, there needs to be sufficient time to not only suggest ideas but also play with the interrelationship of solutions, to explore and fit one aspect of a solution into another. Without the time available to undertake these tasks, the actual quality (the A decision, as discussed on page 212) of the solutions themselves does not have a chance to improve.

The Rule of Sixths, therefore, seeks to create the conditions that allow for committee effectiveness and efficiency by reducing affect, increasing the likelihood of creativity, and developing the conditions where new ideas can successfully be fit to parts of other new ideas to create a solution that is, indeed, of high quality. For especially controversial items, the Two-Meeting Rule is the rule of choice.

The Rule of Three-Quarters

The Rule of Three-Quarters is a thinking rule. It gives the meeting planner a guideline concerning when to send out material to the committee members—three-quarters of the way until the next meeting. More will be said about this material, and the actual way in which the agenda, the minutes, and the reports should be written, in Chapter 29 (The Writing Rules). For now, we need to spend a little time explaining why the Rule of Three-Quarters is so important.

In many of the discussions with committee organizers, the Rule of Three-Quarters generates a lot of questions. "Why can't we just hand stuff out when we get to the meeting? It's so much easier." People misinterpret the Rule of Three-Quarters as a sort of "courtesy" rule, but that really is not the point at all. It's much better thought of as the "thinking" rule. Underlying the Rule of Three-Quarters is the theoretical point that "everything improves if one thinks about it." One's ability to come up with solutions to problems, to consider innovative approaches, are all improved if one has a chance to think through the issues and problems involved. Handing material out at the meeting itself simply does not give individuals a chance to mentally process the material before them. First, most of us can't read that fast, so we skim, pick up on key points, and often try to appear wise by pointing out a typographical error somewhere. Important as typographical errors may be, this level of discussion is not the one that is going to help the committee come up with solutions to difficult problems.

Second, most of us don't think that fast. Under high pressure—and reading something at a meeting and coming up with reactions to it is a distinctive form of high pressure—our most likely response is the conservative "let's do what we've done in the past" approach. This is the tried-and-true one; no one can get into hot water (or so they think) by recommending what's been done before. It's intellectually nonrisky and sounds intelligent.

The Rule of Three-Quarters, then, is essentially a mail-out rule. It is important to follow the Rule of Three-Quarters whether the committee in question is a national committee with individuals coming from around the country, a state or local committee, or even a committee of employees within an office setting. The operative dynamics are the same. Committee members need time to think. When that time is denied them, they react in a knee-jerk, conservative fashion, one that results in a high-quality decision only by chance.

Between the Rule of Halves and the Rule of Three-Quarters is what one might consider the "third quarter" of the intervening period. Between the end of the last meeting and the halfway point between meetings, the meeting manager or planner can gather items for the Rule of Halves. Additional items following the Rule of Sixths might be pulled together so that appropriate attention to the future can be paid. Then an actual agenda is put together, along with appropriate reports and minutes from the previous meeting, and sent out under the Rule of Three-Quarters. The meeting planner should be aware that the third quarter of the intervening period is likely to be a demanding time period. Time can be allocated accordingly.

Intermeeting period

The Rule of Three-Quarters is more than a rule about when to send out material. It allows for thinking, and creates a disciplined approach to group decision making.

The Rule of Two-Thirds

After the material for the meeting has been assembled, a question arises about how to actually organize it. A general rule, the Rule of Two-Thirds, talks about how the meeting is partitioned with respect to the flow of energy and interest, and provides general guidelines for locating items. Chapter 28 (The Agenda Bell) provides specific organizing directions for the actual steps in the agenda.

The Rule of Two-Thirds says that all meetings are divided into three parts and points to the division between the first two-thirds and the last one-third as crucial. There is a beginning period, or "get going" portion, a heavy work portion, and a decompressing portion. Committees, like sports teams and chamber music groups, need time to warm up and articulate with one another. Hence, in the beginning portion of a meeting, individuals are arriving (perhaps some a bit late), finding out what has happened to other members during the intervening period, sharing bits of information on their reactions to world events, and so on. This natural process of group dynamics needs to be taken into consideration in meeting planning. It occupies the initial phase of the meeting itself.

The second meeting phase—the heavy work portion—generally occupies the middle third to middle half of the overall committee meeting. By now, individuals have had the opportunity to warm up and are ready to run together in full stride. This portion of the meeting is a good time for meeting planners to place their action items.

Action items, however, tear at the fabric of group cohesion. The process of building cohesion, which occupied the first portion of the meeting, needs to be undertaken again in terms of rebuilding and "recohesing" the group itself in the last one-third of the meeting. The committee needs some time to interact, where those who have been advantaged and disadvantaged on particular decisions made during the middle course of the meeting can allow for the expression of feelings, resentment, happiness, and so on, without plunging right into some different meeting. Hence, items that require discussion fit well here. Discussion, of course, occurs as well during the decision-making middle phase, but aimed at a decision. In the latter phase, the decompression period, discussion of a creative sort is enacted, and it does not require decision. What is meant by discussion in the latter phase is the serious consideration of issues in a context that does not require decision.

Conclusion

The Fraction Rules provide the committee meeting planner with a set of guidelines and recipes to be used in assembling and organizing material for the meeting itself. As is clear from the basic details covered even in this brief section, there are lots of points to keep in mind. For most of us, these are points we never knew existed, much less kept in mind. However, if followed they will make a strong contribution to the success of the meeting. Still, there are a number of other items that have to be kept in mind as well. Specifically, the actual structure of the meeting agenda discussed in the next chapter (The Agenda Bell) is of great importance.

The Agenda Bell

Introduction

When you think of preparing an agenda, perhaps the concept of a buffet comes to mind. Topics are often plopped onto a page much as a range of foods are placed on a table. There's no particular order to the concept, there are no particular guidelines. Committee members are often left to pick and choose among an array of possible items for consideration. Frequently, the first and most significant part of meetings is spent deciding what the meeting is going to cover and then what the various topics mean. "The finance committee report" is not terribly descriptive, for example. Is one hearing about the finance committee's activities? Does the finance committee have actual items to ask for action upon? Or are there items that the finance committee would like to discuss but that have not yet approached decision status? There are better and worse ways to organize agendas and the items within them. The Rule of Two-Thirds, discussed in the last chapter, provided an introduction to these considerations. The Agenda Bell provides specific directions on how to proceed.

An Underlying Principle

Based on the Rule of Two-Thirds, the Agenda Bell concept suggests that noncontroversial items be introduced in the initial phases of the meeting. The items increase in controversy and conflict potential until the most difficult item is introduced. At about the two-thirds or three-quarters point, decision making is finished for the meeting, and the committee shifts into a discussion mode. Discussion items are introduced in decreasing order of controversy until the end of the allotted time for the meeting, at which point adjournment occurs. The general concept is displayed as a bell-shaped curve, shown in figure 28.1.

The Steps in Agenda Ordering

Committee planners can follow a prescribed set of seven steps for organizing the items in their agenda. The steps have sufficient subparts to take into account the entire range of items that might come up at a meeting. The committee meeting planner follows the outline suggested in figure 28.1.

Category 1: Minutes

The first item on any committee's agenda is action on the minutes of the previous meeting. These will have been mailed out and, as will be discussed in chapter 29 (The Writing Rules), are presented in a way designed to minimize conflict and dispute about what was and was not actually said in the previous meeting. Often, a group that needs a quorum to begin or to approve minutes will not find a quorum present when item 1 is up for action. In that case, it is important not to wait for a quorum to arrive but to begin the meeting promptly and approve the minutes with those who are present. They can be reapproved later (in the latter part of the meeting, under item

Figure 28.1: The Agenda Bell

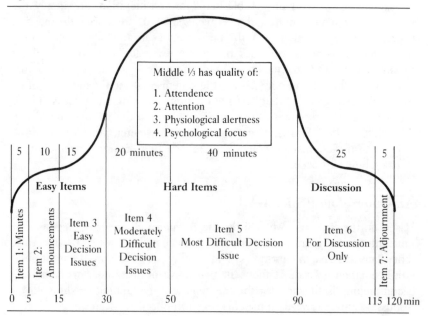

six) when enough people have arrived. It is fatal to wait for latecomers to arrive in order to begin the minute-approval process. If the group does wait, it simply annoys those who have adjusted their schedules in order to get there on time. In the interviews we have held with board members, committee members, and other meeting participants, one of the greatest irritants reported to us is was waiting fifteen or twenty minutes for latecomers. Some members even said that they would "punish" their committee by being obstreperous. Others, perhaps less conscious of their feelings, would act out in obstreperous ways. Rewarding good behavior is always the rule that should be operative in committee meetings. Hence, prompt approval of the minutes is a good first step.

Category 2: Announcements

The second item on most committees' agendas should be a few noncontroversial announcements of general interest. Our interviewees recommend that announcements take up 10 percent or less of the scheduled meeting time. Too many meetings wind up being "oral newsletters." "Newsletter" information can easily be written. If there are more announcements than can be handled by the 10 percent rule, the committee meeting planner should group the announcements into relevant categories (for example, transportation policy, changes in medical coverage) and announce the categories, referring committee members to attachments that detail the issues in question more completely.

Category 3: Decision Issues

There are three groups of decision or action items (Category 3, Category 4, and Category 5). Category 3 items are decision items that are relatively noncontroversial and easy to deal with. The idea behind locating them in Category 3 (and there can be items 3a, 3b, 3c, etc.) is that it allows the group to begin to get into the decision-making harness. This should also allow the participants to clear away some of the decisional underbrush, get some basic work done, and at the same time help coalesce the group.

Category 4: Moderately Tough Decision Issues

Reaching again into the pile of items from the Rule of Halves, Category 4 contains those items of moderate decisional difficulty. These are certainly not the easy ones contained in Category 3, but on the other hand, they do not represent the most difficult item, which belongs in Category 5. These represent a step upward on the scale of controversy and difficulty.

Category 5: The Hardest Decision Item

There should be only one item in Category 5. It should be located somewhere between the 40 percent point and the 65 to 70 percent point on the meeting agenda. We are proposing that Category 5 be given lots of time and that it be strategically located in the center of the meeting. Category 5 is located here for a complex number of reasons: for one thing, late arrivers will have now arrived, and early leavers will not yet have slipped away. Psychological and physical energy is at its highest within the meeting context, so it represents the high point of group energy. The committee-meeting planner can bring all of the available committee resources to bear on the most difficult item. This makes sense. Typically, and almost certainly, Category 5 will have followed the Two-Meeting Subrule mentioned under the Rule of Sixths (Chapter 27). Even though Category 5 is difficult and controversial, it will presumably not be the first time that the group will have seen and discussed the item in question. Indeed, Category 5 on today's agenda might be modified from its previous Category 6 formulation as a discussion item. Committee meeting planners, it is hoped, will have taken account of the comments made in a previous discussion, and will have come back with some ideas for modifications or improvements that will make the decision less controversial and more palatable.

Of course, lots of factors affect how many "controversial" items the meeting manager may have to process. However many there are, Category 5 should be the toughest of the lot.

Category 6: Discussion Items

After the decision making for Category 5 has been completed, the group is now prepared to shift gears. Decision making has torn at the fabric of group cohesion. If the decision making has been tough and rigorous, there are individuals who are feeling good because their views have triumphed, and there are individuals who are feeling poorly because their views have not found sufficient support. The group still needs time to interact, but around items that do not require decision. Thus, discussion items can be placed here. These are items that require committee thought but are not yet at the stage of decision making. Frequently, Rule of Sixths-type items—"blue sky" items—fit here, as well as the more routine items that almost any committee needs to discuss. This allows for a period of decompression. Then, the committee moves on to Category 7, Adjournment.

Category 7: Adjournment

Adjournment is simply a way of wrapping up Category 6 and allowing the group to end on time. It's imperative that the meeting planner work with the chair to end on time. Otherwise, individuals will get restless and become difficult to handle. Once people are kept over the allotted time frame, irritation and anger build up.

A Few Other Considerations

Within this overall ordering scheme, some other principles operate as well. One rule is to order in terms of the needed sequence of decisions. Thus, if item B depends on what was decided in item A, then A should be decided first.

A rule has to do with paying attention to the amount of time for presentation an item needs. For example, an item might become a 4 because it needs more time for presentation.

Additionally, it is possible, in Categories 3 and 4, to "batch process" items under a single heading. So, for example, a grantmaker may have, as a "single" item 3, "small awards." The group may approve them in a batch, rather than discussing each one.

Conclusion

The Agenda Bell provides a way for organizing items according to the degree of difficulty and the political complexity or controversy that is inherent within them. It's the committee planning element that ties the prework done under the Fraction Rules to a specific guideline for what happens in the meeting itself.

However, we cannot rest with just an outline of items. The agenda must be written in specific ways, and the minutes and reports that accompany the agenda must also be handled in specific ways. These considerations lead us to the next chapter, The Writing Rules.

CHAPTER 29

The Writing Rules

Introduction

Planning and organizing the committee meeting is helpful—indeed, essential. But the results must be communicated in visual and concrete forms to committee members. Three kinds of documents are most commonly received by committee members. The first of these is the agenda itself. The Rule of Two-Thirds and the Rule of the Agenda Bell provide ways to organize content, but we still need to focus on what is actually on the page that goes to the members of the committee. Second, the minutes of previous meetings are of obvious importance. And finally, the various reports dealing with agenda items that accompany many mail-out packets need attention as well.

The crucial overall element to keep in mind is to develop a visually attractive package that is informative and not off-putting. An "off-putting" packet has sufficient bulk or size to make an individual hesitate to look at it when she or he gets it, and to set it aside. A colleague of ours said, "When I get a fat packet, I really want to give it the attention it deserves, so I set it aside until I have the time. Considering the large number of packets that are set aside along my desk, I believe it's going to be a posthumous product." An appealing and thin packet is what is needed. The writing rules are aimed at achieving these twin goals, as well as assisting the committee in the decision process. The Rule of Reports is specifically aimed at presenting material in ways that will allow the individual committee members to understand the issues in a more coherent and integrated way. Such understanding promotes better discussion and a higher quality decision.

The Rule of the Agenda

The way to think of an agenda is to use as a model a menu in a fancy restaurant. If the menus in such restaurants were written the way agendas typically are, one would open the menu booklet to find a simple list of very general words, like "meat," "vegetables," "drinks." Experiencing some frustration at such a menu, the patron might call the waiter over and say, "Waiter! I can't order 'meat.' Can you help me out here?" The waiter would reply, "Why, sure! We have 'beef,' 'veal,' 'fish'; what do you want, anyway?" The answer to that question is "dish-specific information." And the model of what we wish for on a restaurant menu is a good one to follow when building an agenda. What our committee members need in order to understand what is coming to them at the upcoming meeting is dish-specific agenda items.

There are some other important features of agenda writing. One of them is the quick summary. Many restaurants will put a one-sentence summary of what the dish actually is below the name of the dish. This gives the patrons enough information to make their decision, and it is a good practice to follow in creating agendas. Hence, there is not only a relatively specific statement of the nature of the item but also a one-sentence elaboration of it as well.

To the right-hand side of the item identification are parentheses, in which the agenda scheduler can put the name of the individual who is responsible for presenting a particular item as well as one of our three key concepts mentioned before under the Rule of Halves and under the Three Characters Principle—*decision, announcement,* and *discussion.* The location of the actual desired action beside each item helps create the "effective thinking context" within which the item will be processed by the recipient, since we think differently about items depending upon the "context of contemplation." It is imperative that we share it with individuals as they receive and begin to process item information.

Last, on the right-hand side of the agenda menu, instead of price we suggest a running clock. Meeting planners try to assess how much time will be required for particular items and allow enough blocks of time for the complicated items and more-restricted blocks of time for less controversial, less complicated items. We are all aware of the tendency that committees and committee members have to expand discussion on relatively trivial items, often as a way to avoid dealing with the more complicated, more conflictual ones. Hence, we seek to use time blocks here as a guideline for members with respect to the importance of the item. Those items that have more time allocated to them are more important than those items that have less time allocated to them.

These four elements—dish-specific item designation, the summary statement, assignment of an individual by name who is responsible, along with the thinking context designation and use of time blocks—are ways in which the meeting planner can use the actual written form of the agenda to enhance committee meetings and to increase their productivity. An example is seen in figure 29.1.

The Rule of Minutes

Most committees take minutes of their activities. These are shared with committee members at the next meeting, where "approval of the minutes" is a commonly requested action. In our case, approval of the minutes is item 1 on our proposed agenda, as outlined under the Rule of the Agenda Bell. However, the way that minutes are taken and presented often does not in-

---

Figure 29.1: A Sample Agenda

Staff Meeting
Family and Children's Service

Friday Morning
8:15–9:45 AM

1. Minutes (Decision)   8:15–8:20

2. Announcements   8:20–8:30

3A. New Recording Forms (Action)   8:30–8:35
   The new forms for recording client contact are ready for final action.

3B. New Minutes Format (Action)   8:35–8:40
   The new minutes format—suggested in our "effective meetings" workshop have been tried and found good. Jim recommends them for approval agency wide.

4. Mileage Reimbursement (Action)   8:40–8:55
   The staff committee on autos recommends that we move to .30 cents for client visits and eliminate the meal reimbursement element. Their report is attached.

5. Quality Assessment Form for Staff (Action)   8:55–9:20
   A staff committee has been working on a form that would allow both workers and supervisors to rate the quality of worker's service delivery. Several versions of this form have already been discussed, and this version is recommended for a trial of one year, to be reevaluated then.

6. Strategic Planning Ideas (discussion)   9:20–9:44
   The agency has not had any service innovations within the past year. We need some new ideas. Perhaps we can just toss out some beginning thoughts here.

7. Adjournment   9:45

---

crease the capability of producing high-quality decisions within a group and, indeed, may serve as a diversionary factor. Partly these problems occur because most of us have never learned how to write minutes. (There's no course in minute writing; it's a topic that receives almost no attention from English teachers and just an occasional nod from those who teach business writing.)

The main problem occurs when one does what is called "process minutes." Process minutes are an attempt to present a running record, often of the "he said, she said" variety, that readers find puzzling and difficult to follow. Re-creating the process of discussion in the minutes often reflects the confusion of the discussion in the meeting itself. This does not mean that the entire consideration of a matter was confused, but rather that as one proceeds through an issue, there's likely to be a bit of back and forth and repetition that does not need to be reflected in the final product, any more than one needs to show the guests at your elegant dinner party the mess in your kitchen.

Content minutes need to be developed. Content minutes focus on the substance of what happens. The recorder listens to and takes notes about the discussions concerning each item on the agenda. Then the recorder, in writing up the minutes, does not simply replicate those notes but tries to provide a synthesis along the lines of the following:

> The van purchase agreement was discussed. Several individuals were in favor of the agreement, arguing that it would provide economy of transportation, among other benefits. Others opposed the agreement on the grounds that the use of private cars, reimbursed as currently, provides the greatest degree of flexibility. Still others felt that it didn't really matter.

In the content summary, relevant points are grouped together without names attached. Then the recorder skips a line, and in capital letters reflects the decision or action in the following manner:

Action

IT WAS DECIDED TO IMPLEMENT THE VAN PURCHASE AGREEMENT PROPOSAL FOR A TRIAL PERIOD OF THREE YEARS. JIM WHITTLESEE AGREED TO TAKE CHARGE OF THE IMPLEMENTATION PROCESS AND AGREED AS WELL TO PROVIDE ANNUAL REPORTS TO THE BOARD ON HOW THIS NEW APPROACH IS WORKING.

This approach focuses the report, provides an organized and intelligible summary for the reader, and headlines the decision at the bottom in capital letters. It is there that names are named, and times and places are specified. It is from this bottom portion that the meeting planner gets items (those that have been tabled) for the agendas of future meetings as well as items for use in the decision audit and decision autopsy procedures. A short example is seen in figure 29.2.

The Rule of Reports

The last pieces of paper that are provided for the committee are the various reports that are used as bases for discussion and subsequent decision making. These reports require a little attention. Two subrules apply here—the Executive Summary Technique and the Options Memo Technique.

The Executive Summary Technique

The Executive Summary Technique requires that all reports, however lengthy, be summarized in a single page, and that it be the single page rather

Figure 29.2: Sample Minutes

Staff Meeting
Family and Children's Service

Friday Morning
8:15–9:30 AM

1. **Minutes**
   The minutes were approved as presented.

2. **Announcements**
   Sheila announced that new keys were ready.
   Elmer mentioned that new grant forms were ready.
   Harold asked for drafts of new announcements for editing.

3A. **New Recording Forms (Action)**
   The new recording forms were discussed; Some felt that the idea of
   paper forms is going out of date and that computerized formats are
   preferred. Others liked the idea of writing.

   THE NEW FORMS WERE APPROVED HAROLD ALSO AGREED TO LOOK INTO
   COMPUTERIZED FORMATS WHICH MIGHT BE USED AS WELL

3B. **New Minutes Format**
   Several concerns about the new minutes format were raised. In
   particular, staff wanted to be sure that there was a clear indication in the
   capitalized bottom portion of **who** agreed to do **what** by **when**.

   THE NEW MINUTES FORM WAS PASSED

---

than the entire report that is mailed out. Certainly, if any committee member wants the entire report, he or she is more than welcome to receive it. However, it has been our experience that the Executive Summary Technique is a better way of providing crucial information for individuals in an attractive and thin package. If a full report must be sent out, it can be done under separate cover. Thus, what the individual receives is a package that is appealing and slender.

Writing executive summaries takes a bit of practice. Typically, we're used to writing more rather than less. Yet, with a little practice, it will be quite possible to do excellent summaries. Since the summaries contain the key issues and elements that will be the focus of the decisions to be taken at the upcoming meeting, the preparation of a summary facilitates this discussion by focusing it, something that is aided even further by the Options Memo Technique.

Figure 29.2: (*Continued*)

4. **Mileage Reimbursement (Action)**
   Differences of view were expressed on this issue. Some wanted the mean allowance continued and the lower mileage rate (.20). Others felt that this forced them to eat, and thus took away from their freedom.

   IT WAS DECIDED THAT EACH STAFF MEMBER COULD CHOOSE WHICH SYSTEM SHE OR HE PREFERRED EACH YEAR

5. **Quality Assessment Form for Staff (decision)**
   This issue of the form for quality enjoyed lots of discussion. Some felt, as had been expressed in the past, that the idea of quality assessment in the human services was silly and a waste of time. Others felt that it was worth a try, especially for a year.

   THE STAFF DECIDED TO IMPLEMENT THE FORM FOR A ONE YEAR TRIAL BASIS

6. **Strategic Planning Ideas**
   The whole idea of innovation was considered in some detail. Staff felt that there just was not enough time to try out new ideas with the overload already present. Others pointed out that there will always be overload. It was felt we first needed ideas on how to find time for new ideas. This item will come up next week.

7. **Adjournment**

The Options Memo Technique

The Options Memo Technique is a way of writing material so as to enhance the committee's ability to discuss issues and improve, therefore, the quality of the decision. Perhaps the best way to illustrate the importance of the Options Memo Technique is to reflect on a typical "report" style in a meeting. Assume for a moment that an issue has come up at a previous meeting, and a subcommittee has been asked to look into it. Jim Smith, the chairperson of the subcommittee, makes his report.

> Ladies and gentlemen, I would like to report on the matter of the Executive Director's salary. The problem was that the Executive Director's salary was too low, in the views of some. Upon investigation, our finding is that it is somewhat low. Therefore, we recommend a $1,000 increase. Are there any questions?

Once this report has been made, the committee is already "in the soup," although it may not realize it. Several problematic elements have been introduced. First, the individual making the report has announced what the recommendation is and asked for questions. From the committee member point of view, however, any question would come off looking like a challenge. If a committee member were to say, "Have you considered this or that option?" it may well look to Jim as a challenge. The recommendation is made definitively, and there is little to discuss, given the way that it was presented. If this meeting is a typical one, very little discussion will occur, the recommendation will be approved, and, after the meeting is adjourned and people are speaking informally, lots of discussion about that particular action will develop. We have all had the experience of using the phrase "Any questions?" and experiencing that uncomfortable period of waiting when no one apparently has anything to say, although plenty is said at a later point.

If a three-step rather than a two-step method is used, however, a great deal of positive discussion can be engendered. The additional step involves the addition of options in the middle of the report. In using the options memo or the options report technique, the first part of the discussion or memo is the same as the one we just mentioned—a statement of the problem. However, after the problem statement, a list of options or reasonable alternatives for action is outlined. Then, in a third step, the individual or subcommittee's recommendation for action is included. It focuses upon which option has been selected for support and explains why. It might look something like this:

> Ladies and gentlemen, our committee has looked into the matter of the Executive Director's salary, as requested several meetings ago. As you may recall, the feeling among some was that the Executive Director's salary was too low.

Our investigation did indeed reveal that, at least within this town, our Executive Director is paid from $1,000 to $10,000 less than individuals holding very comparable slots.

There are several options that we could pursue at this point: (1) Leave things as they are. (2) Provide a raise to our Executive Director to bring that executive to the bottom point of the range. That would be a $1,000 raise. (3) Provide a range that aims a bit more at the middle of the differential rather than at the bottom or top. (4) Other ideas that you may have.

Recommendation: It is our recommendation that we seek over the next six months to bring our executive's salary into the middle of the range. We feel this is important not only for the benefit of the executive but also because of the image that the executive director's salary communicates to others in the community. We want to convey a positive, nonexploitative image. Therefore, this is our recommendation.

The provision of the three-step options technique has several useful features for committee discussion. First, it outlines the options that have been considered, something that groups almost always want to know anyway. If they are listed, people can discuss them without feeling that they have to probe for the obvious. If they are not listed, individuals in the committee tend to feel that they are asking "foolish questions" when they say, "Did you consider this option; did you consider that option?" Hence, questions about options tend not to be asked, and it is these questions that form a large fraction of the postmeeting discussion and sharing.

A second useful role played by the list of options is that of Discussion Pump Priming. Strange as it may seem, committee members often don't know where to begin the discussion of a particular recommendation. If no options are listed, there are an infinite number of ways to start. This wide range of possibilities further confounds members, and, in order to avoid looking foolish, they tend to say nothing. Options provide a way to get into the discussion, to "prime the pump" of group discussion and to set a framework for the discussion. It is for this reason that teachers over the years have included "discussion questions" with assigned readings. That technique occurs not because students are stupid but because they, like the rest of us, wish to avoid looking foolish in front of others.

Priming the pump of group discussion is especially valuable for members who feel less confident about their participation in committee activity. To our surprise, even individuals who spend lots of time in committee activity sometimes report feeling continually intimidated in spite of that participation. There are always "big mouths" who will talk at length on any subject, however irrelevant their contributions may be. Chairpersons frequently tell us, "It was true that the discussion wasn't going very far, but nobody else had anything else to say." That statement is almost always wrong. Other people did have things to say, but weren't sure how to break in, or didn't have a firm conviction about the particular points of view they wished to elaborate and felt it better to be quiet than to look foolish. Therefore, meeting planners and chairs need to help individuals who do not automatically leap into the participatory fray by inviting a set of questions and providing a set of options that might be useful to them.

While the technique of the three-step options-inclusive report is perhaps handiest when the report is written, it is also an excellent model to follow in making an oral presentation. The overall idea of "statement of the problem, key options to consider, and recommended options" is an excellent three-step organizing tool for oral presentations. Not infrequently, presentations before committees involve both oral and written material. Hence, if the presenter follows the written material, the oral report automatically takes on this form. If, however, one does not have written handouts or slides or overheads that provide visual outlining of the problem, the options, and the selected recommendation, then one can follow the form anyway and use it as an organizing tool for public speaking.

Conclusion

The writing rules provide an important component of meeting preparation. All too often preparation of the agenda, preparation of minutes, and the organization and delivery of reports are left simply to chance—whatever happens to cross the meeting organizer's mind at the time that the meeting is being put together. We hope that it can now be clear that a great amount of leverage and influence can be developed by giving some thought to the actual packet of materials that goes out under the Rule of Three-fourths. Small investments here will be amply repaid by smoother, more efficient, and more effective committee meetings, as well as meetings that are a lot more fun to attend.

CHAPTER 30

The Integrity Rules

Introduction

Committees require a certain amount of integrity to function well. What is meant by "integrity" in this context? The definition is simple—doing, in the committee meeting, what was promised on the agenda. That might not sound like a great deal, yet most of us know from experience that there are dozens of times in any given month that people do not do what they said they were going to do. When you, as an individual, are uncomfortable by that failure, you're likely to become angry, even if you don't share those feelings with the offending person or group. That is what happens in committees. We routinely find that, in matters of agenda and time, committees do not follow through on the commitments they have made. Members become angry and sometimes "act out" or "punish" the committee in inappropriate ways. Agenda integrity and temporal integrity are, therefore, important essentials in the functioning of committees.

Agenda Integrity

The definition of "agenda integrity" is simple, yet hard to implement. It means: (1) considering all of the items listed on the agenda and (2) not considering items not on the agenda. Let's spend a moment on each of these precepts.

Given the time that we recommend be spent on agenda preparation and item organization, it behooves meeting planners and committee members to follow through on their investment of time and energy. Indeed, one can view the agenda as a small "contract" made among the committee members. Individuals will spend time reviewing and preparing materials as long as there is some reason to spend that time. Few things irritate a committee member more than to arrive at a meeting, having sacrificed personal time preparing committee business, only to find that, because of somebody else's insistence or personal needs, other matters are being discussed that do not deal with the items on the agenda. All the preparation is wasted, and the individual who has spent personal time sits steaming in a pool of irritation. That individual frequently vows that it's "the last time I'm going to spend my time getting ready for a committee meeting." Time after time, when chairpersons tell us that individuals don't prepare for the meetings, we observe that the actual contents of the meetings do not merit that kind of participation. Furthermore, this cycle becomes vicious—individuals don't prepare, and therefore other topics become prime targets of discussion. The more those topics are in fact discussed, the less individuals feel like preparing. Hence, it is important to deal with items on the agenda. Honoring those expectations will pay great dividends.

The other side of the agenda coin is important as well. Dealing with new items that are not on the agenda means that individuals have not had the chance to prepare. Therefore, discussion is likely to be unfocused and rambling as individuals seek to discover the information they need to answer the questions. Furthermore, discussion of new business (remember the "no new business" principle?) without adequate preparation time often leads to premature action. In those instances when committees take bizarre or unusual positions, it frequently may be due to the lack of thought as an item pops up and people quickly act on it.

Temporal Integrity

Temporal integrity is also relatively simple and straightforward, but again, it's something that is violated with enough frequency to make it a popular pet peeve in our "Pet Peeves of Meetings" list. Temporal integrity involves the following precepts:

1. start on time;
2. end on time;
3. keep a rough time order interior to the meeting; and
4. keep the overall meeting time reasonable and within the limits of what people can tolerate or have agreed to give.

Starting on time requires what must sometimes seem to committee members an heroic act of will. Individuals drag in, and we routinely seem to prefer irritating those who are already present to those who have for some reason not yet shown up. The solution, of course, is to simply do it—"just begin" is the way to set group norms that will reinforce prompt attendance. The longer one waits, the longer the message is conveyed that this group doesn't start on time, anyway. It is important, however, to recall from the Rule of the Agenda Bell that starting with minutes and announcements doesn't mean that those who are a few minutes later are going to miss key items. So there is a recognition that, indeed, at most meetings most people will show up on time, and a few will show up a bit late. However, in order to reinforce the norm that "this group starts on time," one needs to actually do it. Then individuals will alter their schedules. Football games, television programs, and orchestra performances all start at the appointed times. We all manage to adjust to those times—there's no reason why the norm can't be set with respect to meetings. One of the great irritations that committee members report to us is having to sit around waiting for others to show up, when they themselves have made sacrifices and schedule adjustments to get there on time.

Ending on time is equally important. One reason people are late for meetings throughout the day is that earlier meetings don't end when they are supposed to. Our suggested guideline is to simply leave when the appointed time is over. One wants, of course, to be flexible in the application of this rule. A few more minutes may indeed provide useful closure. Nonetheless, it's important for committee members to avoid being "co-conspirators." We have been involved in postmeeting visits among committee members, each of whom complained that the meetings went overtime, but each of whom stayed and participated. Apparently they were expecting that someone else would say, "It's all over," or take the lead. That's rare. It's up to individual members not to tolerate meetings that go on well past the appointed adjournment hour. Frequently, of course, a key reason why meetings end late is that they start late. We've even observed the informal norm in some groups, which extends the adjournment time by a period equal to the length of the late starting time. Meeting planners must remember what they already know—individuals have other obligations and other commitments that must be met throughout the day. We all plan depending upon what we're told is going to happen. Occasional violations of plans are normal and to be expected; regular violations mean that a new set of norms has developed. We need to work against that establishment.

The pattern of putting times on agenda items, suggested under the Writing Rules chapter, helps groups keep a rough time order during the meeting. Poor allocation of time to items is a major reason why meetings run over. A trivial item takes fifty minutes out of an hour-and-a-half meeting, leaving only forty minutes for everything else. While one does not want to be overly rigid about the time allocation and bureaucratize the committee process, one does want to provide some rough guidelines so that members can plan their time accordingly. It helps even those individuals who can't attend the entire meeting. While we don't recommend it, it is sometimes necessary for individuals to join for only a key item. If they have a specific sense of when that item is likely to occur, then they can be more efficient and effective in their own planning.

The final point about temporal integrity involves keeping the meeting within appropriate bounds. Generally speaking, our observation is that meetings usually should not exceed one- to one-and-a-half hours. Three hours seem to be the absolute limit. If one has a three-hour meeting, then breaks at the hour point of about 5 to 7 minutes are appropriate. For a two-hour meeting, a break at approximately the two thirds point will prove to be helpful. For meetings under an hour and a half, breaks are not necessary. People can excuse themselves as necessary. We know people who seem to delight in hosting the giant eight-hour, ten-hour, twelve-hour meeting, in which people are actually glued to their chairs for long periods of time. Under these conditions, we observe that executives have the physical presence of individuals in the meeting room itself, but not their attention. They tune out, they doodle, they draw, they don't contribute. As one humorist said, "The mind can't absorb more than the seat can endure." Therefore, it is important to think of the need to schedule appropriate breaks, and to pace the actual meeting so everyone can contribute maximally.

Conclusion

Agenda integrity and temporal integrity are two crucial elements that will contribute greatly to the effectiveness and success of committees. They not only help to focus committee members' attention on the items in question, but also add importantly in creating a climate that generates commitment and participation. It is the creation of that climate, perhaps more than the organization of content, that will serve to generate effective committee activity.

Committee Evaluation

Quality in product or service is becoming the hallmark of the 1990s. Great energy needs to be put into the whole area of quality development through innovations (big steps) and what the Japanese call *kaizan* (continuous improvement or little steps). Both big, qualitative leaps forward, and small, day-to-day improvements are needed if products and services are to be national and world class.

An important part of quality is evaluation of the products and services that the organization provides to the public. Whether that organization is a commercial entity, a government agency, or a nonprofit/human-service enterprise really does not make much difference. Evaluation is always important.

Evaluation is important for two reasons, and it is hard to tell which is "primary" and which is "secondary." In the near term, evaluation systems are important because they provide information on the actual activities of the organization, product, or service and tell the providers what the customers, clients, or patients want.

Second, the presence of evaluation creates "anticipatory correction" in the behavior of the provider. Knowing that evaluation is going to occur has a "concentrating effect" on the mind of the provider.

Meetings, committees, and boards should be evaluated, too. Good products and services come from good decisions and good implementation, both of which are the responsibility of these groups. Most meetings, committees, and boards do not evaluate anything they do directly. This chapter seeks to provide a corrective perspective to that evasive orientation, as well as specific tools for the meeting, committee and board to use.

CHAPTER 31

Committee Evaluation

Introduction

In American society, various forms of evaluation are increasingly becoming the rule rather than the exception. The human-service field has perhaps been less eager (or less willing, or less able) to perform the kinds of outcome evaluations that are essential to maintain quality of service or product delivered. People, programs, and products are all increasingly being looked at to determine if they actively deliver what they are supposed to deliver. Such an evaluation process, of course, requires a clear understanding from the beginning about "what it is one is supposed to deliver." In executive evaluations done by boards of directors, for example, we have found that one of the most serious sources of difficulty is when board processes never make it clear to the executive what the board wishes the executive to be centrally responsible for and to accomplish in a given time period. Often, these expectations remain at the "I assume he or she knew . . ." level, and this omission leads to problems later.

All sectors of our society are undergoing an increasing demand for qualitative and quantitative evaluation of their activities. Given the problems and difficulties associated with the evaluation of individual problems, people, products, and processes, it is not surprising that committee output, as a "group result," is perhaps lowest on the list of objects of evaluation. Only recently have organizations begun asking whether or not groups (committees, meetings, task forces) have accomplished their stated purposes, and allocating rewards on the basis of whether or not those goals have been achieved. While there are lots of complaints about committees and meetings, as we have mentioned throughout this volume, there is precious little attempt to actually evaluate whether or not goals were achieved, and—if not—what went wrong in the goal-achievement procedures. The purpose of this chapter is to provide some suggestions about ways in which committee activity and output may be evaluated.

Steps in the Evaluation Process

All evaluation processes essentially involve five steps. These steps may be discussed differently by different thinkers, but there is a high level of agreement about how evaluation is to proceed. The steps are specification, monitoring, oversight, assessment, and appraisal.

Specification

The first step in any evaluative process is to specify exactly what the results of the process are to be. Such specification involves standard setting in terms of agreement or assertion about the level of quality that is to be delivered, but it also involves specification concerning the time frames in which that quality is to be delivered, and the levels of mistakes, errors, and other aberrations that will be tolerated. The specification process is often difficult, because it will reveal the difficulties involved in trying to lay out expected outcomes and parameters. However, the saying, "If you don't know where you're going, any road will take you there" applies to the evaluation processes particularly well. If one does not have a sense of the goals to be achieved, then it is very difficult to undertake the remaining steps in the evaluation process. It is even more difficult to apply rewards and sanctions. Specification involves laying out exactly what it is that is to be accomplished.

In committee life, specification involves setting down a committee mandate. It is one of the jobs of the chair to procure or write a mandate. The mandate involves tasks to be accomplished, goals to be achieved, time frames, and so on. Even for the lowly "staff committee," such specification is crucial. It is not enough to answer "What is the purpose of this committee?" with "It's the staff committee—we meet every week. It's a tradition around here." Early specification of exactly what the mission and purpose of the group are will allow the other elements of the evaluation process to fall into place.

Monitoring

Monitoring involves collecting numbers about the ongoing activities of the organization in question. How many clients are seen, how many interviews are held, how many automobiles are produced—these are the kinds of questions that monitoring allows us to answer.

For committees, monitoring may mean simple tabulations about the number of meetings or the number of people in attendance. It may include checkoffs with respect to assignments given and assignments completed.

Oversight

At the oversight level, the process of judgment begins. Data from the monitoring process are compared with other, outside standards, especially those already established in the goals. It allows one to make mid-course corrections and adjustments of activity in order to stay within goal parameters. A simple example of this oversight procedure comes from driving. Almost all of us have had the experience of wanting to be in a particular place at a particular time. We have a number of other pieces of information, including when we must leave, how bad the road conditions are or might become, how fast we usually go, and so on. Taking all of these factors into consideration, we pick a departure time that should allow us to arrive within the desired time frame. However, constant monitoring of progress allows oversight activity to take place. If we have fifty miles to go, and we have completed only twenty-five miles at the thirty-five-minute point, then we may choose to increase speed a bit, take a somewhat speedier route, or perhaps stop and call to change the arrival time.

Assessment

Assessment involves making judgments about program subcomponents. There is a fateful element to it. While adjustments are made in the oversight process, in the assessment process revisions of goals, targets, standards, and resources are made in order to keep the entire project within previously decided-upon specifications.

In committee work, the following assessments can be considered: decisions about sub-areas to continue with or cease pursuing, the confrontation of decision avoidance or premature closure actions (and a discussion about them) and the "up-front" dealing with issues that are preventing the committee from being on a trajectory that would allow it to complete its overall objectives. Assessment can thus focus on not only the substantive elements being discussed by the committee meeting but also committee processes and meeting processes themselves.

Appraisal

Appraisal involves a great deal of judgment, and uses material from specification, monitoring, oversight, and assessment phases to come to a final decision about continuance or non-continuance with a particular person, program, or effort. The word "appraisal" is used in order to invoke its connotation from real estate—a final judgment, taking all factors into account, about what a particular house is worth in a contemporary marketplace. While a variety of elements go into the decision, it finally remains a "judgment call" to put them all together.

For a committee, appraisal involves a sit-down assessment of where the committee has been, where it is going, what accomplishments and lack of accomplishments have characterized this period under review, and processes and procedures throughout. It may then decide to change its specifications, add new ones, redraw its charter mandate or terms of reference, double its meeting time, get more resources, add staff, or, in general, take action steps that either revise its goal expectations or put them into position where those expectations can be reasonably met.

If one were to put this system into an "academic" frame of reference, the specification part would involve a statement of expectations (goals for class/course) and a course statement (class/course procedures) handed out by a professor. There might be actual negotiations with the students about these expectations, along the lines of when papers are actually due and how many quizzes are to be given. However it happens, a statement of expectations is the first step. Students need to know what they need to do. Monitoring may involve a daily or weekly quiz, or the taking of attendance—something that is rather routine and ongoing but lets the instructor know at a minimal level what people are up to. Oversight involves checking student trajectories against due dates and making other kinds of quality assessments. For example, professors often require a brief outline of a paper topic to be completed later in order to assure themselves that the students are—time wise, anyway—where they ought to be. The outline also allows for an elementary quality check. It does not necessarily say that the student is going to write an "A" paper, but problems that would result in poor performance can often be spotted at that early stage. Assessment may involve a midterm exam. While it is not completely faithful, it is not trivial, either, and it allows for the putting and pulling together of a range of activities into a particular product for observation and review. The appraisal element is, in effect, the final grade. It represents taking into consideration material from the monitoring, oversight, and assessment elements, and comparing them with the expectations as laid out in the specifications section.

What Is the "It" That Is to Be Evaluated?

These steps may sound well and good, but the question that immediately pops into mind is "What is it that I'm going to evaluate?" In committee life there are two elements. One has to do with the task aspects of committee operation and the other with the process ones. "Task" simply means "were goals achieved?" But more than that, it involves assessing whether the decisions made by the group were of high quality. Decision-quality assessment has already been discussed, using an A–F grading scheme, and the reader can refer to Chapter 25 for more detailed procedures. If decisions are of high quality, then it is very likely that goals are being met. If decisions are of low quality, then change is necessary.

Apart from the actual quality of the decisions, the interpersonal processes, climate, and "culture" of the committee need to be assessed as well. A simple meeting assessment form, asking for people's reactions, will suffice. The goal is naturally an open, supportive, interpersonal process in which people feel free to share their views without fear of being "put down" but are also themselves sensitive to the level of their own participation and try to neither overparticipate nor underparticipate.

The task and process evaluations should occur often enough in all committees—regular, standing, ad-hoc, advisory—so that the individuals in question can have an opportunity to see where they're going as a group and modify their behavior accordingly.

Decision Audit and Decision Autopsy

Sometimes a more refined analysis is needed in order to help a committee get or remain on track. In these cases, either a decision audit or a decision autopsy might be appropriate. A decision audit simply takes a sample of decisions that have been graded (as already discussed in Chapter 25) and calculates an average score for them.[1] The average grade for decisions is then discussed, and an attempt is made to understand within the group itself how improvements can be made and how problems can be avoided.

Special care is taken in these situations to distinguish between the quality of a decision on the one hand and the quality of the implementation on the others. As most analysts and practitioners know, the final result of the decision involves both a high-quality decision and a high-quality implementation. A good decision can be sabotaged by poor-quality implementation, and a terrible decision can be "saved" by creative implementation. The importance of this dual assessment is clear. If the decision-making system is flawed, then improvements need to be made in it. If the implementation system is flawed, then improvements need to be made in it. At the moment, with respect to committees, we are focusing more on the decision-making system. However, since committees, once they disband, go about the work of implementation, there may need to be attention paid to implementation as well.

1. To refresh readers of the material discussed in chapter 25, a sample of decisions is selected. Each decision is given a grade—an A if everybody wins (although not necessarily equally), a B if there are more winners than losers, a C if there is no gain or loss, a D if there are more losers than winners, and an F if everyone is worse off from the decision having been made than they were before.

A more-detailed analysis occurs in the decision autopsy. In this case, one very good decision (an A or B) and one bad decision (an F or D) is selected for in-depth review. In the case of the A or B decision, the analysis seeks to uncover what went right, and discussion proceeds along the lines of ways in which those positive aspects can be replicated. In the case of the F or D decision, analysis focuses on what went wrong and what steps might be taken to avoid such errors in the future. It is an attempt to learn not only from mistakes but also from successes.

It is imperative in the decision autopsy that both high-quality and low-quality decisions be included. There are several reasons for this necessity. Firstly, if only bad decisions are included, people will perhaps learn what was wrong and try to avoid it, but not learn to do things that are right. True excellence requires the avoidance of making errors, on the one hand, and the proactive doing of things that are appropriate, on the other. Simply avoiding harm does not cure the patient. Alternatively, doing good things while simultaneously doing harmful ones may create a neutral situation with no great result.

Conclusion

The techniques mentioned here are guidelines. They should be adopted as the organization or agency finds them helpful, and adapted as the organization or agency finds it necessary. The central rule of the evaluation process is as follows: It makes less difference *what* system is used than the fact that *some* system is used. In a word, it is the presence of the evaluative impulse rather than the specific mechanisms of any particular kind of evaluation that, in the final analysis, makes the difference. But considering the time, energy, and effort that American society and societies the world over spend in various kinds of committee activity, it is imperative that we evaluate the results of these activities and seek, through the evaluation process, to improve them.

ACHIEVING

DECISION

CRYSTALLIZATION[1]

In spite of the best technical preparation, the field of action often is a place where our best intentions go awry. Events move fast, and we find it hard to think of the things we know to do that will be helpful. This bewilderment is especially present in meetings, committees, and boards because they are so often frustrating, for one thing, and because we frequently know so little about what is really going on, for another.

While space prohibits a detailed discussion of the actual dynamics of the meeting process, two key points will be very helpful to the individual who is seeking to become a meeting master. One is to understand the concept of decision rules, what they are and how they operate in meeting, committee, and board life.

The second is to understand the specific steps

1. Development of the material in this section was supported, in part, by a grant from the 3M Meeting Management Institute, Austin, Tex. The authors want to express their appreciation to the Institute and to Ginny Johnson, Director, for support and encouragement. More information on this project can be obtained by contacting John E. Tropman at The University of Michigan, Ann Arbor, MI. 48109.

that need to be taken to help decision makers "crystallize" a decision within the "boiling pot" of meeting activity. Most frequently, the meeting masters research (Tropman, 1991) suggests that decisions do not occur because members (chairs, members, whomever) do not know the words to say and the steps to take to help groups focus specifically from an ambiguous field of alternatives.

This chapter provides information about both decision rules and crystallization techniques. These perspectives will help the member to both understand more of what is really going on in the meeting and provide techniques to influence that process as well.

Decision Crystallization in Committees

Introduction

One of the great difficulties many committees experience has to do with the decision-making process itself. A majority of complaints suggests that decision avoidance is a key problem: "We talk around and around and around the issues, but somehow we never decide. Then, if we do decide, we revisit it for a whole range of foolish reasons." On the other hand, some individuals complain about decision prematurity: "We go in there, a problem is presented, and right away somebody says, 'Let's do X.' Everybody agrees, and then we leave. There really is no thoughtful approach to the problem." The problem here is the issue of facilitating the decision process itself. Many people are unaware of the steps needed to facilitate the decisions, and the purpose of this chapter is to outline those steps. First we will discuss decision rules. We will then need to discuss the process of, and steps involved in, decision crystallization. We will culminate with a discussion about decision sculpting.

Decision Rules

Decision rules represent the formal and informal agreed-upon ways in which decisions are legitimately arrived at within a group. Competition among decision rules is frequently why decisions don't get made. Most groups have at least five competing decision rules operating simultaneously within them. They are as follows: (1) extensive rule, (2) involvement rule, (3) the implementation rule, (4) expertise rule, and (5) power rule. They are discussed briefly below.

There are competing decision rules because no decision rule is neutral. No decision rule equally attends to all competing interests. Some decision rules favor the breadth of preference within a group, while others favor the interests of those who carry out decisions, those who have experience with particular areas, or those who are affected deeply by the decisions. Still others deal with issues about the role of experts—who know most about the area regardless of whether they are affected by it or feel deeply about it. Lastly, of course, issues of power are never far from the decision-making scene. Each of these concerns evolves into a legitimate basis for making decisions. The problem is that they conflict within the group, and the skilled decision facilitator and crystallizer needs to be aware of them and appeal to them.

The first rule is called the *Extensive Decision Rule*. It is basically historically known as "one person, one vote." This principle has a large degree of acceptance in Western society. Even in the early grades of school a whole range of decisions are made by someone saying, "Well, let's have a show of hands."

A second rule is the *Involvement Rule*, which relates to those who might be deeply affected on moral or other grounds by a particular decision. Minorities are often sensitive to this particular rule since, by definition in many cases, they will not be in the majority. Therefore, if the food being prepared for the company banquet involves only meat, the few vegetarians will seek to secure support on the grounds that, although a minority, their interests are special, and they are deeply affected by the decision of the majority. While they may not get all of the dishes they want, their views may be given greater weight because of the added factor of special need.

Before we go on to the third rule, a word about "consensus" is in order. Members of meetings, committees, and boards often say that they operate from a consensus rule. When pushed, though, it becomes hard for them to define exactly what they mean or what anyone in the group might mean by consensus. One person we talked with about this point finally said, "It's when everyone can live with the decision." From the perspective here, "consensus" usually can be understood as a combination of the extensive rule and the involvement rule. It has aspects of extensiveness in that everyone has to assent. However, because everyone does not have to assent enthusiastically, the involvement rule becomes operative. In essence, the individuals in the group agree because *they do not particularly care about the item in question.* Hence, their "involvement" is low.

Third is the *Implementation Rule*, which focuses on the carrying-out of particular decisions. Frequently we are inclined to give those who must do the task more say in decisions than those who remain on the side. Hence, if someone says, "I've got to prepare the food for the company banquet. Why don't you let me decide what we should have?" he or she is appealing to the implementation decision rule.

Fourth, is the *Expertise Rule,* the appeal to expertise and special knowledge. On medical problems, doctors are given lots of say. The same is true of lawyers and other experts. One difficulty here, of course, is in getting the expert to use his or her expertise only in areas where that expertise is truly present. All too often experts are given some generalized authority, and hence the doctors' or lawyers' view is looked at with special reference even on matters over which they have no greater expertise, involvement, or moral scruples than anyone else.

Finally, there is a *Power Rule* ("What does the *boss* want?"). This rule is illustrated by the clever story of the boss who did, in fact, ask for a vote. Everyone in the room said "Aye," the boss said "Nay." Then, summing up, the boss commented, "The nays have it."

Within the decision-making framework of committees, these five decision-making rules compete simultaneously. To make matters more complex, individuals are likely to advocate a decision rule that they feel will indirectly honor their preference. Thus, they do not have to argue their preference up front. If individuals feel that they have the vote on a particular issue, they are very likely to say "Why don't we just vote, then? It's the American way." If individuals feel they do not have the vote, they might say, "It wouldn't be fair to vote, because some individuals feel deeply, or know more. Therefore, we should pay greater attention to those preferences." And so it goes. Individuals facilitating the committee process—especially staffers and chairs, but also members and others—need to be aware of the competition among decision rules and seek to nullify their cross-cutting impact. By "cross-cutting impact" we refer to the fact that if all decision rules hold equal legitimacy simultaneously and do in fact favor different outcomes, the committee decision process is often stalled. Not infrequently, such stalling results in an appeal to power, and "the boss decides"—but not without a lot of grumbling and complaining. It is sometimes helpful at the beginning of a discussion if a facilitator or chair suggests the decision rule that should have the greatest dominance for this particular discussion. It must be done, however, at the beginning of the discussion, before its specific effect on the preference ordering of outcomes can be clearly seen. Otherwise, individuals will think of it as a ploy. The decision rules will be called upon in the process of decision crystallization.

Decision Crystallization

What we typically call a "decision" in committees is really a decision mosaic, a decision "picture" made up of smaller decision elements, discrete decision "bits" that are built into a final-decision mosaic. Typically, the committee proceeds, element by element, to build a decision. When the final-decision picture is established, decision sculpting is undertaken.

The decision facilitator begins by identifying a key element as the first topic of discussion. For purposes of this illustration, let us think of a decision that is needed on what food to serve at the agency picnic. Obviously, the "decision" about what to serve is comprised of a number of decision elements, among them what meat to serve, what vegetables to serve, what drinks to serve, and what time to serve them. All of these items need to be decided one by one and then built into a final-decision mosaic.

The first step in decision facilitation is to identify the range of different elements and suggest that the committee proceed element by element through them. This will prevent a discussion that involves some individuals talking about meat, some about vegetables, some about drinks, and some about time, all simultaneously contributing their "bit" to the discussion. The problem with that kind of discussion is that it never builds to a conclusive result. In this case, we can assume that the decision facilitator has identified the meat course as the appropriate place to begin, and discussion has commenced.

In groups, decision elements are approached by "rounds" of discussion. A round of discussion occurs when one has gone "around" the group and asked for contributions, and each person has made, or has had the chance to make, one contribution. There will be a lull at this point in the group. The chair or facilitator may ask a question like "Anything else to say? Anyone else have a view?" and there will be a silence. At this "trough" in the discussion, it is important that a series of three steps be taken. If taken, a decision is likely to result, or at the very least substantial progress toward a decision is likely. If these steps are not taken, individuals will begin to repeat themselves, and the committee will be caught in a "wheel-spinning" exercise.

Summative Reflection

The first of the three steps is *summative reflection*, provided by the decision facilitator or chairperson. A summative reflection involves organizing and feeding back in appropriate categories what the group has said thus far. A typical summative reflection in the case under consideration might be: "Well, we have several people who want hamburgers, a few who want hotdogs, some who want fish, and some who prefer to bring their own food." It must be remembered that the group doesn't know what the group as a whole thinks until they've had a chance to hear it. Without a summary, individuals in the group may not sense what the committee, as a committee, would like. That is the purpose of the summative reflection.

Action Hypothesis

Following upon the summative reflection is the decision or *action hypothesis*. Here the facilitator or chairperson suggests an action derived from the summative reflection that seems reasonable and prudent. It should be emphasized that the offer of action is made for the benefit of the group, not because it is the speaker's own preference. Often groups are not clear about what they actually want or don't want to do until somebody says "it" out loud. We have all been in situations where we are waiting to go out to dinner with a group. Various people are saying "It doesn't matter to me," "Anything is okay," and then someone says, "Let's have Chinese food." At that point, someone says, "Oh no! I'm allergic to Chinese food." And others concur. It was not until a course of action was specifically expressed that individuals understood something of the internal structure of their own preferences. It is for that same purpose that the decision or action hypothesis is offered.

Discussion Refocus

Let us assume that the group nods and "hmms" its agreement. At that point, the decision facilitator or chairperson goes to the next step, *discussion refocus,* and says, "Fine. Let's now move on to a discussion of the vegetables," and suggests as the next topic of discussion the next logical item in the decision-element array.

In this way, decisions are built, element by element, until the total decision mosaic is assembled. At that point we engage in decision sculpting. But before discussing decision sculpting, let's see what happens if things don't go so well. It's not unlikely that in the decision or action hypothesis stage someone says "No, no!" and there is general disagreement. That is perfectly okay, and the decision facilitator or chairperson is prepared to accept the psychological cost of that "rejection." After all, the purpose of suggesting action was to see where the group was. If it appears that the group will not accept the proposed action hypothesis, then the decision facilitator or chairperson suggests another round of discussion on the same topic, but with a slight difference. The difference is that the more extreme of the proposals (perhaps, in the example given, those who wanted to bring their own food) are set aside, and an attempt is made on expanding the reasonable, central core of options already on the table. In addition, the chairperson or decision facilitator may wish to add considerations that have escaped attention thus far. In the example given, since no attention was paid to vegetarian staff members, that might be the sort of topic mentioned. A second round of discussion occurs, followed by an attempt at crystallization, followed by discussion refocus.

During the decision action hypothesis stage, it is helpful if the chairperson or decision facilitator can appeal to two or more decision rules in the actual statement of the action hypothesis. For example, the chairperson or decision facilitator might say, "Well, it seems like hotdogs have pretty good support [extensive decision rule], and they're not hard to make [implementation decision rule], and the kids love them [intensive decision rule], and I know the boss doesn't care [power decision rule]." In a sense, in this seemingly innocent phrase, support is being sought on the basis of a variety of different decision rules. The best decisions wind up being those that can satisfy two or more decision criteria at the same time. Because decision rules conflict, the need to satisfy several at once is important. However, because of the conflict, decision rules may cancel one another out. Thus, a metarule— a previously agreed-upon ordering rule—needs to be invoked.

For example, many groups try for "consensus" first, and then, failing that, "vote." However, it is frequently the case that chairs, when they fail to get "consensus," don't invoke one of the *other* rules. Chairs often say things like, "Where are we?" hoping, in effect, for someone else to take the emotional heat of forming and saying an action hypothesis. One of the most important points for chairs to know, therefore, is the different decision rules, and he or she has to be prepared to invoke them in some sequence.

Decision Sculpting

Decision sculpting involves looking at the decision mosaic and seeing whether all the parts are there. If, for example, only alcoholic beverages have been planned for and no soda, that omission can be rectified during a decision-sculpting phase. Decision sculpting allows the committee to look at the overall decision once it is provisionally in place. Of course, one always wants to see how things fit together, but it is very difficult to see how they fit together until all the provisional pieces are present. Too, it's hard to be sure all the pieces are in place, but many can be.

Conclusion

This brief discussion provides the rudiments of a discussion of the process of facilitating decisions within committees. It is important to understand that decision making requires proactive, energetic participation in the group process, but from the point of view of assisting the group in understanding what its preferences are, exploring the values and virtues of those several preferences, and selecting among them. Most of the time, this process is left to accident. Decisions emerge—when they do emerge—by the luck of the draw. We can and must do much better than a reliance on "maybe it will happen and maybe it won't." By understanding the inner dynamics of the decision-approach process, and the ways it can be facilitated, we can assist the group in making high-quality decisions.

Naturally, decisions can also be manipulated. Like most techniques, decision facilitation can be used for positive or negative ends. It is our professional view that decision facilitation should be used to further the ends of the group, not as a way to get one's own interests brought to the forefront.

Decision crystallization sounds easier than it is. Like other "arts," what looks simple actually requires lots of practice. Readers should not be discouraged when the initial attempts don't work out as well as hoped. In time, they will. But these skills, unlike some of the rules, require more dynamic than mechanical application. The results will be well worth it.

THE VOLUNTARY
BOARD OF
DIRECTORS

Boards of directors are going to play an increasingly crucial role in America's future. The ability of boards to understand their role and to function well within that role is of ever-increasing importance to the functioning of society. Why is that? Because boards of directors are one of the types of small groups that are increasingly being relied upon by American society for the accomplishment of social purpose. John Naisbett outlines this direction clearly in his book, *Megatrends: Ten New Directions Transforming Our Lives* (1982). Three of the ten trends he talks about are particularly germane here. One is a movement from centralization to decentralization. A second is a movement from institutional help to self-help. And a third is a movement from representative democracy to participatory democracy. Each of these trends speaks to the overall movement away from large-scale bureaucratized control of our lives, whether that control is public or private, to small or more human-scale organizational forms that permit individuals to control and shape their own destiny.

The importance of a particular type of social activity, however, is no guarantee that people necessarily will do it well. It is not even any guarantee

that people will have basic knowledge about what is required. This is
the case with boards of directors. Many of us have conventionalized
and ritualized sets of expectations about what boards of directors are
supposed to do in general, how those goals are to be accomplished,
and what our particular role as a board member might be in assisting
the boards to accomplish those goals.

CHAPTER 33

The Board of Directors

Boards have seven basic responsibilities. First, boards are legal corporations, and as such have special legal responsibilities as corporations. Second, boards are trustees of civic purpose. They are the repository of community hopes and aspirations for accomplishing social goals and, as such, have an equally powerful but less easily specific responsibility to the community as a whole. Third, boards are decision makers. They have a legal responsibility, in civic terms, to make decisions affecting the agency. Fourth, boards have a responsibility for role appropriateness. They must organize themselves properly to accomplish the decisional purposes that they were set up to achieve. Fifth, boards have a responsibility as trainers and developers. They need to pay attention to the growth of their own members as individuals and the growth of the board's corporate capability for decision making. Sixth, they have to find and hire an executive director. Seventh, they have a responsibility for entrepreneurship and strategic planning.

Boards as Legal Corporations

It is often thought that since board members are giving of their time for civic purposes, directors are free from liability. This is not likely to be the case, and each board should consult an attorney experienced in incorporated non-profits' matters so that the rules and regulations of the state that govern their operation, and the responsibilities and potential liabilities that they might incur under them, are fully understood.

Basically, board members have three legal responsibilities. The first of these is diligence. In the case of a charge against a particular board of directors, courts are likely to check whether the board members have been diligent in the performance of their duties—in the holding of regular meetings, and in their attendance at the meetings, at the very least. If board members never come to meetings, they cannot be said to be diligent. A second standard is prudence. Board members are required to be prudent in the carrying-out of their duties. Prudence means that the board director must show the same care in looking after corporate interests as a reasonable man would exercise in looking after his own interests. William Zelman (1977) comments as follows:

> The exercise of prudence as well as diligence is associated with the satisfactory performance of board duties. In contrast to the concept of diligence, which involves positive action, prudence involves the avoidance of acts demonstrating lack of loyalty or good faith. In this context, lack of loyalty refers to refraining from acting in one's self-interest in any manner that may interfere with corporate business, good faith refers to the exercise of honest and reasonable judgment to perpetuate the best interest of the organization. To avoid liabilities resulting from lack of reasonable prudence, board members should bear these definitions in mind as well as the following precept: they may not gain private profit from their official position and may not deal with the organization from an adversary position acting as or for a competitor. (P. 272)

Zelman's last point suggests a third rule a director should bear in mind—avoiding conflict of interest. Many directors have a range of business interests that may occasionally come into conflict or be involved with the board of directors' interests. While state law may vary on this point, it is generally accepted practice to expect that the director with an intersecting interest to declare it to the other directors publicly, such that it can be recorded either by letter or in writing, and the other directors can take that interest into account in making the decision.

These cursory points are not a complete outline of directors' legal responsibilities. They may, however, pique interest in finding out in more appropriate detail, and with respect to one's individual board, exactly what the legal situation and potential liabilities might be.

Boards as Trustees of Civic Purpose

Organizations set up to provide help to others carry a social responsibility perhaps parallel (if more vague) to the legal responsibility. This role is the "trustee" role, and it represents the community's relatively undefined sense of what it would like the board to do. Directors, therefore, must be sensitive to the fact that they have a "triple constituency": themselves; the agency's staff and clients; and the community. The community constituency is often ignored because it is hard to define or pinpoint. (There are multiple ones—ethnic communities, communities of donors, clients, etc. Often they overlap.) While it is not possible to state what the community constituency is, what can be done is to outline ways in which it can be tapped. A generally broad-based representation should be the goal.

One such way is to have the board of directors broadly composed of key community actors who express interest in board activities. The human service organization community should be "represented" on the board of directors as well. Such "representation" cannot be thought of as official in any sense, but it does provide ways to tap into important subcommittees within the community as a whole.

A second way that community interest can be tapped is through the establishment of an advisory committee or body of interested delegates to the organization. All too often, organizations wait until a vacancy occurs on the board of directors, and then go on a vigorous "search" process to find somebody who is willing to offer the time. On the other hand, it is also true that when the term of a director has been completed, boards often feel embarrassed to not reappoint that individual, since there is no "place" that that person can go, no particular structural role that he or she can take so that the director's experience and perspective can continue to be useful to the agency, but in a capacity different from a director of the agency. The establishment of an advisory committee or delegate body can help overcome both of these problems as a place for interested persons to connect into, and exit from, the organization's board. The delegate body or advisory group should consist of all persons who have expressed an interest in joining with the organization, and those who have had the opportunity to serve with the organization. The group can be fairly large, perhaps up to fifty members, and can meet once or twice a year. From it the board of directors can draw membership on some committees, secure additional help, and so on. It provides a way in which people can become involved with and linked to the organization, and at the same time learn about the organization. Therefore, when the opportunity comes for them to be invited to a directorship, they can perform that role in a knowledgeable way without having that invitation be their first contact with the organization.

The advisory group is also a way the organization can secure the inputs and perspectives of members of the community-at-large, and can do so from a broader base than is typically possible if board membership is the sole vehicle available.

An advisory group means that recruitment is an ongoing process. One should not wait until a particular point in the year and then seek to recruit new board members. Rather, one should be continually adding people to the organizational stable of interested and committed individuals, and begin a process of involving and using their services on an ongoing basis.

Boards as Decision Makers

Boards of directors have the responsibility to make decisions. All too often we find that this central and most essential function of the board of directors is one that is handled casually and cavalierly. Decisions are delayed, denied, or not made with any reasonable eye toward the information and perspectives needed. Boards frequently have no mechanism for assessing the quality of their decisions and for checking the impact that their decisions have had in subsequent months and years. Boards should therefore take it upon themselves to set up a reasonable set of procedures for ensuring the making of quality decisions. The last section of this chapter will speak explicitly to that point. (Also see Chapter 15.) Suffice it to say that quality procedures (rules) and quality processes (crystallization) as well as quality reviews are needed for high-quality decisions.

Board Responsibility for Role Appropriateness

There are *two* aspects to role appropriateness that concern boards of directors. One is internal and one is external. Material already reviewed in Part IV covers much of the material on Role Appropriateness. A brief review, focusing specifically on boards, would be helpful here.

Externally, boards are actors in a theatre of community organizations, and as such there are three major external responsibilities that they must fulfill: information sharing, coordination with other organizations, and implementing community decisions.

First, they share information about their own program and activity with other boards in the community. There is no requirement in the sharing function that adjustments need to be made in the program to accommodate other organizations. That might come or it might not. Rather, the point here is to make programmatic information available on a sustained basis.

Second, boards do have some responsibility to consider coordination among other agencies, and between agencies and constituencies. This is an outgrowth of sharing. Everyone can't and shouldn't do everything. Organizations have special competencies, interests, and constituencies. These need to be articulated with the activities of other organizations so that a community level of efficiency and effectiveness can be approached (we wouldn't even consider using the word "attained"). All too often, boards act in isolation from other similar organizations in communities, and directors should recognize that this is improper role performance.

Third, boards need to assist in the implementation of community decisions. Here, again, a cooperative rather than a coercive posture carries the day. Communities may, in their larger priority-setting and goal-determining functions, seek to set certain overall directions that are helpful for them.

Boards, as members of those communities, and directors, as members of boards, should try insofar as possible to articulate their efforts with community-wide goals and priorities. Finally, boards play an advisory function to the community as a whole. They may send representatives to a community-wide planning organization that seeks to set overall community guidelines, or respond to community events and let their view and perspective be known. We call this function "advisory" because it is sending board opinion to other units within the community system, and is not an area in which the board has legal responsibility. However, its views can be helpful and should be transmitted.

Internally, the board needs also to attend to three main functions: decision making, oversight, and, occasionally, administration. Decision making has already been mentioned. The other two are central to board operation. Once decisions are made, it is often assumed that "it" will happen. The old dichotomy between "policy" or "politics" and "administration" suggests that the old decision will somehow automatically be carried out. All of us who have had experience in the decision-making field know that this is not the case, that decisions are chains of events, not single events, and that administration is a process, not a point in time. It is true, of course, that the executive director of the organization has responsibility for carrying out decisions made by the board. That statement assumes that "carrying out" is a mindless, thoughtless task, something that could perhaps be done by an automaton.

The truth, of course, is far from it. While there are certain elements easy to implement, many may be hard. This array of implementation decisions leads to a very important function called the decision oversight function, and it involves joint participation between the executive director and the board of directors to deal with issues of interpretation, clarity, and others that come up during the implementation process. This decision oversight function sometimes merges with supervision of the executive director, which is also a crucial responsibility of the board of directors. Often, directors feel that the boards essentially ignore them until some problem or difficulty arises, and then come down fairly hard on the situation. When one talks to boards in these kinds of situations, one hears the lament from the directors that the executive never took time to relate to them. Hence, decision oversight is a board function shared by the executive, in which both work together for the implementation of decisions.

Occasionally, the board must administer the agency. This situation occurs when there is a sudden transition of the executive and an acting executive cannot be found. Sometimes the executive leaves or is fired. Sometimes organizations in their earliest founding days use board members to do administrative tasks (a pattern that's hard to get out of). In any case, the situation means that the board acts as a sort of task force.

The Board as Trainer and Developer

Boards of directors of non-profit organizations need to grow and improve both collectively and individually. This responsibility is often not even recognized by the board members themselves. The board somehow feels that growth and improvement in board functioning will occur automatically, if it needs to occur at all. Unfortunately, boards of directors, like other organizations, tend not to improve automatically, but rather tend to decline, if special attention to growth and improvement is not taken. Hence, our rule of thumb is that the board, as part of its responsibility, should set a goal of board training and improvement as a part of and vehicle through which other aspects of its responsibility can be developed. This prescription is not an unusual one. Most agencies or organizations have such a perspective for their employees, and look kindly on the activities of the employee aimed at self-development and personal improvement. Often, the organization will provide financial support for special courses, meeting attendance, or interactions with professional organizations aimed at this kind of personal improvement. A similar perspective should be extended to the board, and, as a rule of thumb, the board should encourage at least one personal or collective group experience per year. Such an experience could involve a board-sponsored training session or annual retreat for the members, in which all participate jointly, or it could involve supporting individual board members going to individual meetings or undertaking individual growth experiences and programs. Whichever model is chosen, board performance will improve as a result.

Hiring the Executive

One of the crucial board activities is hiring the executive director or the president of the organization. We have left this responsibility till last because it is so often thought of first. Directors with whom we have talked often say, "Our responsibility is to hire the executive, and let him or her do the job we expect to be done." Nothing, in our judgment, could be father from the truth, and in making that statement we do not wish to underrate at all the importance of hiring the director. However, one cannot and should not take the position that responsibility ends there, as indicated by the first section of this chapter. Legal responsibilities exist in any case, and there are responsibilities for providing strategic guidance for the executive and the agency.

How does one go about finding an executive director? Typically, a search committee is established, a job description prepared, and the vacancy posted in professional journals and around the community. One needs to pay attention to rules of affirmative action, both because it is right to do so and because ignoring them can lead to serious and difficult complications. Applications are received, reviewed by the search committee, and a number of possible candidates are developed for further study. At about this same time, the search committee usually has developed a set of criteria that will help it, but should not limit it, in a search for a new executive. Often these criteria are expressed through the job description.

Further attention is then given to the smaller group of selectees. At this point, courtesy demands, though practice often denies, that a letter of rejection be sent to those whose names will not be held for further consideration. From the group of selectees, a smaller group, often called the "short list" of individuals, is invited for interviews. Some individuals will be very knowledgeable about the organization and may be currently a part of it. Others may come from far away, and the interview session becomes also a briefing and exchange of idea session.

At this point, we'd like to enter a word of caution. Many search committees put a great deal of emphasis on the interview itself and on the statements and assertions made at the interview, as well as the general style, composure, and "smoothness" of the individual in the interview situation. While it is in appropriate to minimize this evidence, it's worth noting that the interview situation is a highly unusual one, and from a scientific point of view (if one were thinking, for example, of sampling) an awkward and odd sample of an individual's behavior. There have been too many situations in which the interview has been misleading in fundamental ways, resulting in the hiring of individuals who later prove to be bad choices, and, we are sure, the unfortunate rejection of individuals who seemed to be less impressive but who would, in fact, have been outstanding. A corrective here is the detailed and intensive investigation of candidates on the short list by calling those people who know the individuals and seeking information about them. This information should be given equal if not greater weight than the interview itself.

Entrepreneurship and Strategic Planning

Boards of directors have a responsibility for entrepreneurship and strategic planning. It might sound strange to think of a board as being responsible for entrepreneurship. One might ask, "What can this mean?" In this particular case, entrepreneurship means the development and implementation of new ideas. We believe it takes three kinds of resources to run modern organizations (voluntary and otherwise): money, people, and ideas. Most organizations spend a great deal of time on money, a lesser amount of time on people, and almost no time on ideas. For this reason, many organizations have ample financial and personnel resources, but are in some sense conceptually bankrupt. In the long run, this neglect could affect the organization's financial status and people resources. Therefore, one of the board's most important tasks is to see to it that there is an ongoing consideration of new ideas, some emphasis on risk, and a share of failures. That prescription may sound strange, but without failures there is no risking, and without risking there is insufficient development of the new-idea process. As emblems and leaders of the organization, boards embody these "characterizations." Hence, the following discussion of "organizations" is here, in the chapter on boards, because boards signify the organization and are the first and final arbiter of it.

Organizations might be classified in four general types, three of which are at least somewhat problematic, and only one of which is ideal. The four types are: *conservative organizations, traditional organizations, entrepreneurial organizations,* and *overboard organizations.* Let us say a word about each of these types, and some of their problems and difficulties, with a special emphasis on the relationship of these organizational types to the new-idea process.

The *conservative organization* is one that actively opposes new ideas. It is set in its ways and quite convinced that the way it has always done things is the way things should be done. The phrase, "If it ain't broke, don't fix it," is frequently heard, with no recognition that "if it ain't broke now, it will be soon." Such organizations often punish innovators. They seek to root them out and remove their "unfortunate influence" from the organization. Indeed, innovation is unsettling; there's no question about it. But these are organizations that will, in the course of time, find themselves without clientele, without resources, and without support. As much as organizations dislike change, they must continue to change at least at the rate that the environment is changing, or they will be left behind. The fact that the environment changes slowly and sometimes imperceptibly, especially to members of conservative organizations, does not mean that the environment is not changing at all. Over time, the distance between what the environment needs and what the organization provides grows ever larger. Finally, there will be some shocking or cataclysmic event that will reveal to all in inescapable terms the difficulties in which the organization would now find itself. Nonetheless, the time frames here are certainly extended, and nothing dramatic is going to happen on any day, except, of course, the final Armageddon-type day when the organization suddenly goes out of business.

Boards of directors of conservative organizations are often among those elements of the organizations that take the lead in their conservatism. In these organizations, it is our experience that sometimes the staff is pressing the board, and the directors within the board, to take a more up-to-date or a more change-oriented view, and they are often rejected. If a board assessment reveals an opposition to change, then steps should immediately be taken to change this perspective. Unless one begins with an appreciation of change, the other specific changes that may be purposed will all fall by the wayside. Board leadership in setting expectations for innovation is a key step.

The *traditional organization* is the most common form of organization, and it is one that does not actively oppose change; but it does not actively promote innovation, either. It allows individuals within the organization who are interested in change and development to pursue and push ideas. These organizations eventually do change. The problem with them, however, is that the change process is essentially random. If the organization has within its ranks one or more individuals who will take upon themselves the cost—personal and social—of promoting change within the organization, it is fortunate. Many organizations have such change-oriented individuals within their structure, but these individuals are not willing to take the risks of actually pushing change. Readers will be all too aware of how, in the typical committee, a new idea is brought up to a chorus of "It won't work," "It can't work," "We tried that once and it was a failure." Only the most intrepid are going to pursue new ideas in the face of such a cacophony. Further, the ego strength required to sustain that kind of criticism is reasonably rare. Hence, what the organization requires for change to become an actual reality is great individual sacrifice on the part of those few members willing to take that risk. Unfortunately, in many organizations either the individuals are not present, or, if present, too frightened to speak up or just get "too weary" of promoting change. Hence, many of these agencies fall by the wayside and often are replaced by new organizations. Boards of directors need to protect and support the innovator, set up programs so that the innovator has some access to resources, and try to work in ways to help share with the innovator the costs of innovation. To the extent that this kind of posture can be established, the organization has moved into the entrepreneurial category.

The *entrepreneurial organization* is the one that makes change and innovation as an ongoing part of all of its daily activities. This attitude or philosophy penetrates the entire organization from the board of directors to professional and support staff. Innovation is supported at all levels—policy, program, and production.

In short, the organization stimulates innovation rather than receives it. It seeks to be proactive with respect to innovation rather than reactive. When a culture of innovation is present, the risk to any individual of suggesting any particular innovation is vastly lowered. This increases the rate of suggestions, and while any given suggestion may not work out, it may remain in a sort of innovation pool to be combined with other suggestions later. We all know that any one suggestion may not carry with it the total solution to a complex problem. Several pieces of a puzzle may need to be put together before an effective solution is reached. Yet if these pieces are not ventured, then it is unlikely that the puzzle will ever be finally put together. The board of directors in an entrepreneurial organization structures itself and helps to structure the agency so that support for these kinds of innovations can be present. With respect to its own activities, the board may try creative new approaches, different meeting styles, different meeting locations, different ways of processing information. Again, there is an attempt to model, at the board level and with support from the board level, innovative activities.

There are organizations, however, that in their rush to change have so many irons in the fire, so many kinds of developments going on at any one time, that it is more of a kaleidoscope of chaos than an organization. These organizations we call *overboard organizations*. The overboard organization is typified by the response one author got when asking an executive of such an organization, "What's really going on in your shop?" The executive replied, "Your guess is as good as mine." This executive had taken openness to such a point that there was almost no organization. No one knew anything, no one could give any permission for anything, no one could order anything—it was indeed chaotic. Innovation was stifled for an opposite reason than was true in the conservative organization. There, innovation underload was the problem. Here, innovation overload is the problem. The board of directors in the overboard organization often seeks to "let it all hang out," which, not infrequently, "it" does—to the disadvantage of everyone concerned. Leadership here involves emphasizing stability.

An overall perspective, then, suggests that directors in the not-for-profit sector (and in the profit sector) move their organization toward the entrepreneurial center. Conservative and traditional postures should be avoided. Overboard postures should be eschewed as well. One way to make this movement is through the strategic planning process.

It is imperative that organizations engage regularly in the strategic planning process, which helps the organization articulate where it's going and what it wants to do, how it can get there, and to delineate its goals while assessing the difficulties and environmental changes besetting the organization that need to be addressed. It is the role of boards, during board meetings, to take the proactive leadership responsibility for being sure that their organizations are continually moving to assess and review—"environmentally scan"—the world around them and making those proper adjustments.

When article after article talks about the problems in American corporations and not-for-profit enterprises during the latter part of the twentieth century, one wonders what the boards were doing while this decline was going on. Anyone who has sat through a board meeting has a pretty good idea of what was going on—highly orchestrated performances that were dominated by the executive staff (the top team of the organization) did not create an atmosphere of board vigor. It was the absence of this vigor that, in many ways, was the predisposing cause for organizational decline.

There are a variety of ways that boards can initiate the process of moving toward an entrepreneurial stance. The SWOT analysis is one of the best. It stands for assessment of organizational strengths and weaknesses (S and W) and reflects as well the threats and opportunities (T and O) with which the organization must deal.

This section is not the place to go into a detailed analysis of a strategic-planning exercise. That is available elsewhere in considerable detail (Tropman, 1991, for example). Suffice it to say there that a SWOT analysis is an essential tool for the making of high-quality decisions at the board level. All too often, the authors have received calls from boards inviting them to facilitate at a "board retreat." And, because of poor planning on the part of the board and executive, these calls come one to two weeks before the actual retreat. When questions about the kind of preparation and agenda development that has been done by the board in preparation for the retreat arise, the individuals making the request usually demur, indicating that this was just going to be "an informal get-together to explore problems." Having had our share of "informal get-togethers to explore problems," we usually try to discourage the board from continuing with its retreat plan until proper preparation has been undertaken. Get the information and people you need ahead of time, so that the meeting will be worthwhile. This is consistent with the Rule of Halves. Following that rule with respect to an annual retreat would suggest that a half year before the retreat is actually scheduled should be the time when potential agenda items for the retreat are assembled. That allows the executive staff, as well as any volunteers involved, a three-month data-gathering period during which a SWOT analysis or other relevant data can be collected, assembled, processed, analyzed, and put into a format—following the Rule of Reports, of course—that allows for a profitable discussion.

We can all recognize the unprofitable meeting, the unprofitable retreat, where time is spent wishing that data had been collected. Many, many, many meetings end with the promise and injunction to get data that should have been gathered ahead of time.

Boards' responsibilities, therefore, involve entrepreneurship and strategic direction of the organization. Without a constant influx of information, these responsibilities are unlikely to be met. Yet, unless the board meeting is set up to allow time for this information to be discussed, it's not going to do any good to have it. That's the purpose of the Rule of Sixths. The Rule of Sixths, it is recalled, suggests that one-sixth of the board agenda (or any meeting agenda) be devoted to "blue sky"-type items—new possibilities, new problems, new opportunities, new threats. The Rule of Sixths, in effect, makes the strategic planning process go on at *each* board meeting. The reason that this kind of "partialization" is important is that it allows people to explore new ideas—to move away from conservatism and traditionalism toward entrepreneurism in gradual steps, making them much more palatable. On the other hand, when it's in the overboard mode, a board needs structure. Specific discussion about specific and focused items introduces an element of needed discipline.

Overall, then, the board's responsibility for entrepreneurship and strategic planning occurs both on an annual basis (at a retreat, or other annual meeting event) and on an ongoing meeting basis. Both are needed. Both are crucial.

Conclusion

These responsibilities are perhaps greater and more extensive than any director had previously thought, and it is appropriate that for interpersonal organizations there be an expanded and enriched list of responsibilities. We have approached the matter of directorship too casually. As society moves toward increased reliance on the smaller organization at the community and state levels, and decreases confidence in and responsibility of bureaucracies and mega-bureaucracies, the performance of these organizations becomes a matter of public and social concern. It is not simply a matter of casual donating of "voluntary" time to good causes but now becomes central to the function of the organization, the community, and the society itself.

However, saying that responsibilities are present and providing ways in which these responsibilities can be usefully carried forward remain two different things. Certainly recognition is a first step. But directors, presidents, and executive directors need some assistance and guidance in setting up the kind of operating structure that is going to make the carrying through of these responsibilities a reality. This requirement brings us to a discussion of the meeting organization: making meetings more effective is the central way in which these responsibilities are, in fact, met.

EPILOGUE

While this revision adds new and important material to that in the first edition, it retains the essential thrust of our initial work, *viz.* that meetings are a crucial social form through which the country's business is accomplished—whether they be regular staff meetings, special advisory group meetings, informal ad hoc meetings, or board meetings. What doesn't happen in companies, government agencies, and social agencies often can be laid at the foot of faulty meetings. Decisions weren't taken. Information wasn't available, etc., etc. The list is virtually endless. But like most tools, committees and meetings are two-edged swords. They can be used to help, but they can also be used to harm. Like most tools, they need to be used properly in order to achieve maximum effectiveness. The purpose of both editions of this volume has been to provide some crucial insight needed by meeting goers, meeting chairs, and meeting observers to understand how meetings go wrong and what it is we can do to make them go better.

BIBLIOGRAPHY

Allen, Fleet D. *Advisory Committee Organization, Role and Utilization.* Ed.D. dissertation, North Carolina State University at Raleigh, 1971.

Altman, Stan. "Performance Monitoring Systems for Public Managers." *Public Administration Review* 39, 1 (Jan./Feb. 1979).

American Management Association. *Leadership in the Office.* New York: Haddon Craftsman, 1963.

American Management Association. *Top Management Committees.* New York: AMA, 1961.

Anderson, John. "What's Blocking Upward Communication?" In *Current Perspectives for Managing Organizations,* Bernard M. Baas and Samuel D. Deep. (Eds.). Englewood Cliffs, NJ: Prentice-Hall, 1970.

Angell, Donald L., and DeSau, George T. "Rare Discordant Verbal Roles and the Development of Group Problem-Solving Conditions." *Small Group Behavior* 5 (Feb. 1974): 45–55.

Argyris, Chris. "Individual Actualization in Complex Organizations." In *Organizations and Human Behavior: Focus on Schools,* Fred D. Carver and Thomas J. Sergiovanni (Eds.). New York: McGraw-Hill, 1969.

Argyris, Chris. *Reasoning, Learning, and Action: Individual and Organizational.* San Francisco: Jossey-Bass, 1982.

Armstrong, Thomas O. *Staff Department Services and Line Management.* New Wilmington, PA: Economics and Business Foundation, 1946–47.

Arvey, Richard D., and Neel, C. Warren. "Moderating Effects of Employee Expectancies on the Relationship between Leadership Consideration and Job Performance of Engineers." *Journal of Vocational Behavior* 4 (April 1974): 213–222.

Ash, Phillip. "The Many Functions of Discussion." *Supervisory Management* 16 (March 1971): 21–24.

Auerbach, Arnold J. "Aspirations of Power People and Agency Goals." *Social Work* 6 (Jan. 1961): 66–73.

Auger, B. Y. *How to Run More Effective Business Meetings.* New York: Grosset and Dunlap, 1964.

Baker, John C. *Directors and Their Functions.* Boston: Division of Research, Graduate School of Business Administration, Harvard University, 1945.

Baker, Robert (Ed.). *The Stress Analysis of A Strapless Evening Gown.* Englewood Cliffs, NJ: Prentice-Hall, 1982.

Bales, Robert F. "In Conference." *Harvard Business Review* 32 (March–April 1954): 44–50.

Bales, Robert F. *Interaction Process Analysis: A Method for the Study of Small Groups.* Reading, MA: Addison-Wesley, 1950.

Bennis, Warren G. "RX for Corporate Boards." *Technology Review,* 81, 3 (Dec./Jan. 1979): 12; 86.

Bennis, Warren G. "The Crisis of Corporate Boards." *Technology Review,* 81, 2 (November 1978): 11–12.

Bernard, C. *The Functions of the Executive.* Cambridge, MA: Harvard University Press, 1968.

Berry, Waldron. "Beyond Strategic Planning." *Managerial Planning* 29, 5 (March/ April 1981).

The Board of Directors: New Challenges, New Directions. Conference Report No. 547. New York: The Conference Board, 1972.

Boyce, M. W. "Management by Committee." *Personnel Practice Bulletin* 20 (June 1964): 47–51.

Bradford, Leland P. "A Dozen Reasons Some Meetings Bomb—And Others Work Wonders." *Training and Human Resource Development* (May 1978).

Brenner, Sten O., and Hjelmquist, Erland. "Verbal Interaction in Small Groups Related to Personality: A Presentation of the VEGA Project." *Göteborg Psychological Reports* (University of Göteborg, Sweden) 3, 7 (1973).

Bureaucrat X. *Cover Your Ass: or How to Survive in a Government Bureaucracy.* Edmonton: Hurtig Publishers, 1977.

Capen, Julia, and Huckins, M. Esther. *Suggestions for Training Courses for Board and Committee Members.* New York: The Woman's Press, 1935.

Carroll, Daniel T. "Boards, and Managements: Ten Challenges and Responses from the Board Room." *Harvard Business Review* 59, 5 (Sept./Oct. 1981): 60–66.

Cohen, Michael D., and March, James G. *Leadership and Ambiguity: The American College President.* New York: McGraw-Hill, 1974.

Cohen, Michael D.; March, James G.; and Olsen, Johan P. "A Garbage Can Model of Organizational Choice." *Administrative Science Quarterly* 17, 1 (March 1972): 1–25.

Cohn, Martin M. "The Role of Research in Federation and Agency Planning: A Critical Analysis." *Journal of Jewish Communal Service* 42 (Fall 1965): 82–91.

Collins, B., and Guetzkow, H. *A Social Psychology of Group Processes for Decision Making.* New York: Wiley, 1964.

Colton, Olive A. "The Responsibility of the Board to the Community." *Public Health Nursing* 26 (April 1934): 181–186.

Cooke, Edward F. "Research: An Instrument of Political Power." *Political Science Quarterly* 76 (March 1961): 69–87.

Cooley, Charles H. *Social Organization.* New York: Scribner's, 1920.

Coon, Horace. *How to Be a Better Member.* New York: New American Library, 1956.

Cox, Fred M.; Erlich, John; Rothman, Jack; and Tropman, John E. (Eds.). *Strategies of Community Organization.* 3rd ed. Itasca: Peacock, 1979.

Cox, Fred M.; Erlich, John; Rothman, Jack; and Tropman, John E. (Eds.). *Tactics and Techniques of Community Practice.* 2nd ed. Itasca: Peacock, 1984.

Daft, Richard L., and Bradshaw, Patricia J. "The Process of Horizontal Differentiation: Two Models." *Administrative Science Quarterly* 25, 3 (Sept. 1980): 441–456.

Dale, Ernest. *Management: Theory and Practice.* 3rd ed. New York: McGraw-Hill, 1978.

Dale, Ernest, and Urwick, Lyndall. *Staff in Organization.* New York: McGraw-Hill, 1960.

Davis, Evelyn K. "Board and Staff Relationships." *Public Health Nursing* 29 (Aug. 1937): 466–471.

Davis, Keith. *Human Relations in Business.* New York: McGraw-Hill, 1957.

Davis, Michael M. "Ten Duties of Board Members." *American Journal of Nursing* 29 (June 1929): 644.

Dean, Alan L. "Advantages and Disadvantages in the Use of Ad Hoc Commissions for Policy Formulation." Paper presented at the 47th Annual Meeting of the American Political Science Association, Sept. 6, 1951, at San Francisco. Mimeographed.

Dearborn, DeWitt, and Simon, Herbert. "Selective Perception: A Note on the Departmental Identifications of Executives." *Sociometry* 21, 2 (1958): 140–144.

Dolliver, Barbara. *The Intelligent Woman's Guide to Successful Organization and Club Work.* Philadelphia, PA: Chilton, 1962.

Donahue, Harold W. *How to Manage Your Meeting.* Indianapolis, IN: Droke House, 1955.

Doyle, Michael, and Strauss, David. *How to Make Meetings Work.* New York: Jove Publications, 1977.

Drucker, Peter F. *Management: Tasks, Practices, Responsibilities.* New York: Harper and Row, 1974.

Drucker, Peter F. "Deadly Sins in Public Administration." *Public Administration Review* 40, 2 (March/April 1980): 103–106.

Drucker, Peter F. "Managing the Public Service Institution." *Public Interest* 33 (Fall 1973): 43–60.

Drucker, Peter F. *Practice of Management.* New York: Harper and Bros., 1954.

Dunham, Arthur. "The Modern Board Member." *Public Health Nursing* 29 (Nov. 1937): 629–633.

Dunsing, Richard J. *You and I Have Got to Stop Meeting This Way.* New York: American Management Association-Amacom, 1978.

Edson, Jean B. "How to Survive on a Committee." *Social Work* 22 (May 1977): 224–226.

Fenn, Dan H., Jr., "Executives as Community Volunteers." *Harvard Business Review* 49, 2 (March/April 1971): 4–19; 156–157.

Fiedler, F. E., et al."Organizational Stress and the Use and Misuse of Managerial Intelligence and Experience." Bibl., *Journal of Applied Psychology* 64, 6 (Dec. 1979): 635–647.

Filho, Paulo de Vasconcellos. "Strategic Planning: A New Approach." *Managerial Planning* 30, 5 (March/April 1982).

Ford, Charles H. "Management by Decisions, Not by Objectives." *Business Horizons* 23, 1 (Feb. 1980).

Ford, Charles H. "MBO: An Idea Whose Time Has Gone?" *Business Horizons,* 22, 6 (Dec. 1979).

Forester, J. "Critical Theory and Planning Practice." Bibl., *American Planning Association Journal* 46, 3 (July 1980): 275–286.

Fowler, Glenn. "Community Board Wrap-up." *New York Affairs* 6, 1 (1980).

Fowler, Phyllis A. *The Committee as an Interacting Small Group.* Dissertation, Wayne State University, 1972.

Freeman, Linton C.; Fararo, Thomas J.; Bloomberg, Warner, Jr.; and Sunshine, Morris H. "Locating Leaders in Local Communities: A Comparison of Some Alternative Approaches." *American Sociological Review* 28 (Oct. 1963): 791–798.

Frohman, Alan L., and Ober, Stephen P. "Establishing Leadership: How to Analyze and Deal with the Basic Issues." *Management Review* 69, 4 (April 1980): 46–50.

Giermak, Edwin A. "Individualism vs. the Committee Process." *Advanced Management* 25, 12 (Dec. 1960): 16–19.

Glass, Joseph G. *How to Plan Meetings and Be a Successful Chairman.* New York: Merlin Press, 1951.

Goffman, E. *The Presentation of Self in Everyday Life.* New York: Doubleday, 1959.

Greenleaf, Robert K. *The Institution as Servant.* Cambridge, MA: Center for Applied Studies, 1972, 1976.

Greenleaf, Robert K. *Servant-Retrospect and Prospect.* Cambridge, MA: Center for Applied Studies, 1980.

Greenleaf, Robert K. *Trustees as Servants.* Cambridge, MA: Center for Applied Studies, 1974, 1975.

Greenleaf, Robert K. *The Servant as Leader.* Cambridge, MA: Center for Applied Studies, 1970, 1973.

Griffiths, Daniel E. "Administration as Decision-Making." In *Organizations and Human Behavior: Focus on Schools,* Fred D. Carver and Thomas J. Sergiovanni (Eds.). New York: McGraw-Hill, 1969.

Groobey, John. "Making the Board of Directors More Effective." *California Management Review* 16, 3 (Spring 1974).

Gummer, Burton. "A Framework for Curriculum Planning in Social Welfare Administration." *Administration in Social Work* 3, 4 (Winter 1979): 385–395.

Haft, Robert. "Business Decisions by the New Board: Behavioral Science and Corporate Law." *Michigan Law Review* 80, 1 (Nov. 1981): 1–67.

Haga, W. J. "Managerial Professionalism: Reply to Lorant" *American Journal of Economics and Sociology* 39, 4 (Oct. 1976): 420–421.

Hall, Jay. "Decisions, Decisions, Decisions!" *Psychology Today* 5, 6 (Nov. 1971): 51–58.

Hamby, Russel. "Gender and Sex-Role Behavior in Problem Solving Groups." *Sociological Focus* 11, 3 (Aug. 1978).

Handbook for Legislative Committees. The Council of State Governments, Chicago, IL (Jan. 1963).

Harari, Ehud. "Japanese Politics of Advice in Comparative Perspective." *Public Policy* 22, 4 (Fall 1984).

Harper, Ernest B., and Dunham, Arthur. *Community Organization in Action.* New York: Association Press, 1959.

Hartogs, Nelly, and Weber, Joseph. *Boards of Directors.* Dobbs Ferry, NY: Oceana Publications, 1974.

Heffernan, W. Joseph, Jr. "Political Activity and Social Work Executives." *Social Work* 9 (April 1964): 18–23.

Hegarty, Edward J. *How to Run a Meeting.* New York: McGraw-Hill, 1952.

Herbert, W. R. "Effective Time Management." *Public Management* 61 (Jan. 1979): 9–10.

Herman, Edward. "Greening of the Board of Directors?" *Quarterly Review of Economics and Business* 12 (Autumn 1972): 7–93; and *Social Policy* 3 (Nov./Dec. 1972 and Jan./Feb. 1973): 56–63.

Hewett, Thomas T.; O'Brien, Gordon E.; and Hornik, John. "The Effects of Work Organization, Leadership Style, and Member Compatibility upon the Productivity of Small Groups Working on a Manipulative Task." *Organizational Behavior and Human Performance* 11 (April 1974): 283–301.

Hilkert, Robert H. "The Board Member—Opportunity for Service." *Child Welfare* 44 (March 1965): 156–163.

Holloman, Charles R., and Hendrick, Hal W. "Adequacy of Group Decisions as a Function of the Decision-Making Process." *Academy of Management Journal* 15, 2 (June 1972): 175–184.

Homans, George C. *The Human Group.* New York: Harcourt, Brace, 1950.

Houle, Cyril O. *The Effective Board.* New York: Association Press, 1960.

Hunt, Edward E. *Conferences, Committees, Conventions, and How to Run Them.* New York: Harper and Bros., 1925.

Hurd, Baruch. "The Audit Committee: A Guide for Director." *Harvard Business Review* (May–June 1980): 174–186.

Huseman, Richard C., et al. "Planning for Organizational Change: The Role of Communication." *Managerial Planning* 28, 6 (May/June 1980).

Ingalls, John D. *A Trainer's Guide to Androgyny.* Rev. ed. Washington, DC: U.S. Department of Health, Education and Welfare, 1973.

Janis, Irving L. "Groupthink." *Psychology Today* 5, 6 (Nov. 1971): 43–46.

Janis, Irving, and Mann, Leon. *Decision Making: A Psychological Analysis of Conflict, Choice and Commitment.* New York: Free Press, 1977.

Jay, A. "How to Run a Meeting." In *Tactics and Techniques of Community Practice,* Cox, F. et al. (Eds.). Itasca, IL: Peacock, 1977.

Jones, C. "'If I Knew Then . . .' (A Personal Essay on Committees and Public Policy)." *Policy Analysis* 5, 4 (Fall 1979): 473–480.

Juran, J. M., and Louden, J. Keith. *The Corporate Director.* New York: American Management Association, 1966.

Kahalas, Harvey. "A Look at Major Planning Methods: Development, Kantor, R. *Men and Women of the Corporation.* New York: Basic Books, 1977.

Kaufman, Debra, and Fetter, Michael. "Work Motivation and Job Values among Professional Men and Women: A New Accounting." *Journal of Vocational Behavior* 17, 3 (Dec. 1980).

Keith-Lucas, Alan. "The Political Theory Implicit in Social Casework Theory." *American Political Science Review* 471 (Dec. 1953): 1076–91.

Kent, Glenn H. "Team Management of Pension Money." *Harvard Business Review* 57, 3 (May/June 1979): 162–167.

Kernberg, O. F. "Regression in Organizational Leadership." *Psychiatry* 42, 1 (Feb. 1979): 24–39.

King, Clarence. *Social Agency Boards and How to Make Them Effective.* New York: Harper and Bros., 1938.

Klein, Harold E., and Newman, William H. "How to Integrate New Environmental Forces into Strategic Planning." *Managerial Review* 69, 7 (July 1980).

Klopfer, Frederick J. *Decision Rules and Decision Consequences in Group Decision Making.* Dissertation, Texas Tech University, 1975.

Koontz, Harold. *The Board of Directors and Effective Management.* New York: McGraw-Hill, 1967.

Kotter, J.; Schlesinger, L.; and Sathe, V. *Organization.* 2nd ed. Homewood, IL: Irwin, 1986.

Leavitt, Harold J. *Managerial Psychology* 3rd ed. Chicago: University of Chicago Press, 1972.

Lees, John D. *The Committee System of the United States Congress.* London: Routledge and Kegan Paul, 1967.

Levinson, Daniel, and Klerman, Gerald L. "The Clinician Executive." *Psychiatry* 30, 1 (Feb. 1967): 3–15.

Levy, Leslie. "Reforming Board Reform." *Harvard Business Review* 59, 1 (Jan./Feb. 1981): 166–172.

Likert, Rensis, and Likert, Jane Gibson. "A Method for Coping with Conflict in Problem-Solving Groups." *Group and Organizational Studies* 3, 4 (Dec. 1978).

Lindblom, C. E. "The Science of Muddling Through." *Public Administration Review* 19, 2 (Spring 1959).

Lohmann, Melvin R. *Top Management Committees, Their Functions and Authority.* New York: American Management Association, 1961.

Long, Fern. *All About Meetings: A Practical Guide.* Dobbs Ferry, NY: Oceana Publications, 1967.

Mace, Myles L. *The Board of Directors in Small Corporations.* Boston, MA: Division of Business Administration, Research, Graduate School of Harvard University, 1948.

Mace, Myles L. *Directors: Myth and Reality.* Boston, MA: Division of Business Administration Research, Graduate School, Harvard University, 1971.

Machlowitz, Marilyn. *Workaholics.* New York: Mentor, 1980.

Maeroff, Gene L. "Trustee Choice: Reform Urged." *New York Times* (March 11, 1980).

Maier, Norman R. F. *Problem Solving and Creativity in Individuals and Groups.* Belmont, CA: Brooks/Cole, 1970.

March, James G., and Simon, Herbert A. *Organizations.* New York: Wiley, 1958.

Mazzolini, Renato. "How Strategic Decisions Are Made." *Long-Range Planning* 14, 3 (1981).

McCarthy, Gary, Personal Communication, 1989.

McLean, Francis. *The Family Society: Joint Responsibilities of Board, Staff and Membership.* New York: American Association for Organizing Family Social Work, 1927.

Messeha, Refaat Fayek. *A Critical Analysis of the Board of Directors: Selection, Election, Structure, Performance, and Compensation.* Dissertation, University of Wisconsin, 1966.

Michael, Stephen R. "Feedforward Versus Feedback Controls in Planning." *Managerial Planning* 29, 4 (Nov./Dec. 1980).

Mileti, Dennis, et al. "Structure and Decision Making in Corporate Organizations." Bibl., *Sociology and Social Research* 63, 4 (July 1979): 723–744.

Moore, Joan W. "Patterns of Women's Participation in Voluntary Associations." *American Journal of Sociology* 66, 6 (May 1961): 592–598.

Moore, Mark H. "Policy Managers Need Policy Analysis." *Journal of Policy Analysis and Management* 1, 3 (Spring 1982): 413–418.

Morris, Seymour, Jr. "Managing Corporate External Affairs." *Management Review* 69, 3 (March 1980).

Mueller, C. R., Jr., and Mueller, S. "How to Find Out Everything You Wanted to Know About Your Organization But Were Afraid to Ask." *Corrections Today* (March 1980).

Muller, Robert K. *Board Life: Realities of Being a Corporate Director.* New York: AMACON, 1974.

Naisbett, John. *Megatrends: Ten New Directions Transforming Our Lives.* New York: Warner Books, 1982.

National Information Bureau. "The Volunteer Board Member in Philanthropy." New York: National Information Bureau, 1979.

National Organization for Public Health Nursing. *Manual for Board and Committee Members of Public Health Nursing.* 2nd ed. New York: Macmillan, 1937.

Naylor, Thomas H. "How to Integrate Strategic Planning into your Management Process." *Long-Range -Planning* 14, 5 (1981).

Naylor, Thomas H., and Neva, Kristin N. "Design of a Strategic Planning Process." *Managerial Planning* 28, 4 (Jan./Feb. 1980).

North, Joan. "Guidelines and Strategies for Conducting Meetings." *POD Quarterly* 2, 2 (Sept. 1980).

Ouchi, William. *Theory Z: How American Business Can Meet the Japanese Challenge.* New York: Avon, 1982.

Parsons, Talcott. "Suggestions for a Sociological Approach to the Theory of Organizations." In *Complex Organizations: A Sociological Reader,* Amitai Etzioni (Ed.). New York: Holt, Rinehart and Winston, 1961.

Pascale, R. T., and Athos, A. *The Art of Japanese Management: Application for American Executives.* New York: Simon & Schuster, 1981.

Peter, Laurence J., and Hull, Raymond. *The Peter Principle: Why Things Always Go Wrong.* New York: William Morrow, 1969.

Peter, Laurence J. *The Peter Prescription.* New York: Bantam, 1973.

Pogrebin, Letty C. *How to Make It in a Man's World*. Garden City, NY: Doubleday, 1970.

Price, James L. "The Impact of Governing Boards on Organizational Effectiveness and Morale." *Administrative Science Quarterly* 8, 3 (Dec. 1963): 361–378.

Prince, George M. "How to Be a Better Meeting Chairman." *Harvard Business Review* 47, 1 (Jan./Feb. 1969): 98–108.

Purham, John C. "Non-Profit Boards under Fire." *Dun's Review* 114, 4 (Oct. 1979).

Quick, Thomas L. "The Many Uses of a Task Force." *Personnel* 51, 1 (Jan. 1974): 53–61.

Reeser, Clayton. "Tactical Planning." *Managerial Review* (Nov./Dec. 1981).

Rice, George H. "But How Do Managers Make Decisions?" Chart, *Management Decision* 18, 4 (1980).

Riedel, J. A. "Citizen Participation: Myths and Realities." *Public Administration Review* 32, 3 (May/June 1972): 211–219.

Rittel, Horst W. J., and Webber, Melvin M. "Dilemmas in a General Theory of Planning." *Policy Sciences* 4, 2 (June 1973): 155–169.

Ross, Aileen D. "Control and Leadership in Women's Groups: An Analysis of Philanthropic Money-Raising Activity." *Social Forces* 37, 2 (Dec. 1958): 124–131.

Ross, Aileen D. "Philanthropic Activity and the Business Career." In *Social Welfare Institutions,* Mayer Zald (Ed.), New York: Wiley, 1965.

"Run a Meeting That Gets Things Done." *Changing Times* 23 (Sept. 1969).

Schmidt, Richard. *The Relationship Between Inside-Outside Representation on Boards of Directors and Selected Measures of Economic Performance, Financial Structure, and Business Policy*. Dissertation, New York University, Graduate School of Business Administration, 1974.

Schwartz, Felice N. " 'Invisible' Resource: Women for Boards." *Harvard Business Review* 58, 2 (March/April 1980): 6–18.

Selznick, Philip. *Leadership in Administration: A Sociological Interpretation*. New York: Harper and Row, 1957.

Senor, James M. "Another Look at the Executive-Board Relationship." In *Social Welfare Institutions,* Mayer Zald (Ed.), New York: Wiley, 1965.

Seward, Jack. *The Japanese*. New York: William Morrow, 1972.

Simon, Herbert A. *The New Science of Management Decision*. Rev. ed. New York: Harper and Bros., 1977.

Simon, Herbert A.; Smithburg, David W.; and Thompson, Victor A. *Public Administration*. New York: Knopf, 1950.

Simpson, E. H. *The Mechanics of Committee Work. An Essay on the Tasks of a Committee Secretary*. Brussels: International Institute of Administrative Sciences for the United Nations, 1952.

Singer, G., and M. Wallace. *The Administrative Waltz or Ten Commandments for the Administrator*. Oxford: Pergamon Press, 1976.

Snadowsky, Alvin. "Member Satisfaction in Stable Communication Networks." *Sociometry* 37 (March 1974): 38–53.

Sorensen, Roy. *The Art of Board Membership*. New York: Association Press, 1950.

Stenzel, Anne K., and Feeney, Helen M. *Volunteer Training and Development: A Manual for Community Groups.* New York: Seabury Press, 1968.

Stern, Alfred R. "Instilling Activism in Trustees." *Harvard Business Review* 58, 1 (Jan./Feb. 1980): 24–32.

Strauss, Bertram W., and Frances. *New Ways to Better Meetings.* Rev. ed. New York: Viking Press, 1964.

Thelan, Herbert A. *Dynamics of Groups at Work.* Chicago: University of Chicago Press, 1963.

Thierauf, Robert J. *User-oriented Decision Support Systems: Accent on Problem Finding.* Englewood Cliffs, NJ: Prentice-Hall, 1988.

Thomson, William. "Eliciting Production Possibilities from a Well-Informed Manager." *Journal of Economic Theory* 20 (June 1979).

Tillman, R., Jr. "Problems in Review: Committees on Trial." *Harvard Business Review* 38, 3 (May-June 1960): 6–12; 162–173.

Tocqueville, Alexis de. *Democracy in America.* New York: Harper and Row, 1966.

Tropman, John E. *A Comparative Analysis of Welfare Councils.* Ph.D. dissertation, University of Michigan, 1967.

Tropman, John E. "The Effective Committee Chair: A Primer." *Directors and Boards.* (Summer 1980).

Tropman, John E. *Effective Meetings: Improving Group Decision-Making.* Beverly hills, CA: Sage Publications, 1980.

Tropman, John E. *The Board of Directors.* Vermont Youth Services Institute, 1981.

Tropman, John E. *Meetings; How to Make Them Work for You.* New York, NY: Van Nostrand Reinhold, 1985.

Tropman, John E. *Development and Direction for Boards of Directors.* Toronto: Canadian Center for Philanthropy, 1991, 88ff.

Tropman, John E., Dluhy, Milan; Lind, Roger; and Vasey, Wayne (Eds.). *Strategic Perspectives on Social Policy.* New York: Pergamon, 1976.

Tropman, John E.; Johnson, Harold R.; and Tropman, Elmer J. *The Essentials of Committee Management.* Chicago: Nelson-Hall, 1979.

Utterback, William E. *Committees and Conferences—How to Lead Them.* New York: Rinehart, 1950.

Veatch, Jeannette. "Learning, Training and Education." *Young Children* 29 (Jan. 1974): 83–88.

Vogel, Ezra. *Japan as Number One: Lessons for America.* Cambridge, MA: Harvard University Press, 1980.

Vroom, Victor H., and Yetton, Phillip W. *Leadership and Decision-Making.* Pittsburgh, PA: University of Pittsburgh Press, 1976.

Wagner, Russell H., and Arnold, Carroll C. *Handbook of Group Discussion.* Boston, MA: Houghton Mifflin, 1965.

Weschler, Irving R. *Issues in Human Relations Training.* Washington, DC: National Training Laboratories, National Education Association, 1962.

Willie, Charles V. "Community Leadership in the Voluntary Health and Welfare System." In *Applied Sociology,* Alvin W. Gouldner and Seymour M. Miller (Eds.). New York: Free Press, 1965.

Wills, Garry. *The Kennedy Imprisonment: A Meditation on Power.* New York: Atlantic Monthly Books, 1982.

Yarborough, Joanne. *Women in Management: Selected Recent References.* Washington, DC: U.S. Dept. of Labor Library, U.S. Government Printing Office, 1978.

Zald, Mayer, and Denton, Patricia. "From Evangelism to General Service: The Transformation of the Y.M.C.A." *Administrative Science Quarterly* 8 (Sept. 1963): 214–234.

Zander, Alvin. *Making Groups Effective.* San Francisco, CA: Jossey-Bass, 1982.

Zelman, William. "Liability for Social Agency Boards." *Social Work* 22, 4 (1977): 270–274.

Ziller, Robert C. "Four Techniques of Group Decision Making under Uncertainty." *Journal of Applied Psychology* 41, 6 (Dec. 1957).

Zimbalist, Sidney E. "Welfare Planning Research: Master or Servant"? *Social Work* 2 (July 1957): 41–44.

Index

Accountability, 8, 179–83, 194, 216–18
  and the chairperson, 13
  and constituency, 13
  and private bodies, 175
Action hypothesis, 267
Administration, 9, 49. *See also* Task force
Advisory committee, 275
Affirmative action, 204–9
Agenda, 9, 23, 35, 56, 100–101, 225
  agenda bell, 235–39
  arrangement of items on, 78–79, 230, 236–39
  and daily schedule, 80
  following, 57–58
  of general advisory committee, 129
  hidden, 7, 200
  integrity, 249–50
  items for discussion only, 80, 238
  material for, 81
  number of items on, 78, 236–39
  preparation of, 77–80, 236–39
  rule of the, 241–42
  sample, 242
  using the clock, 79, 239

Analysis, 36–37, 96
Annual report, 69
Appraisal, 257–58
Assessment, 257
Attendance, 53, 55–57
Authority
  chair person, 166
  formal, 119
  legal, 119
  of policy-implementing committee, 142–43

Banfield, E., 126
Board of directors, 41–51, 149–50, 271–84
  accommodations for meeting, 47
  authority of, 119, 273–74
  changing membership, 50–51
  and decision making, 276
  development of, 45–46, 278
  education of, 45–46
  entrepreneurship, 279–84
  external vs. internal roles, 276–77
  infrastructure, 45
  as legal corporation, 273–74
  on letterhead, 47

Board of directors (*continued*)
  and mission of agency, 45
  and policy-overseeing committee,
      157–58
  reimbursements, 47
  relationship with executive, 44–45,
      47–48
    hiring, 278–79
  relationship with staff person, 47–
      48
  role appropriateness, 276–77
  sensitivities of, 46–47
  strategic planning, 279–84
  as trustees of civic purpose, 274–75
Brookings Institution, 127

Chairperson, 5–15
  accepting position, 5–8
  accountability, 13
  active posture, 89
  as administrator, 9
  appointment, 13
  appointment by high vote getter, 12
  authority, 166
  boss model, 166
  committee election, 12
  constituency, 12
  coordinator model, 166
  duties, 8–11
  inadequate, 30–31
  and leadership, 8–9
  legal appointment, 11
  and mandate, 6
  mediator model, 166
  as meeting presider, 9–10
  and meetings, 85–86
  and membership, 6–7, 91
  neutrality of, 88
  opposition to, 12
  and participation, 87
  partisan problems, 12
  and policy advisory committee,
      131–32
  and policy-coordinating committee,
      137
  and policy-deciding committee,
      152, 153

  and policy-implementing commit-
      tee, 145–46
  and policy-overseeing committee,
      159–60
  and policy-sharing committee, 124
  relationship with officers, 19–20
  relationship with staff person, 37,
      93
  as representative, 10–11
  roles, 8–11
    role flexibility, 14
  rules of the game, 101–2
  selection, 5, 11–13
  seniority appointment, 11–12
  style, 99
  and task force, 165–66
  and time assessment, 7–8
Change
  costs of, 214
  through advocacy, 141
  through community organization,
      141
  through education, 141
  through negotiation, 141
Charge, 100, 103–4
Chief executive. *See* Executive
Clearing process, 49–50
Committee. *See also* Committee pro-
      cess
  auspice, 173–78
  broad vs. narrow focus, 189–90
  composition, 199
  constraints, 104–5, 110
  difference of view, 199
  elected vs. appointed, 170, 179–
      83
  geographical domain, 185–89
  horizontal vs. vertical, 170, 185
  mechanics, 35
  mission, 13
  objectives, 105
  preparation, 77–84
  progress of, 110
  public vs. private, 170, 173–78
  reputation, 14
  role of, 13
  scope of, 170, 184–91

selection, 189
types of, 117–20. *See also specific
    types*
interorganizational vs. intraorgan-
    izational, 118–19
policy-related, 118, 120. *See also*
    Policy issues
Committee election, for chairperson,
    12
Committee etiquette, book of, 2
Committee for Economic Develop-
    ment, 127
Committee member, 21–31. *See also*
    Committee member, new
accepting position, 21–22
and chairperson, 6–7
and committee process, 24–25, 89–
    92
conferences among, 83
discretion, 26–28
divided loyalties of new members,
    207–8
duties, 21–28
meeting preparation, 22–23, 89
at meetings, 89–92
participation, 21, 23–35, 89–92
personality vs. committee process,
    21
and policy advisory committee, 132
and policy-coordinating committee,
    138
and policy-deciding committee, 153
and policy-implementing commit-
    tee, 146
and policy-overseeing committee,
    160
and policy-sharing committee, 124
posturing, 180
and procedures, 103
providing feedback, 26, 92
public positions, 180
reading background material, 22
representation, 28–29
responsibility, 26–28
roles, 21–28, 30
    role confusion, 29–30
scheduling time, 22

special assignments, 25–26
submitting written comments, 22
task force, 166–67
Committee member, new
locating new members, 205–6
suspicion of new members, 207
training new members, 206–7
Committee on Congressional Over-
    sight, 156
Committee process, 24–25
balancing formality and informality,
    102
dynamics of, 73–116, 95
evaluation, 215–16, 253–60
events in time, 74, 250–52
and information, 36–37
mechanics of, 53–71, 95
rules of, 221–34, 240–48
staff person's support, 35–36
Committee tone, 8
Common Cause, 177
Communication, 111–12
and national committees, 189
Community calendar, 56–57
Community power, 144
Compromise, 90, 143
COMSAT, 173
Conferences, 82–84, 106
among members, 83
among nonmembers, 83
among staff persons, 83–84
and policy-deciding committee,
    152
report conference, 115
Consensus, 264
Conservative organization, 280–81
Constituency, 170, 179–83
and accountability, 13
of chairperson, 12
and committee member, 29
future, 198
past, 198
present, 198
Consultants, 112–13
Cooptation, 200
Coordinating committees, 119, 120,
    134–39

Crisis, 24, 43, 162–63
Cuban missile crisis, 24

Data collection, 36–37, 96
Decision audit, 259
Decision autopsy, 259–60
Decision crystallization, 261–69
Decision making, 24–25, 87–88,
    261–69
  action hypothesis, 267
  and board of directors, 276
  and compromise, 90
  decision audit, 259
  decision autopsy, 259–60
  discussion refocus, 267–68
  facilitator, 266
  happiness criterion, 213
  and information, 219–20
  policy advisory committee, 131
  policy-coordinating committee,
    137
  policy-deciding committee, 151–
    53
  policy-implementing committee,
    144–45
  policy-overseeing committee,
    158–59
  policy-sharing committee, 123–24
  quality of, 211–14, 227
  rules for, 263–65
  sculpting, 268
  summative reflection, 266
  task force, 165, 166
  those affected by decision, 200
  vs. agreement, 90
Decompression, 165
Delegating responsibility, 19
Discrimination, 207
Discussion, 86, 267–68. See also Par-
    ticipation
  refocus, 267–68
Distributing the packet. See Prepara-
    tion
Dominance, structure of, 2

Effectiveness, 214, 219–34. See also
    Committee process

Efficiency, 219–34. See also Agenda;
    Committee process
Entrepreneurial organization, 281–
    82
Entrepreneurship, 279–84
Evaluation, 194, 215–16, 253–60
  appraisal, 257–58
  assessment, 257
  monitoring, 256–57
  oversight, 257
  process aspects, 258–59
  specification, 256
  task aspects, 258–59
Executive, 41–51, 163–64
  balancing staff and board of direc-
    tors, 50
  duties, 41–48
  hiring, 278–79
  issues, 48–51
  and policy-deciding committee,
    152
  policy leadership, 42–43
  as professional, 42
  recommendations of, 44
  relationship with board of direc-
    tors, 44–45, 47–48, 278–
    79
  relationship with staff person, 47–
    48
  roles, 41–48
Executive committee, 158
Executive director, 39. See also Exec-
    utive
Executive secretary, 39. See also Exec-
    utive
Executive summary technique, 244–
    45
Expertise rule, 265
Experts. See Consultants
Extensive decision rule, 264
External relations, 10, 160, 276–77

Facilitator, 9
Fact finding, 36–37
Feedback, 26
Finance committee, 158
Financial reports, 23

Follow-through. *See* Postmeeting activity
Fraction rules, 228–34

Gardner, John, 177
Goffman, Erving, 3, 222
Graphics
  format, 67
  organization, 67–68
  type, 67
Group dynamics, 36

Hand outs, 63
Hidden agenda. *See* Agenda

Identification tags, 59
Implementation rule, 264–65
Implementing committees, 119,
  140–48
Individual responsibility, 218
Information, and the committee process, 36–37
Integrity rules, 249–54
Interorganizational considerations,
  105–8, 118–19, 200
  following another committee, 107
  preceding another committee, 107
  working with organizations, 107–
  8
  working with other committees,
  106
Intraorganizational considerations,
  118–19, 150
Introductions, 59, 99
Involvement rule, 264
Issue conceptualization, 8. *See also*
  Policy issues
Issue resolution, 24. *See also* Policy
  issues

Joint task force, 106

Kennedy
  John F., 24
  Robert F., 24–25
Khrushchev, Nikita, 24

Leadership, 8–9, 85
Leaks, 33
Letterhead, 47
Local committee, 185–86
Loyalty
  of committee member, 26–28
  of staff person, 33–34

Mandate, 6
Media, 10
Meetings. *See also* Committee; Committee process;
  Participation; Preparation
  background materials, 23, 81–82,
    100–101, 240
  and chairperson, 85–86
  fraction rules, 228–34
  initial, 74, 98–109
  location, 53, 164, 208
  and members, 89–92
  postmeeting activity, 97, 114–15
  principles of efficiency, 221–27,
    228–34
  scheduling, 56–57, 99–100, 101,
    164–65, 208
  setting, 53, 61–64, 208
  and staff person, 92–97
  vs. social gathering, 59
  writing rules, 240–48
Megatrends: Ten New Directions Transforming Our Lives
  (Naisbett), 271
Membership of committee. *See* Committee member
Memos, 22, 37
  options memo technique, 246–48
Minutes. *See* Record keeping
  rule of, 242–44
Mission, 13, 33, 45–46, 100
Monitoring, 256–57

Nader, Ralph, 177
Naisbett, John, 271
Name placecards, 59
National Advisory Commission Report on Civil Disorders, 126

National committee, 188–89
Networks, 205–6
Neutrality, of chairperson, 88
"No More Reports" principle, 225–26
"No New Business" principle, 224–25
Notices, 55
    two-media rule of contact, 56

Officers, 16–20. *See also specific office*
    acceptance of the officership, 17
    duties, 16–17
    purpose of the corps, 19
    relationship with chairperson, 19–20
    roles, 16–17
Old boys networks, 205–6
Options memo technique, 246–48
Orchestra principle, 223
Organizational contexts, 169–91. *See also* Committee
Orientation, 99, 123, 206
Overboard organization, 282–83
Oversight, 257, 277. *See also* Policy-overseeing committee

Packet. *See* Meetings, background material; Training package
Parliamentarian, 102
Parliamentary rules, 102. *See also Robert's Rules of Order*
Participation, 23–25, 86–87, 89–90
    appropriate, 21, 23–24, 250–52
    facilitating, 113–14
    level of, 23
    limiting, 113–14
    quality of, 54
    restricted, 94
    self-appraisal, 24
    of special groups, 193–94, 204–9
    of staff person, 38–39
    symmetry, 205
    of the underrepresented, 193–94, 204–9
Partisan problems, of chairperson, 12

Passive resistance, 26
Personality vs. committee process, 21
Personalized folders, 59
Personnel committee, 158
Planning rules. *See* Fraction rules
Policy-administering committee. *See* Task force
Policy advisory committee, 126–33
    decision making, 131
    general policy, 129–30
    specific issue, 128–29
    technical advice, 130–31
Policy-coordinating committee, 134–39
    basis for plan, 137
    decision making, 137
    issues of cost, 136
Policy-deciding committee, 149–54
    appointments, 152
    budget, 153
    decision making, 151–53
    information vs. action, 150
    mission, 152
    policy vs. administration, 150
    resource issue, 151
    yearly conference, 152
Policy-implementing committee, 140–48
    authority of, 142–43
    and change, 141
    compromise, 143
    cooperative, 142
    decision making, 144–45
    factions, 143
    mission, 143
    partisan, 142
Policy issues, 43, 49, 118
    policy advisory committee, 126–33
    policy-coordinating committee, 134–39
    policy-deciding committee, 149–54
    policy-implementing committee, 140–48
    policy-overseeing committee, 155–61

policy-sharing committee, 121–25
    task force, 162–67
Policy loyalty. *See* Loyalty
Policy-overseeing committee, 155–
    61
    budget, 158
    decision making, 158–59
Policy-sharing committee, 121–25
    categoric, 121
    decision making, 123–24
    mutuality of, 122
    orientation, 123
    sharing information, 122
Political reconnaissance, 7
Postmeeting activity, 97, 114–15
Power, 201
    community power, 144
    vs. competence, 201
Power plays, 48–49
Power rule, 265
Premeeting activity, 77–84
Preparation, 77–84. *See also* Fraction
    rules
    of agenda, 77–81
    distributing the packet, 81–82
    for meetings, 89
    writing rules, 240–48. *See also*
        Agenda
Presentation, 36–37
*The Presentation of Self in Everyday
    Life* (Goffman), 3, 222
Press, 10
Private bodies, 175–76
Pro-activity principle, 226
Procedural suggestions, 24
Professional developments, 42
Public Administration (Simon et al.),
    214
Public bodies, 174–75
Public funds, 177
Public utility, 177
Punctuality, 58–59, 250–52

Quality
    of decision making, 211–14
    vs. substance, 213–14
Quasi-public bodies, 173, 176–78

Rand Corporation, 127
Reciprocal relationship, 9
Record keeping, 215–16
    at meetings, 96–97
    of meetings, 36
    for public bodies, 175
    of reports, 68–69
    rule of minutes, 242–44
    sample minutes, 244–45
Refreshments, 62–63
Regional committee, 186–87
Report conference, 115
Reports, 36–37, 57, 65–71, 112
    acceptance of, 70
    action on, 69–70
    annual, 69
    approval in principle of, 70
    approval of, 70
    binding, 68
    discussion only, 69–70
    format, 67
    graphics for, 67
    "No More Reports" principle,
        225–26
    organization, 67–68
    pagination, 68
    progress, 217
    quality of, 66
    receipt of, 70
    record keeping for, 68–69
    report conference, 115
    reproduction of, 68
    rule of reports, 244–45
    summary of, 69
    type for, 67
    types of, 69
Representation, 197–203
    delegated, 198
    and judgment, 198
    and special interest, 198
Representativeness, 197–203
    role stereotyping, 202
    vs. representation, 202
Reputation, 14
Robert M. La Follett Institution of
    Public Affairs, The, 218

Robert's Rules of Order, 10, 91, 102,
    220
Role flexibility
    of chairperson, 14
    of committee member, 28–29
Role inversion, 2
Role playing, 86, 222–23
    interacting roles, 223
Role principle, 222–23
Role stereotyping, 202
Rule of halves, 225, 228–30
Rule of minutes, 242–44
Rule of reports, 240, 244–45
Rule of sixths, 230–31, 284
Rule of the agenda, 241–42
Rule of three-quarters, 232–33
Rule of two-thirds, 233–34, 235

Search committee, 279
Secretary, 17–18
See also Meetings, committee
Simon, Herbert, 214
Smithburg, D., 214
Social contexts, 169–91. *See also*
    Constituency
Special assignments
    committee member, 25–26
    staff person, 35
Special groups, 204–9
Specification, 256
Staff person, 32–40
    acting as committee, 38
    acting for committee, 38
    acting on behalf of committee, 38
    from agency, 32
    and committee process, 95
    committee process support, 35–36
    conferences among, 83
    duties, 33–37
        level of tasks, 39
    expressing opinions, 94–95, 138
    loyalty, 33–34
    and meetings, 92–97
    neutrality, 138
    and policy advisory committee,
        132–33

    and policy-coordinating commit-
        tee, 138
    and policy-deciding committee,
        154
    and policy-implementing commit-
        tee, 146–47
    and policy-overseeing committee,
        160–61
    and policy-sharing committee,
        124–25
    and procedures, 103
    relationship with board of direc-
        tors, 47–48
    relationship with chairperson, 34,
        37, 93
    relationship with committee, 34–
        35, 37–38
    relationship with executive, 47–
        48
    roles, 33–37
    special assignments, 35
    task force, 167
    time available, 34
State-wide committee, 187–88
Stationery, 47
Strategic planning, 279–84
Study committee, 144
Subcommittees, 26, 82, 156
Summary report, 69
Summative reflection, 266
Sunshine laws, 174
SWOT analysis, 283
Synthesis, 36–37, 96

Tabling, 87
Task force, 162–67
    decision making, 165, 166
    legal authority, 163
    staff person, 167
Temporal integrity, 250–52
Thompson, V., 214
Three-characters principle, 224
Time assessment, 7–8, 22, 24, 34,
    110, 250–52
Traditional organization, 281
Training package, 206

Treasurer, 18
Two-media rule of contact, 56
Two-meeting rule, 231

United Fund, 177
Urban Institute, 127

Vice-chairperson, 17

Warren, Roland, 185
Work in tandem, 106
Writing rules, 240–48
Written comments, 22, 23, 90